The Working Sovereign

Axel Honneth

The Working Sovereign

Labour and Democratic Citizenship

Based on the Walter Benjamin Lectures 2021
Centre for Social Critique, Berlin

Translated by Daniel Steuer

polity

The translation of this book was supported by a grant from the Goethe-Institut.

Polity Press
65 Bridge Street
Cambridge CB2 1UR, UK

Polity Press
111 River Street
Hoboken, NJ 07030, USA

ISBN-13: 978-1-5095-6128-5 – hardback

A catalogue record for this book is available from the British Library.

Library of Congress Control Number: 2023952087

Typeset in 11.5 on 14 Adobe Garamond
by Fakenham Prepress Solutions, Fakenham, Norfolk NR21 8NL
Printed and bound by CPI Group (UK) Ltd, Croydon, CR0 4YY

For further information on Polity, visit our website:
politybooks.com

In memory of
Georg Lohmann (1948–2021)
and
Lothar Fichte (1946–2022)
– friends who passed away too early

Contents

Preliminary Remarks

One of the major deficiencies of almost all theories of democracy is that they persistently ignore the fact that most members of their beloved sovereign people are workers.[1] We suppose rather fancifully that citizens keep themselves busy by engaging in political debate; the reality, however, is quite different. Most people spend day after day, and many hours a day, in paid or unpaid work. Because of the subordination, underpayment and strain that work entails, workers find it almost impossible even to imagine playing the role of an autonomous participant in the processes of democratic will formation. This blind spot in democratic theory is, in fact, an inability to acknowledge something that precedes democratic theory, and yet finds its way into every nook and cranny of the theory's object: the social division of labour of modern capitalism. By allotting very different positions to different individuals, the division of labour determines the extent to which each person can influence the processes of democratic will formation. This fateful neglect of the division of labour and its effects means that democratic theory is unable to acknowledge one of the few means by which a democratic state based on the rule of law can influence the conditions that are necessary to maintain it. For apart from education, the social world of work is the only institutional sphere in which most citizens have experiences and learn lessons that exercise a decisive influence over the social and moral views and attitudes of a political community. By shaping working conditions, a democratic state can foster behaviours that are beneficial to democracy, namely cooperative behaviours, or that run counter to it, namely egocentric behaviours.[2] The only other area in which the state can exercise such influence is education policy.

The connection between democracy and the social division of labour is the subject of this book. Initial preparatory work for it was done in the academic year 2018/19, during which I was a visiting professor at the School of Social Science of the Institute for Advanced Studies in

Princeton. Having no teaching duties, I was able to acquaint myself with the vast body of literature on the topic. I am very grateful to my friend and colleague Didier Fassin, then head of the School of Social Science at IAS, for providing me with the opportunity to develop the plan for the book. I used an initial draft of the book for the Walter Benjamin lectures in 2021, which, because of the Covid pandemic, I delivered outdoors on three consecutive evenings in Berlin's Hasenheide park. My thanks go to the two directors of the Centre for Social Critique at Humboldt University, Berlin – Rahel Jaeggi and Robin Celikates. Their invitation stimulated me to return to my reflections about the role of work in modern societies, reflections that go a long way back, and which I have now revised and provided with a new theoretical framework.[3] I have fond memories of the evenings in Hasenheide park, not least because of the generous and cordial hospitality of Rahel, Robin and their team – and the weather played along too! Eva Gilmer provided invaluable help with the difficult task of transforming the script for the lectures into a book. Her linguistic sensitivity and sense for textual balance and succinctness have helped to ensure that this monograph is much clearer, leaner and more concise than the original version. I owe her the most heartfelt thanks for her work. The same applies to Daniel Steuer, who has translated this book into English with the finest feeling for nuances of meaning; I hardly think it is possible to produce a better translation of my text. I'm extremely grateful to Daniel for his marvellous work. During my time as visiting professor at the Centre for Social Critique, and in the following months, a number of people pointed out weaknesses and gaps in my arguments. I am grateful for the advice, objections and valuable help of Rüdiger Dannemann, Timo Jütten, Andrea Komlosy, Bernd Ladwig, Christoph Menke, Fred Neuhouser, Emmanuel Renault, Ruth Yeoman, Christine Wimbauer, Rahel Jaeggi and Robin Celikates. For some of them, I suspect, what follows will not be radical or bold enough. They can lay the blame for my somewhat cautious intellectual attitude at the feet of my new academic environment, the Philosophy Department at Columbia University, where John Dewey taught for almost three decades as a pragmatic social reformer and meliorist of the highest rank.

PART I

Normative Beginnings:
Labour in Democratic Society

In liberalism, we speak of rights, liberty, and community. We also discuss the self-governing forms of subjectivity or agency, and the range of abilities of deliberation, judgement, discussion, and action required in the exercise of rights, liberty and community in practice. Yet, when we examine our producing practices we see that the way they are organized, and so the forms of subjectivity and the types of abilities they foster, undermine the development of agency and abilities necessary to engage in liberal practices of rights, liberty, and community.

James Tully[1]

Over the course of the eighteenth century, the Western world saw the emergence of both a new understanding of society and an entirely new set of ideas about the value of human labour. In the wake of the Enlightenment, societies were no longer seen as hierarchical systems in which, on the basis of an allegedly God-given class structure, small minorities could exercise political power over the vast majority. Instead, they were understood as voluntary associations of citizens with equal rights in which, in principle, membership was sufficient to give someone the right to political participation. This revolutionary reinterpretation of what constitutes the legitimacy of a social order necessarily brought about a fundamentally different understanding of the work someone did to secure their livelihood. Work could no longer be seen merely as a duty owed to a political ruler. Rather, it had to be regarded as an expression of the willingness to actively contribute to the common good and prosperity of the political community. Alongside the nascent idea of the sovereignty of the people, then, there emerged the idea that a society is a cooperative association in which each must contribute as much as they can to societal prosperity, and in this way show that they are worthy members of the political association. This is still the guiding idea today. What happened in the eighteenth century was a decisive intellectual step that established a close connection between the concept of political democracy and the concept of a fair division of labour.[2]

With this step, the ancient, and dismissive, idea of work as a matter of mere individual need and as a sign of political immaturity was finally overcome, at least in theory. Before the bourgeois revolution, the individual's work was seen as essentially a burden, and nothing more: the daily toil that betrayed their position as a dependent member of a particular estate. In the 'new age', it became a condition of free existence and full membership in society. Suddenly, what had once simply signalled one's need to make a living became a symbol of social emancipation and freedom. No one expressed this connection between political equality and social cooperation as succinctly as Hegel in his *Elements of the Philosophy of Right*, published in 1821. Hegel devotes a whole chapter to the new significance of work as a condition of membership in a legally constituted corporation. Every (male) member of bourgeois society, he writes, '*is somebody*' – that is, possesses the full social status of a citizen – because of his 'competence and his regular income and means of support', and in this recognized existence as a tradesman he has 'his honour'.[3]

However, Hegel's confident claim was not borne out, of course, in the social reality of early capitalism. Around 1800, the daily working lives of the vast majority of people in Western Europe took the form of the oppression and unfreedom of workers in the early industrial factories, the dependence of domestic servants in the homes of rich bourgeois and aristocratic families, or the misery of agricultural day-labourers on the farms.[4] The discrepancy between these wretched conditions and Hegel's promise – that employment would henceforth be the uncoerced expression of personal honour and social cooperation – is obvious. On the one hand, there was drudgery, unchecked exploitation, subordination and enforced labour contracts – conditions that prompted Marx, in 1849, to speak of the resurrection of 'slavery'.[5] On the other, there was the new, modern ideal of work as 'free' and self-determined and as the route to a secure social status. This contradiction between social reality and normative idea, between facticity and validity, forms the subject matter of this book. In it, I pursue three questions. How should the ideal of free labour, of work that is no longer forced upon the individual, be understood in normative terms if it is meant to guide us in our search for political change (Part I)? What were labour relations like in the capitalist past, and what do they look like today (Part II)? And what can be done, under present conditions, to reduce, or perhaps close altogether, the stark gap between the aspirational idea and the reality (Part III)? In addition, two excursuses will aim to clarify two concepts that are crucial to substantiating the claim that there is a mutual dependence between democratic participation and sufficiently good working conditions. The first of these concerns the concept of social labour: how must we understand this term if it is to capture all those activities that are seen to be necessary in society and must thus be governed by publicly justifiable regulations? The second discusses how we should view the genesis and functioning of the social division of labour if we are to understand it as the primary means of facilitating broader political participation through the improvement of labour conditions.

1

Three Resources for a Critique of Contemporary Labour Relations

This introductory chapter addresses the question of how the modern idea of free, dignified labour should be understood if it is to be used as the guiding principle of a critique of contemporary labour relations. This is no simple task. Various competing conceptions of what counts as a normatively 'good' or appropriate organization of social labour have been around for quite some time. There are many diverse perspectives from which work can be considered as a good for the individual or society – as something that transcends the mere satisfaction of needs and the provision of sustenance – and there are just as many traditions that advocate ways of improving, transforming and even revolutionizing working conditions. I therefore start by distinguishing and evaluating three modern schools of thought that offer critiques of capitalist working conditions but on the basis of very different ideas about the good or correct organization of social labour. In Chapter 2, I then take a closer look at the most promising and plausible of the three, the one that looks at labour as a social good and considers the impact of working conditions on democratic practice and participation. This approach once was taken for granted by some social theorists but unfortunately has since been almost completely forgotten. Chapter 3 is a systematic attempt at justifying the normative perspective from which the remainder of the book discusses the contemporary and future condition of social labour. I hope that, by the end of that discussion, it will have become clear why my argument focuses on the complementary relationship between a fair division of labour and political democracy.

Before the great transitions that took place between 1750 and 1850, there were few theories of how best to arrange labour relations. Premodern works contain only scant remarks about possible marginal improvements to the quality of daily activities in the crafts, the household or agriculture. The reason for this lack of utopian imagination is that, as I have already mentioned, work was held in such low regard: from antiquity to the early modern period, any activity that counted as work was so strongly associated with pure necessity, humiliating drudgery and low social status that criticizing it seemed as superfluous as thinking about how to improve it. According to the historian Moses Finley, 'neither in Greek nor in Latin was there a word with which to express the general notion of "labour" or the concept of labour "as a general social function"'.[1] But this contemptuous attitude began to change in the wake of the Protestant work ethic, bourgeois emancipation and the legal assertion of 'free work',[2] and it gave way to the idea, articulated by Hegel, that labour is a means of securing individual independence, social status and honour.[3] In the nascent capitalist countries, there soon emerged, alongside the critique of existing labour relations, ideas of a completely different world of work. It was only at this point, after work had become 'free' in the sense that it was no longer tied to personal tutelage and membership of a particular estate,[4] that the idea of work was also 'free' to become associated with hopes for something better, more agreeable, more just or more in tune with human nature – in short, with normative ideas of a 'liberated' form of labour. Such visions for the future of social labour were fuelled either by historically specific ideals of certain 'free' and 'self-determined' kinds of activity or by the discrepancy between actual working conditions and the promise of democratic liberty. Some believed that all work could be as cooperative and fulfilling as the work of craftsmen or artists; others believed that the ideals and principles of democratic participation should also govern labour relations. Over the first half of the nineteenth century, employees became ever more conscious of the misery created by the new capitalist working conditions, and this period therefore saw the increasing dissemination of ideas of liberated and humanely organized forms of labour. Workers and craftsmen formed associations in France, the British Isles, the German states and North America, and these groups began to combine their criticisms of working conditions with proposals for improvement. If we are to determine what normative framework governed this complex mixture of social outrage, moral critique and utopianism, we need first to ask what, in each case, these critics saw as wrong, reprehensible or immoral. Doing so will allow us to explicate the normative bases of the various demands for a reorganization of social labour. Proceeding in this way, we can identify three movements that were critical of capitalist labour relations. The object of each movement's critique – what exactly was considered wrong, immoral or ethically suspect – will allow us to determine, indirectly, the movement's arguments in favour of another, better, more just organization of the sphere of labour. This historical reconstruction enables us, in turn, to identify three normative paradigms that, as I see it, may be employed in a critique of labour relations today.

(a) Estrangement[5]

The first of our three movements emerged just two decades after the French Revolution, and thus at the same time that Hegel's *Elements of the Philosophy of Right* first appeared. At the time, some early socialists were criticizing working conditions in the privately owned factories. Their point was not just that workers were exploited to the point of complete exhaustion, that they were not given any security or that they were subject to the harshest forms of discipline; their main accusation was that the new regime of work deprived workers of the ability to experience their activity as a part of themselves – as an externalization of their own personality.[6] The theme was picked up by the early Marx in his *Economic and Philosophical Manuscripts*; combining it with Hegelian ideas, Marx created one of his most enduring theoretical motifs, that of estranged labour.[7] According to this idea, what is truly scandalous about capitalist relations of production is that they dissect communal work into quantifiable pieces that can then be assigned to individuals and traded as commodities on the market. Marx is convinced that if labour becomes such a commodity, it loses all those properties that make it valuable to us; we are no longer able to experience labour as a productive use of our specific powers and skills as species-beings for the benefit of the social community. As it appears in Marx's early writings, the idea of estranged labour rests on questionable assumptions and contains a number of inconsistencies, and the early writings therefore demand significant interpretive effort. It is not clear, for instance, whether Marx wants to claim that in its original, uncorrupted form labour necessarily involves the translation of one's intentions and capacities into a tangible product. Such a claim would imply a highly problematic exclusive focus on material products, and it may well rest on untenable idealist premises. It is also unclear whether work that involves the productive – even pleasurable – exertion of the powers that we possess qua species-beings is possible only collectively or whether it can also be performed by a single subject. We would therefore be justified in interpreting non-estranged labour as just as much an ideal of individual self-realization as an ideal of un-coerced cooperation.[8] Despite the concept's inherent difficulties, the core of Marx's idea – that labour under capitalist conditions is estranged because it can no longer be experienced as the exertion of the capacities we possess qua species-beings – quickly became popular in the emerging labour movement. And not only there: the British Arts and Crafts movement and other reform movements also soon picked up on the idea that, for work to again become a cooperative or individual exercise of specifically human capacities, as it still was in the arts and crafts, it was necessary to battle against the prevailing conditions of production.[9]

With this popularization, the philosophical elements of Marx's thesis gradually receded into the background, but the idea's intuitively plausible core – that the capitalist economy 'estranges' labour and turns it into something separate from the labourer, something 'thing-like' – nevertheless became one of the most influential paradigms in the critique of labour relations.[10] The chief accusation is that capitalist working conditions do not allow the labourer to identify with his activities as an expression or exertion of his specifically human abilities – a fact that Marx, in the *Economic and Philosophical Manuscripts*, describes in Hegelian terms as the 'worker' no longer being 'at home' in his work, which is now traded as a commodity.[11] The worker therefore cannot see work as an end in itself, as a productive 'objectification' done for its own sake, but only as a 'means of physical subsistence'.[12] Marx's insight is still alive today, even if it is not necessarily expressed in his terms – terms that derive from the world of Hegelian thought. Today, work is described as 'meaningless' rather than 'estranged', which helps to avoid the idealist assumption of a fixed human nature that consists in uncoerced, pleasurable work – an assumption that now seems untenable. But despite this softening of the rhetoric and change of emphasis, the phenomenon is the same: other-directed work that is treated as a profitable commodity cannot be experienced as gratifying and meaningful, but only ever as estranged. But what would meaningful, non-estranged work be like? And how might we justify the normative demand for such work?

Contained in this way of talking is the thesis that non-estranged labour, as a specific form of human activity, possesses a unique intrinsic value. On this view, work *itself* is valuable; it is not valuable simply because it creates goods that are external to it, such as the achievement of socially defined goals or social recognition. If work was valuable simply in virtue of the creation of such external goods, it would suffice to ensure that work had some meaningful purpose, or to improve wages, or to accord the work more recognition, and we would not need to ensure that the work processes themselves were meaningful and gratifying.[13] To justify the demand for meaningful work processes and to guarantee their implementation, we must maintain that work has intrinsic qualities that imply that work activities be designed in a certain way. Without reference to such intrinsic qualities we would have no criteria for deciding whether a given labour process satisfies the necessary conditions for meaningfulness and the absence of estrangement. It would not be enough to point to subjective evaluations, because this would open the door to arbitrary individual judgements about what constitutes meaningful work.[14] The idea of estranged or meaningless work requires us to identify the objective intrinsic qualities of work, which alone allow us to determine whether the desired conditions are actually given in social reality.[15]

It is very difficult, however, to identify among the numerous ideas about the intrinsic values of work those that are objective, rather than a matter of personal or collective preference. In more recent intellectual history, many ethically desirable qualities have been attributed to work as such, from its disciplining effects to the way in which it strengthens community.[16] But within the Marxian tradition, there is widespread agreement on the way to objectively determine work's intrinsic value. Work allows us to exercise the skills and abilities that characterize us as human beings and which we can realize only through work. Of course Marx, as we have seen, added a few other elements to this idea. In his early work, he adopted Hegel's conception of genuine work as activity that objectifies one's intentions and talents in an object and thus makes them visible.[17] But we may leave aside this claim, which plays hardly any role in his later work. Marx tells us that the intrinsic value of work is objectively given by the fact that it allows us to make uncoerced and collective use of the powers that are peculiar to the human being. Among the advocates of this first normative paradigm, there is also widespread agreement about what these 'powers' or 'abilities' are: the capacities to constructively plan, to design or to set purposes – capacities that can be realized only through work. However, if we ask for a normative justification as to why work should always take a social form in which its intrinsic value can be realized, answers begin to differ. Marx's own argument is almost Aristotelian. He claims that the capacity to work on and transform nature purposefully and creatively is part of the essence of man, so the exercise of this capacity is a central condition for the successful realization of the human form of life. More recent proponents of the view that there is a moral obligation to ensure that work is meaningful argue more cautiously. They point out that human beings have a deep-seated need for meaningfulness in everything they do and that this need must also be satisfied in the world of work.[18] Despite these differences, the various versions of the first paradigm all agree that a good and appropriate organization of social labour must allow every employee to exercise distinctively human capacities such as the ability to rationally formulate purposes, engage in cooperative action and creatively shape their activity and environment.

(b) Autonomy

The second normative paradigm is autonomy, which has been, and still is, an important concept in the critique of labour relations. This paradigm does not rely on any assumptions about the intrinsic value of work, and it does not look to a future of meaningful work that is free from estrangement. Instead, it asks how we are to rid work of any kind of paternalistic domination or arbitrary rule. The social movement that first formulated this aim emerged around the same time as the socialist movement in Europe, but surprisingly this social movement was located on the east coast of the United States – a country that many European commentators would later claim, somewhat condescendingly, could never produce an organized, socialist workers' movement.[19] The craftsmen, workers and self-employed small businessmen who came together in Philadelphia, New York and Boston in the early nineteenth century to revolt against the new capitalist forms of wage labour drew on the normative promises contained in their country's republican constitution. It had been only a few decades since they had battled,

successfully, to ensure – through the First Amendment to the constitution – that the state could no longer exercise power over the formation
of its citizens' political opinions. Now, the question was over the fate
that their newly won freedoms were suffering in the manufacturing halls
and factories that gradually began to emerge along the east coast during
industrialization.[20] The position of the state was that the employees of
those factories were free because they could *freely* decide, without being
in any way coerced, whether to accept their work contracts.[21] But wage
labourers soon found that such freedom did not go very far, for they were
dependent on the entrepreneurs in various ways. They could reject the
work contract on offer only if they could find alternative work and had
sufficient savings – and that was rarely the case. Once they had entered
into a contract, the factory owner enjoyed an almost unlimited right
to determine the work processes. And workers had no legal or other
means of seeking redress if they were fired. The groups that began to
rebel against such conditions soon invented a term that encapsulated
all these forms of dependence: wage slavery. In this, they anticipated
Marx, who would later repeatedly claim that wage labour was a new
form of slavery.[22] The intention behind the phrase was not to present
the working conditions of wage labourers as on a par with the slavery
still suffered, at that time, by the African-American population. It was
clearly understood that slave owners legally owned the whole person of
the enslaved individual whereas the capitalist was legally entitled only
to the output of the worker's labour. Still, for American labour leaders
of the 1820s and 1830s, the manifold forms of dependence involved in
everything from contracts to working conditions were enough to justify
talk of a new form of slavery. Their pitch to the masses was that, in a
democratic republic, wage labour was intolerable: it exposed employees
to the whims of entrepreneurs in a way that was incompatible with the
newly established principle of individual independence and freedom.[23]

Among the leadership of the labour movement, however, there was
more agreement about what they did not want than about what they
did. There was a more or less general consensus that the conditions
of the wage labour system contradicted the principle of independence
from arbitrary rule. But when it came to possible alternatives to the
capitalist labour market, the picture was rather different. The proposals
for agricultural cooperatives put forward by Robert Owen when he

toured the US in the 1820s were met with scepticism: the proposals were seen as having limited benefits for the majority of wage labourers, and implying a great degree of dependence on wealthy and philanthropically minded individuals.[24] Some leading figures of the movement suggested a broader distribution of the ownership of productive capital across the population, which it was supposed would ensure that wage labourers were better able to participate in discussions about contracts and labour relations. Yet another faction believed that the evil of wage labour could be overcome only if the factories were the property of the employees and run as cooperatives.[25] But none of these proposals matured into a clear programme that convinced the majority of the population. Any hopes for rapid improvement ended once and for all with the beginning of the American Civil War, which shifted public attention on to the question of the legitimacy of the old, genuine slavery.

Shortly after the end of the Civil War in 1865, the labour activists' battle against wage labour was rekindled. The basic argument had not changed. They still insisted that workers' dependence on the good will of the owners of capital was incompatible with the republican promise of freedom. But they had sharpened their ideas about the economic order that would put an end to this unfreedom. The new watchword was the 'cooperative commonwealth'. Its aim was to put the whole system of industrial production into the hands of worker cooperatives that would peacefully compete over market profits.[26] Over two decades, these radical demands even found support among organized labour. Even politically minded intellectuals like John Dewey came to believe that the project of a democratic republic was incomplete without the democratization of the economy – albeit, in Dewey's case, against the background of a different concept of freedom.[27] However, these impulses soon died down again with the establishment of a national trade union in 1886, when the influence of the more radical wing of the labour movement began to wane significantly.

Today, the republican paradigm for the critique of labour relations is experiencing a revival. Several authors, among them Elizabeth Anderson, invoke the tradition of the early 'Labor Republicans' (as Alex Gourevitch calls them) in their arguments against private capital's control over labour power.[28] To reiterate the point, this argument is not about the nature of work – whether it is meaningful or estranged – and still less is it about work's intrinsic qualities. Rather, the argument is that, as long as workers cannot autonomously determine the details of their work contracts and conditions of work, or at least participate in the relevant decision processes, they are subject to the arbitrary rule of private employers. As these two alternatives indicate, there are more and less radical versions of the argument. Some advocates of this paradigm are convinced that a genuine liberation from arbitrary rule in the sphere of social labour requires the total abolition of wage labour and the total self-administration of businesses by employees. Others believe that the principles of republican freedom would be satisfied by rights that guarantee participation in the formulation of contracts and the determination of working conditions.[29] These different approaches appear to result from different evaluations of the economic efficiency of self-administered businesses. Whether one inclines to one or the other republican position will depend on one's assumptions about the feasibility of running an economy without private investors and the incentives of market competition.

Within this paradigm, the demand for the absence of paternalism and arbitrary rule in the sphere of social labour is also justified in two different ways. And a justification is needed here, for those who defend the liberal market economy can easily insist that working conditions and the aims of a business should be a matter for the business owner – the person who bears the risk. One republican argument against this position is that the right of every person to be independent of the arbitrary will of other persons or institutions must not end when they clock in at work. Even at work, 'you are subject to no one's arbitrary and unaccountable will', because such autonomy is a universal right of every individual[30] and because 'exercising autonomy', as Anderson says, 'is a basic human need'.[31] The other argument is of a more immanent character. It claims that there is a contradiction between the political sphere, where the principle of freedom from paternalism and arbitrary rule is long established, and the area of social labour, where this principle is yet to be introduced. If autonomy is legally guaranteed in the sphere of politics, there can be no justification for the absence of this guarantee in the economic world. Notwithstanding the differences between these two normative justifications, the normative principle of the second paradigm is always the same: the social organization of labour is only good, fair or justifiable if employees are no longer exposed to the arbitrary rule of business owners and employers.

(c) Democracy

The third paradigm for a critique of labour relations differs from the other two in decisive respects. Where the republican tradition ignores the question of whether work might have ethical value, and the question of work's intrinsic qualities more generally, the third paradigm takes work to be an important social good. Unlike the first – Marxian – paradigm, however, the third paradigm does not take this good to be an end in itself or to be intrinsically valuable. Rather, social labour is seen as valuable because it serves another, more important purpose. The third paradigm is thus characterized by the fact that it sees work as a valuable social practice, but one that is valuable only because it is useful for the achievement of a higher good. Like the second paradigm, it does not investigate work's positive intrinsic qualities, but unlike the second paradigm it takes work to be valuable, if only as a means and in a mediated fashion.

According to the third paradigm, the purpose that makes work an instrumental good is political will formation among the citizens of a particular community. On this view, social labour should be organized such that it facilitates an intrinsic good, namely the greatest possible and most effective participation of all members of a society in the processes of democratic self-determination. By the same token, work is seen as bad, wrong or inappropriate if it does not promote such participation. However, as we shall see, for this tradition the social division of labour's contribution to successful democratic will formation is not just of random or contingent instrumental usefulness. Of course, many conditions must obtain if all citizens are to be included in the processes of political deliberation: for instance universal suffrage and a functioning public sphere.[32] These conditions are more than just instrumentally valuable for the realization of democratic inclusion and participation; they are the foundations of democratic life, and thus represent essential and constitutive conditions for inclusion and participation. What distinguishes the third normative paradigm is the claim that the same is true of a well-organized and fair division of labour. Like universal suffrage and the integrity of the public sphere, sufficiently well-organized social labour is seen as an integral and irreplaceable precondition for the inclusion of all citizens in the processes of democratic will formation. The fair division and appropriate organization of social labour is not only of instrumental but of constitutive value for the democratic process.[33]

Perhaps surprisingly, concerns about the detrimental effect that the mechanization and fragmentation of work might have on politics were already being voiced by Adam Smith. In *An Inquiry into the Nature and Causes of the Wealth of Nations*, Smith mentions in passing his worry that, with increasing division of labour, the workers' monotonous, meaningless tasks would lead to such an impoverishment of sentiment and understanding that informed participation in political life would become impossible.[34] Some fifty years later, Smith's aside became the key to Hegel's analysis of the modern market economy. In the chapter on labour in *Elements of the Philosophy of Right*, Hegel says that the working estates are capable of 'universal life' – and thus of active participation in the 'reasonable whole' that is society – only if their professional activities are sufficiently complex and protected, and only if the working estates are organized in trade-specific corporations that celebrate their particular professional ethos.[35] We can now formulate the third paradigm's fundamental claim: the division of labour within which the majority of the population works must satisfy the normative condition that it provides all employees with the self-confidence, knowledge and honour that enable them to take part in opinion formation in society at large without shame or fear. After Hegel, this rough idea gave birth to a whole tradition of thought, albeit one that mostly exercised its influence under the surface. In France, this tradition began with Émile Durkheim's 'organic solidarity'; in Britain, G. D. H. Cole's guild socialism, which influenced the English labour movement, played a similar role.[36] Both shared the idea that a flourishing democracy requires a fair, inclusive and conscious division of labour, and that an attitude of democratic cooperation depends on various mechanisms that promote a shared awareness of the mutual dependencies that result from the division of labour. The normative argument for this complementary relationship between democracy and a fair division of labour can already be found in Hegel: only those with a profession that is worthy of recognition, and that is in fact recognized, can possess the cognitive abilities and psychological self-confidence that are required for a level of effective participation in social will formation, in line with the idea of active citizenship. Socially necessary labour is considered to be organized appropriately, or at least well enough, only if it does not constrain employees' ability to take part in democratic life. Of course, what that claim means for the detailed organization of the vast number of activities that make up social labour depends on empirical assumptions about the aspects of actual working conditions that are particularly detrimental to participation in political will formation. The representatives of this third position may therefore come to very different conclusions about how the situation might be improved. But the essence of their critique is always the same: the criticism takes aim at those conditions that make it impossible for the majority of the working population to fully take part in deliberative exchange in democratic society – conditions such as excessive physical or psychological strain, the excessive fragmentation of work processes, a lack of recognition or an absence of secure integration in the social division of labour.

We have sketched the three most important versions of the critique of capitalist labour relations. The first critique takes aim at the fact that individuals are forced to perform meaningless, objectively non-gratifying tasks; the second at the fact that they are subjected to the arbitrary rule of private actors; and the third at the fact that they cannot develop the physical and psychological preconditions that would allow them to participate as equals in processes of democratic will formation. I shall now critically compare these three versions of the critique, with a view to preparing for our discussion of contemporary labour relations. I begin again with the Marxian paradigm, which I shall call the 'critique of estrangement'. According to this critique, a non-estranged relationship with our work activities is possible only if we can see these activities as an expression or representation of talents and abilities that are specific to the human species.

The obvious strength of this paradigm – its plausibility and clarity – is at the same time its greatest weakness. Setting aside the metaphysical connotations of Marx's version of the critique of estrangement,[37] the idea that all work should express specifically human abilities and capacities is undoubtedly attractive and, to that extent, convincing. Activity that allows agents to creatively materialize their intentions and feel that they are effective actors in their physical environment is the paradigm of action – action that is an end in itself and that is gratifying for its own sake. Even if we weaken the conditions for non-estranged activity – that is, drop the requirement that an object must be transformed, leaving only the condition that a specifically human capacity must be exerted – the paradigm does not lose much of its original appeal. Work that does not involve the transformation of an object, for instance delivering mail, teaching young people or caring for the elderly, will be all the more attractive and gratifying if the workers can freely express their own abilities and talents.

We must bear in mind, however, that we are talking not about subjective feelings or impressions – merely being happy with one's work – but about the fulfilment of an 'objective' standard. It is not enough that people experience their own activities as 'meaningful' or that they feel them to involve the exertion of specifically human abilities; rather, the activities must be such that they are actually, or 'objectively', the instantiations of one or more of these abilities.[38] But at this point it becomes immediately clear that it will be extremely difficult to apply this criterion to individual cases among the multitude of work activities. Everything will depend on what we mean by a 'specifically human ability'. Is, for instance, the capacity to do basic arithmetic such an ability? If so, it would follow that working at a supermarket checkout, even if such work is monotonous and physically and psychologically stressful, counts as non-estranged labour. If we are to avoid arbitrariness, we need to define specifically 'human' abilities – those that, for Marx, might represent the 'powers of our species-being' – as narrowly as possible. But if we define them narrowly, the number of abilities that count as eminently human reduces, and the sphere of work activities that might count as 'non-estranged labour' shrinks. Ultimately, this narrowing down runs the risk of forcing us into a kind of ethical perfectionism: the normative demands are raised to such a level that the majority of necessary work falls short. Whether a building inspector, auto body painter or worker at a laundrette is paid fairly for their work becomes irrelevant, as do the level of safety at work and whether the work makes them happy. Regardless of those issues, if the work does not realize one of the capacities that truly characterize us as humans – the ability to create complex plans, be creative, set goals or cooperate – it must be considered estranged. The critique of estrangement thus seems to end up in a cul-de-sac, because its criteria for non-estranged work must be either too strict or too relaxed. If they are too relaxed, almost any work activity must qualify as non-estranged, because, trivially, some rudimentary elements of human ability are always involved. If they are too strict, only very few kinds of labour can potentially count as non-estranged. On this second, perfectionist version of the view, most kinds are work that are necessary now, and will be necessary in future, do not qualify as non-estranged. We can also put this extreme view differently: the demand that socially necessary work activities must always be carried out for their own sake and must 'objectively' express our highest capacities is based on a tendency vastly to overestimate the plasticity and modifiability of socially necessary work.[39]

The fact that the critique of estrangement ends up in this cul-de-sac is not the only problem associated with it. Even in the early Marx, it is not clear whether the description of estranged labour applies only to the work of individual subjects or whether it applies also to the joint activities of groups. The relevant passages in the *Economic and Philosophical Manuscripts* sometimes speak of the activity of an individual subject, and sometimes about cooperation, and Marx never really makes it clear whether the question of estranged labour concerns the future well-being of individuals or that of whole communities.[40] I would argue that this indecision is typical of the critique of estrangement in all its forms. Representatives of this paradigm generally leave open the question of whether meaningful, non-estranged labour would benefit individual subjects or the whole community. The fact that little effort is made to establish a firm link between the non-estranged labour of individuals and the well-being of the social community speaks in favour of the first possibility. The idea that meaningfulness and non-estrangement depend on cooperation, and thus are likely to benefit the community, is usually not explicitly expressed and tends to play only a minor role. This gives rise to the second problem with the critique of estrangement: its marked tendency towards ethical individualism. The primary focus is on forms of work that might benefit the individual, and the idea that good or just labour relations are important for societal well-being recedes into the background. The suggestion that actual labour relations may threaten family life, active citizenship or participation in the public sphere seems to play almost no role at all. In sum, the critique of estrangement ends ultimately in an inescapable quandary, because it has to opt for a criterion for non-estranged labour that is either too weak or too strong, and it is overly focused on individual well-being. All of that suggests that the paradigm of estrangement is not suitable as a point of departure for the critique of contemporary labour relations.

The second – republican – paradigm also runs into some problems, but they are of an altogether different kind. The issue is not that the paradigm implies inflated, perfectionist expectations regarding the transformation of work – indeed, it has only a limited interest in the substance, scope and effort associated with individual work activities. As I explained above, thinkers in this tradition focus their critique almost exclusively on the fact that wage labourers in private businesses are not guaranteed the same freedom from arbitrary rule that they are granted as a matter of course in the sphere of politics in a democratic society. An obvious objection to this normative view is that there needs to be some further justification for the thesis that the same moral principles should apply to the economy as apply in the area of political and democratic action. At the very least, this view needs a convincing response to the counter-argument that the discrepancy between the two spheres is the price we pay for economic wealth and efficiency, which depend on our handing over the control of business, production processes and investment to private actors, who, because they put in their own money, have a natural interest in maximizing profits and thus in the flourishing of their businesses.[41] Of course, there are a number of convincing objections to this thesis, which is a mainstay of market liberalism, but the conception of two completely separate political and economic sub-systems, each of which follows different functional rules, would first need to be refuted before the normative principles of republican freedom could be transferred from the political to the economic sphere.

But there is another, more serious objection to the republican paradigm, as we saw briefly above. The republican's response to the question of how labour relations might be improved can only ever be that all employees must be liberated from paternalism and the arbitrary rule of private entrepreneurs. Depending on the republican's political leaning, this will mean either giving employees extensive rights to participation and social security, or transferring ownership rights to employees so that businesses can be autonomously self-administered.

But whichever position the republican adopts, practically nothing is said about how work itself can be improved, how the pressures of work might be reduced or how individual tasks can be made more complex and varied. From the republican perspective, the only serious injustice is the private exercise of power; it closes its eyes to the increasing mechanization, one-dimensionality and isolation of work. The first problem with republicanism concerns the organizational form of social labour, the second the detailed design and scope of work. There is no feedback relation between these two dimensions: even when the organizational form of social labour changes, the activities and substance of individuals' work may stay the same, and even with substantial changes in the scope and substance of individual activities, the form of the social organization of labour may, in principle, remain unchanged.[42] But the republican view seems to assume that the liberation of wage labour from paternalism and arbitrary rule would automatically bring all the other ills associated with contemporary labour relations to an end. Republicans therefore do not ask whether improving working conditions would require not only changing the organizational form of labour but also restructuring the social division of labour and the delimitations and material substance of different fields of work.[43] The weakness of the republican tradition is therefore its almost exclusive focus on employees' dependence on private rule, which makes it blind to the qualitative aspect of labour relations. An account of the injustice and disadvantage created by monotonous, back-breaking and draining work would require a much richer moral vocabulary than republicanism's simple distinction between freedom and unfreedom is able to provide.

The two paradigms discussed so far home in on just one normative principle and hope to identify all necessary changes to existing labour conditions on the basis of that principle: for the first normative paradigm, the liberation of individual work from all estrangement and meaninglessness; for the second, the liberation of work from all forms of rule that have no democratic legitimacy.[44] By contrast, the third – democratic – paradigm is not attached to any single principle; its view of how labour relations might be improved is based on what is required to increase the likelihood that employees can participate in democratic will formation. This important difference is a consequence of the fact that the democratic paradigm treats changes to labour relations only as a means, albeit an indispensable means, for achieving an overarching end – namely the inclusion of society's members in the democratic process. At any given moment in time, the appropriate measures for improving labour relations can be established only by taking the idea of democratic participation as the normatively guiding principle.[45] The subordinate norms that should govern labour relations are identified through a reflective application of this overarching principle to the historically changing world of work. The paradigm is therefore not committed to the idea that one particular intervention is required to bring about just employment relations and working conditions. Rather, on this view a measure is appropriate if it increases the likelihood, under the given historical circumstances, that employees will take an active part in democratic will formation. Whether reform should aim to address the material substance of work, the lack of participation, low wages, the absence of recognition or simply the length of the working day will depend on which factors represent particular obstacles to democratic will formation at a given point in time.

Because of its particular normative structure, the third paradigm has two significant advantages over the other two paradigms. First, because the guiding principle leaves open the question of which norms should govern labour relations, any aspect of work can become the focus of attention: the question is simply whether it hinders employees' active participation in democratic processes. Potential obstacles to such participation could include work activities that degrade workers' intellectual abilities, workers' acute fear of unemployment, the experience of powerlessness in the workplace or a lack of recognition of workers' achievements. If such conditions impede employees' democratic participation, the democratic paradigm must consider them an evil to be removed. This also implies that there should be no exclusive focus on particular measures. Instead, the appropriate measure will be the one that is a suitable remedy for a specific ill in a certain historical situation. This essential flexibility means that the democratic approach can draw on the critique of estrangement or the republican tradition as normative resources if these can assist in identifying the defect in question and finding suitable remedies for it. If, for instance, the exercise of democratic rights is somehow being hindered by the volume and character of the work activities themselves, there is no reason not to adopt the normative vocabulary of the critique of estrangement as a diagnostic tool and therapy. If, by contrast, the problem lies more with the organizational structure of businesses and their associated form of rule, it makes sense to use the normative vocabulary of the republican tradition. Both resources can be useful and they should be seen as complementing each other. But an exclusive focus on just one of them threatens to move less visible sources of the work-related impairment of democratic participation out of sight.

The second advantage the democratic paradigm enjoys over its two competitors is that it allows for intermediary cases between what is 'wrong' or 'unjust' on the one side and 'right' or 'fair' on the other. The critique of estrangement and republicanism operate with all-or-nothing normative concepts, and so lack the theoretical means for formulating such intermediary cases. The tradition I label 'democratic', by contrast, consciously adopts a different model. According to this tradition, the principle of democratic participation in the sphere of work can be introduced only gradually, and this process can moreover never be considered complete because there is no criterion for the complete realization of the principle. This characteristic is also the result of the framework in which an overriding principle is applied to specific circumstances. Within this framework, we cannot predict which adaptations will be required as a result of changing circumstances, and for this reason alone there can be no final, comprehensive compliance with the guiding principle. As John Dewey might have put it, the democratic paradigm is only ever guided by the 'ends in view' – that is, the goals that are visible and can be achieved under current historical conditions – because unlike the other two positions, it does not pretend to know what a perfectly satisfactory and well-ordered world of work would look like. At each historical moment, a detailed empirical investigation can help us to identify measures that would bring us closer to a world of work that supports democratic life, but for principled reasons we can never anticipate the new possibilities that will arise from the new conditions, and so we cannot know what next steps might be required. We will have new experiences, in the light of which our original ideal might appear in new and unexpected ways. It is therefore pointless to see it as a fixed final end to be achieved or as a perfect condition to be realized. Rather, the ideal pursued by the democratic paradigm is a regulative one. It allows for the formulation, at each stage, of tangible goals that seem achievable given the knowledge available at the time – no more, no less. The idea that we can know what the ideal conditions will look like is altogether alien to this paradigm.[46]

By now it should be clear that I prefer the democratic paradigm over the critique of estrangement and the republican approach. As I have said, it has two advantages: it offers a broader view of the range of ills that affect the world of work, and it does not take itself to be pursuing a fixed final end. In what follows, I therefore assume that the best way to understand the idea of a good and appropriate organization of social labour is in terms of the pursuit of the conditions that allow workers to participate actively and self-confidently in the processes of democratic will formation, or conditions that at least do not prohibit such participation. Of course, I have not yet provided a systematic justification for this position. The justification will be presented in Chapter 3. First, I wish to provide more detail about a few aspects of the prehistory of the democratic paradigm within the tradition of political thought.

2

A Forgotten Tradition

The industrial system ... is in great measure the key to the paradox of political democracy. Why are the many nominally supreme, but actually powerless? Largely because the circumstances of their lives do not accustom or fit them for power or responsibility. A servile system in industry inevitably reflects itself in political servility and in a servile Society.

G. D. H. Cole[1]

I mentioned above that Adam Smith's *Wealth of Nations* contains a passing reference to the close link between the quality of someone's work and their ability to participate in political communication. Book 5 of that work, which lists the duties of a community's political leaders, contains a section titled 'Of the Expense of the Institutions for the Education of Youth'. Smith writes that 'in the progress of the division of labour, the employment of the far greater part of those who live by labour ... comes to be confined to a few very simple operations'. This leads, Smith continues, to a 'torpor' of the mind and a general withering of the ability to conceive 'any generous, noble, or tender sentiment' – a development that is detrimental to the well-being of a 'civilized society', which relies on its members being able to acquire 'intellectual' and 'social' virtues.[2] According to Smith, these virtues are necessary for civilized social life because every adult member of society must be able to form a judgement concerning the 'great and extensive interests of his country'.[3] This was not an obvious position to adopt in an age that was still far from affording workers – 'the labouring poor, that is, the great body of the people'[4] – a right to form a political opinion, let alone a right to democratic participation. Why, then, did Smith believe that it was necessary to avoid a situation in which the monotony, tedium and strain of work made it impossible for people to form a judgement about the general concerns of their country? Smith's answer is surprisingly clear: because otherwise those who govern cannot count on the ability of people to understand and accept the laws they pass. In the 1770s, well before the French Revolution, Smith thus provided a straightforward articulation of why governments need to pay attention to work and employment conditions within their jurisdictions: because such conditions determine whether workers can fully understand the laws, accept them on rational grounds and embrace their meaning. The apparent implication of Smith's view is that the less tiring, monotonous and tedious work is, the greater are the chances that individuals can form an appropriate view of the politically urgent tasks their country faces, and thus come to at least a basic judgement about the quality of the measures taken by the government.[5] But this does not lead Smith to propose direct political interventions in the labour market to make employees' individual activities more complex and varied and less tiring. Instead, he suggests that the dangers he identifies can be counteracted through indirect educational measures that would be external to businesses. Adhering closely to his belief that market processes should be interfered with as little as possible, he advocates state-financed educational institutions that would help to mitigate the intellectual degradation caused by wage labour.[6] What begins as a promising observation about the negative impact of the division of labour on politics and civilization thus ends with a return to Smith's economic liberalism, with which he is simply unable to part.

In *Elements of the Philosophy of Right*, Hegel initially adopts Smith's optimistic view about the beneficial effects of the market, but when it comes to the point at which politics and the division of labour cross over, his approach is very different.[7] Unlike Smith, Hegel places the measures that are meant to counteract the increasing degradation and one-dimensionality of social labour in the institutional sphere of market society itself. He suggests that employees be organized in trade-specific associations, which he calls 'corporations'. Apart from guaranteeing their members' livelihoods,[8] the tasks of the corporations are mainly to ensure the social value of labour and to maintain an awareness of the mutual dependence of everyone who is participating in the market.[9] These recommendations were way ahead of their time, and it is clear that the aim of such professional groups is to guarantee something that the new economic formation should have been able to provide by itself: that workers not only receive an income that secures their subsistence but are able to develop an awareness of the actual social value and importance of their activities within an increasingly opaque division of labour.[10] Even the slightest tendency towards the simplification, specialization or impoverishment of labour is anathema to Hegel, because it increases the ever-present danger that the mass of people who live off their labour will not possess the necessary mental, intellectual and cultural abilities to make full use of the liberties and rights of modern society. In a rather inconspicuous place in *Elements of the Philosophy of Right*, Hegel concisely expresses the mutual dependence between social participation and the form of the social division of labour. If, he says, 'the specialization [*Vereinzelung*] and limitation of particular work ... increase, as do likewise the dependence and want of the class which is tied to such work', then 'this in turn leads to an inability to feel and enjoy the wider liberties, and particularly the spiritual advantages, of civil society'.[11] It is not simply one's level of income or savings but the quality of one's workplace and work activities that determines one's opportunities to participate in social life. For Hegel, the opportunity to enjoy the civil liberties and cultural blessings of modern society depends on a social division of labour that provides employment of sufficient quality. With this view, Hegel does not arrive at the belief that democratic rule depends on a just and transparent division of labour, for unlike Kant he lacks insight into the intrinsic relationship between the rule of law and public will formation, and thus cannot take this decisive next step. However, no other early nineteenth-century thinker expressed with the same clarity the fact that the political liberties of the new age would have a 'fair value',[12] to use John Rawls's term, only if the social division of labour provided secure, socially recognized and sufficiently complex and varied forms of employment.

The importance of a fair division of labour for democracy and political participation was made clear about seventy years after Hegel by the sociologist Émile Durkheim. It is often forgotten that Durkheim was the first to clearly state that democratic will formation presupposes good and fair conditions of social labour. He gets close to this idea in his first book, *The Division of Labour in Society*, which applies the biological model of the living organism to modern society and asks how modern society's highly complex division of labour must be organized if it is to protect the social cohesion that is necessary for society's reproduction. Durkheim's answer already contains, in rough outline, the idea that interests us here, namely that such social cohesion comes about only if people voluntarily agree to their working conditions, are offered good, sufficiently complex and varied work, and have a clear idea of the position of their activities within the overall structure of the division of labour.[13] This conception does not yet contain an explicit reference to democratic will formation, but Durkheim increasingly made the link clear throughout his intellectual development. In his lecture course on the sociology of morality, which he delivered regularly from 1896 until his death in 1917, his final position begins to crystallize. It becomes clear that Durkheim believes that a flourishing public sphere depends on the fair, inclusive and transparent organization of social labour.[14] Accordingly, he comes to emphasize that the democratization of the professional sphere is *a precondition* of broad participation in political debate, and he proposes that all sectors of socially divided labour be organized into professional groups that will support this democratization. Like Hegel's corporations, the purpose of the groups is to introduce practices of self-administration into the workplace and thus narrow the gap between a person's private life and their status as a citizen.[15] With this approach – a democratic version of Hegel's conception of market society – Durkheim founded French solidarism and syndicalism.[16]

Only a few decades later, a movement that aimed to democratize the world of work emerged in England. It had a much more socialist orientation than the movement inspired by Durkheim, and its protagonist was George Douglas Howard Cole, already mentioned above, who is unfortunately often forgotten today, like many of the other intellectuals associated with the workers' movement, even if their ideas are as relevant as ever. Cole began as a member of the Fabian Society, remained a lifelong admirer of William Morris, and early on in his life recognized a fundamental flaw in any purely political understanding of democracy. He described this flaw as a 'paradox': democracy means that all citizens have equal rights and equal opportunities to participate in political opinion and will formation, but the dependence, toil and subordination associated with capitalist labour relations mean that the majority cannot do so.[17] Cole believed that working-class people are unable to play an active role in civil society because, such is the low status of their activities, they lack the self-confidence and discursive habits that are required for effective participation. In this way, Cole's theory was motivated by the same concern that led Hegel and Durkheim to warn against the dissociative powers of the capitalist labour market and propose the introduction of professional groups and corporations. And like Hegel and Durkheim, Cole was worried that demoralizing, humiliating working conditions make it difficult for workers to make use of their right to democratic participation, and so sought alternatives to existing labour relations. His search soon led him to Robert Owen's workers' cooperatives as a source of inspiration. Cole's preferred model was not unlike Hegel's trade-specific 'corporations' or Durkheim's plea for a more cooperative market based on professional groups, but it came with a much stronger criticism of capitalist private property. His idea was that workers could become accustomed to the processes of democratic will formation by involving them in the administration of their businesses, or even by giving them autonomous control over them.[18] From the start, what he had in mind was an economic formation in which worker cooperatives sold their products and services, and so strove for economic gain, but in which profits flowed back to the employees. But Cole's rather unfortunate label for his programme – 'guild socialism', an intentional allusion to the mediaeval guilds – did little to help popularize his ideas.[19] Hegel shied away from the use of the term 'guilds' as a label for his 'corporations' on the grounds that guilds were based on forms of privilege and exclusion that were incompatible with modern universal liberties.[20] But despite the misleading name he gave to his lifelong cause, during the first half of the twentieth century Cole became one of the most important proponents of democratizing labour relations and so enabling workers to participate in processes of political will formation.

The tradition of thinkers who, like Hegel, Durkheim and Cole, believed democracy depends on appropriate labour relations did not end after the Second World War. Although the power and cultural importance of the workers' movement gradually ebbed, various voices continued to call for working conditions that would support the inclusion of all members of society in processes of general will formation.[21] In Anglo-Saxon countries, it may have been John Stuart Mill's plea for worker cooperatives or John Dewey's occasional flirtation with the idea of 'industrial democracy' that kept alive the idea of a necessary connection between political democracy and fair working conditions even after the slow decline of the workers' movement.[22] On the continent, the ongoing influence of Durkheim's solidarism and the continuing reverberations of Marx's writings ensured that the idea endured. As before the war, there were marked differences of opinion as to precisely how labour relations would have to be configured if they were to conform to the normative requirements of a dynamic democracy. People differed as to whether the core of the problem lay at the level of the quality and volume of work or at the level of its organization, and accordingly different reforms were proposed: for instance, trade unions' proposals for the 'humanization' of the world of work[23] or the pilot projects for self-administration that were carried out in Yugoslavia.[24] Nevertheless, in this search for solutions all sides were motivated by the same thing, and it was the very fact that had irritated Hegel, Durkheim and Cole: that employees are somehow expected to suddenly become politically aware and able citizens once they enter the polling station. For this tradition, this is a chimera, born of the liberal fiction that all members of society have the same opportunities to participate in democratic deliberation. What this fiction ignores, out of a mixture of moral idealism and social arrogance, is that the ability to act as a self-confident, sovereign political individual, as the idea of democracy demands, depends on material, temporal and psychological preconditions.

As the twentieth century progressed, the belief that political democracy had to be complemented by a fair division of labour became increasingly restricted to the margins. With the triumphant march of liberalism, the conviction that the two issues had little to do with one another prevailed, such that so-called democratic theory could confidently be practised without any discussion of labour relations. In the next chapter, I discuss the conceptual reasons for this blind spot in contemporary democratic theory and provide a novel systematic justification for the position just sketched – one that is independent of these older, often forgotten traditions.

3

Democracy and the Question of a Fair Division of Labour

An economic system is not only an institutional device for satisfying existing wants and needs but a way of creating and fashioning wants in the future. How men work together now to satisfy their present desires affects the desires they will have later on, the kind of persons they will be. ... Since economic arrangements have these effects, and indeed must do so, the choice of these institutions involves some view of human good and of the design of institutions to realize it. This choice must, therefore, be made on moral and political as well as on economic grounds.

John Rawls[1]

For the representatives of the tradition just described, it was obvious that political democracy depends on good and fair labour relations. It is therefore somewhat baffling that the connection between political democracy and labour relations seems to have been forgotten today. The representatives of the old tradition saw the intrinsic link between the two spheres in the normative substance of a mode of political sovereignty whose security depends not only on all members of society being legally included in democratic will formation, but on the social division of labour providing fair and sufficiently good conditions for enacting that sovereignty. The argument for this complementarity thesis is that the intensification of the division of labour brings with it mental and cultural disadvantages for the working population that may prevent individuals from exercising their right to political participation. The representatives of our tradition therefore insist that democratic states have a duty to ensure that the quality of labour relations in their territories is sufficient to give employees the possibility to participate fully in the public processes of democratic will formation. None of the authors holds, however, that the differences between the political and economic spheres should be removed altogether – that the organization of both spheres should depend on what the majority in a public assembly decides, as the more radical wing of the workers' movement believes. The authors in our tradition believe that this more radical solution cannot work, for the specific tasks of the two spheres differ too much to be subject to the same method of normative regulation. The task of politics is the democratic negotiation of legitimate legislation, in which all citizens must be included. The task of the economy, by contrast, is the social coordination of the economic performance of employees, whose activities relate to each other under the conditions of the division of labour, so that employees can contribute to the well-being of the community as efficiently as possible. Considerations of economic efficiency lead the representatives of our tradition to resist the suggestion that the principles of direct democracy should be simply transferred to the sphere of the division of labour. They believe that, from the perspective of economic efficiency, it would be risky for businesses, public bodies or state and corporate administrations to be organized on the model of collective autonomy. They differ widely, however, on the question of the degree to which the sphere of work should be reorganized in trying to secure its interaction with the democratic principles of the political sphere. Their positions range from Hegel's and Durkheim's reformism to John Dewey's meliorism. Dewey believes it should be left to the economy to find out, through trial and error, how far the economic sphere can be democratized without harming economic efficiency.[2] Along this path, the question necessarily arises of whether the standard of 'economic efficiency' is in fact as neutral and objectively valid as economic theory claims it is. As discussions of this question progressed, it became clear that the answer depends on how economic efficiency is measured: is it in terms of the amount of capital gain, or is it in terms of productivity, that is, the relationship between productive effort and the amount of consumer goods produced?[3]

Quite apart from these questions, which indicate the full breadth of the positions within my preferred tradition, we may note that the central argument for fair and good working conditions is of a purely immanent character: in a democratic regime, the requirement that all members of society must participate in political decision-making implies that working conditions be subject to normative rules that enable every employee to make use of this right to participation. This thesis may sound obvious, plausible and convincing, but contemporary democratic theory takes no

– or very little – notice of it. This oversight surely cannot be attributed to simple ignorance or a lack of empirical knowledge. Rather, it must be connected to basic conceptual decisions that obscure the importance of a good and fair organization of work for successful democratic participation. In what follows I analyse the conceptual reasons for this blind spot, and I shall at the same time try to provide further justification for the fundamental assumptions of the thesis of complementarity.

In arguably the two most important attempts at establishing the moral foundations of the modern state under the rule of law – John Rawls's theory of justice and Jürgen Habermas's discourse theory of law – there is one line of thought in each that comes very close to the idea that democratic politics must be complemented by working conditions that are conducive to it.[4] In Rawls, it is the insight that equal rights to liberties must possess a 'fair value', which means that the actual exercise of these rights is tied to the removal of social and economic inequality.[5] In Habermas, it is contained in the normative demand that the practice of democracy must continually establish that the factual conditions for equal participation in its own procedures actually obtain.[6] The fact that motivates both authors to insist on the removal of existing inequalities is obvious: a discriminated against or socially disadvantaged person or group will be unable to participate in the processes of public will formation on an equal footing with everyone else, as the idea of the democratic state under the rule of law normatively requires. Both authors, however, abruptly break away from this line of thought before the deleterious effects of existing labour relations come into view. Neither Rawls nor Habermas asks whether a person's ability to participate in democratic will formation on an equal footing with others might depend not only on the education system but on the way social labour is organized.[7]

Of course, it is not a coincidence, and nor is it down to mere negligence, that these influential thinkers mostly fail to mention the organization of work and professions.[8] In both cases, the omission of this important sphere is the consequence of certain background assumptions; we must first uncover these before deciding whether we have good reasons to reject them. Two assumptions in particular may have persuaded Rawls and Habermas not to pay too much attention to labour relations as a factor that influences opportunities for democratic participation.[9] First, both authors are inclined to see the labour market, with its economic incentives, as an indispensable – even if not ideal – tool for the efficient allocation of employees in complex societies, and they do not consider any possible alternatives.[10] This tendency is evident in Rawls's view that economic incentives are suitable means of convincing individuals to pursue demanding occupations with extensive training requirements, occupations that would, absent these incentives, be left unfilled, because no one would take them on voluntarily – leaving only the unacceptable option of compulsion. The same tendency expresses itself in Habermas's view that the labour market's function of distributing the tasks that must be carried out among groups of willing individuals, a function that is necessary for the reproduction of the system, can be performed only if the labour market is not burdened with moral demands that are so excessive as to put the reproduction of society at risk.[11] This first background assumption is thus roughly the same in Rawls and Habermas: in societies with a pronounced division of labour, there are not really any feasible functional alternatives to the labour market as an allocation mechanism. However, the assumption that the distribution of socially necessary work to certain groups of individuals can be achieved only via the mechanism of supply and demand does not imply that the labour market cannot be shaped or regulated by law. Rawls and Habermas do not exclude the possibility of state intervention in the labour market in principle. On the contrary, if such interventions contribute to the removal of violations of the legally enshrined principle of equality, they are essential on normative grounds. In cases of discrimination – when a private or public employer pays someone less, gives them a workplace of lesser quality or does not hire them at all because of their gender, skin colour, cultural background or sexual orientation – the state must, as Rawls and Habermas see it, take legal action against such social disadvantage.[12] However, this equation of social disadvantage with unequal treatment or discrimination conceals a second background assumption that the two authors seem to share: that the opportunities for democratic participation depend solely on someone's position vis-à-vis all other members of society. According to this view, a person is 'disadvantaged' only if they are worse off or treated less well, in one or several respects, compared to another group of people that is considered the standard case. However, this one-sided focus on the principle of equality has unfortunate consequences as far as the world of work is concerned. Here, the quality of the work or the level of remuneration may themselves explain why an appropriate level of participation in democratic will formation is not possible – quite independently of any comparison with the situation of others. Thus, the idea of a 'minimum wage' expresses the correct insight that an individual's income can be too low, in 'absolute' and not just in 'relative' terms, to allow for participation in certain social practices that are considered valuable. In such cases, the issue is not the removal of a form of discrimination that others do not suffer, but the reorganization of individual areas of activity or work structures such that employees are in a position to participate freely in the democratic processes of public discussion and will formation. Equality and the provision of adequate conditions are two normative principles that belong to very different normative registers, and they can therefore lead to very different perceptions of the same social reality. If we apply the first principle, we see only those – many – social disadvantages that result from discriminatory treatment. If we apply the second, we see those social disadvantages that result from conditions that fall below minimum requirements. What speaks in favour of the second principle is that, to paraphrase a famous line from Harry Frankfurt, it is whether a workplace conduces to participation in democratic practices, not how it compares to others, that is important.[13]

Of course, this is not to say that the principle of equality, or of equal treatment, therefore has no normative relevance for the organization of labour relations. It is the appropriate standard in all cases in which, on the basis of certain personal qualities, individuals receive less income, are treated less well in the workplace, or find it harder to enter certain professions, offices or positions. And democratic participation frequently also suffers when this is the case. In societies where people are still subjected to degrading and disparaging treatment on the grounds of their skin colour, gender identity, disability or sexual orientation, there are many such cases of discrimination.[14] But not all work-related disadvantages that affect free and self-confident participation in democratic processes involve the unequal treatment of specific groups of people. If work is too tiring for one to think about political events at the end of the day, if a job does not pay enough for one to have a life that includes political activity, or if one is so dependent on one's superiors that one is required to constantly demonstrate good conduct, these are deficiencies that result from the fact that one lacks the resources and capacities that are necessary for democratic participation. 'Too tiring', 'not enough', 'so dependent' – these formulations already indicate that we are dealing here not with a relative but with an absolute lack of important resources and goods. Because of Rawls's and Habermas's tacit assumption that social equality in the labour market is, as far as this sphere is concerned, enough to meet the normative demand for the possession and potential use of democratic rights, 'absolute' deficiencies related to the type of employment or quality of the workplace are outside their field of vision. In the absence of a standard for comparison, they cannot see how a particular type of employment or a given work structure might have to be changed to adapt it to the needs of democratic participation. Autonomous and self-confident participation in democratic practices depends equally on the social equality of all citizens and the availability of a number of basic capacities and resources for which minimum requirements cannot be established via a comparison between individuals. One could go further: the second condition must precede the first. Only those who have the necessary abilities and resources can see themselves as equal members of a group.

Taken together, the two background assumptions that guide Rawls's and Habermas's theories of justice explain why the social conditions for the exercise of political rights or democratic participation – the organization and form of the social division of labour – do not really figure in their reflections. The first assumption rules out the possibility of alternatives to the labour market as an efficient allocation tool. The second limits the scope for normative regulation of the labour market to measures that secure equality and equal treatment. As a result, the need to complement processes of democratic will formation with work structures that support them is recognized in only one respect, namely in the belief that the conditions for the equality of all citizens must also be guaranteed in the labour market. For the reasons I have given, our two authors cannot entertain the possibility that further, much broader conditions might be required on the grounds that given working conditions reduce, or even entirely undermine, opportunities for democratic participation.[15] Entertaining this possibility means positing some thresholds below which a work activity cannot be said to allow for participation in processes of political will formation in a normatively satisfactory way. In what follows, I want at least to sketch the dimensions with regard to which such thresholds must be established. We must keep in mind, however, that it is almost impossible to determine precisely where the thresholds should lie in each case, because the actual thresholds will depend to a large degree on specific cultural and economic conditions, and it is thus almost impossible to make any generally applicable statements about them. For each dimension, the boundary between sufficient and insufficient resources and abilities can be precisely determined only on the basis of a detailed understanding of the history of the relevant political community. When in what follows I shall identify five dimensions of a person's position in the social division of labour that to a large extent determine that person's opportunities for participating in processes of public will formation, these dimensions should therefore be understood as constituting a heuristic framework that still needs to be filled in with political detail. This framework seeks to identify the aspects of work that may undermine democratic participation.[16] The five dimensions are economic, temporal, psychological, social and intellectual in nature, and I shall present them in turn. In each case, the dimension relates to conditions or resources of which a sufficient minimum enjoyed by all is far more important, for the purposes of political participation, than a person's enjoyment of these resources relative to others'. In that sense, the following list also clarifies what it means to talk of 'fair' or sufficiently good labour relations in the context of a democratic community. In a 'fair' social division of labour, all the activities that make up the division of labour satisfy the condition of not hindering – with regard to any of the five dimensions – the exercise of the democratic rights of those who carry out these activities.

1. The first and foremost condition for participating in public political debates is economic independence. Having no control over the decisions of the people to whom one owes one's livelihood means that one will, whether voluntarily or instinctively, behave in such a way as to ensure that the steady stream of income will not cease. This can be so preoccupying that there is little opportunity to reflect on the political aims one supports without at the same time taking into account the expectations of third parties and without worrying about one's own well-being. Such dependence does not permit free and autonomous participation

in processes of public will formation. The situation lacks the existential trust in a secure future that is necessary for one to be able to reflect on alternative ways of organizing one's political community. As long as most people's livelihoods are tied to gainful employment, a secure, adequately remunerated job is therefore a fundamental condition for participation in the processes of democratic will formation. Guaranteed employment, a decent minimum wage and adequate unemployment benefits are minimum requirements if we are to free individuals from anxieties about the security of their income.[17] But they alone do not suffice. If securing your livelihood means accepting any working conditions, even if you would never freely endorse them, you are subject to arbitrary decisions beyond your control, and potentially unable to articulate your personal interests in the context of political will formation. In this case, too, your decisions remain dependent on powerful others in a way that makes it impossible to participate as freely and autonomously in the processes of democratic will formation as the idea of the democratic legitimization of political authority demands. Real economic independence also requires that workers have some power to negotiate working conditions. If this requirement is not fulfilled, workers will be forced in times of economic need to accept labour relations that are completely determined by others and disadvantageous to the workers. As a consequence, they will lack a belief in the public significance of their own will. They will perceive themselves as second-class citizens among the allegedly equal members of the body politic, for they will feel that their own views about their role in social cooperation do not count. The common phrase, made popular by Hans Fallada, about the impotence of the 'little man in the street' – and, we should add, the 'little woman' – 'who can be treated whatever way one likes' reflects how many dependent employees regard their own position.[18] This group of people has little or no say in deciding what work and what working conditions are considered acceptable. These people thus cannot develop the mindset necessary for participation in political practices, for they do not think that their intentions or interests have any influence on the political public sphere.[19] A further necessary condition for economic independence is therefore that workers must have individual or collective bargaining power that is sufficient for them to negotiate working conditions in a fair and participatory way. Even a workplace that was perfectly safe and secured by the state's welfare policies would remain a dull and unfulfilling place to work without the guarantee of such participation, because the workers would still be exposed to the whims of those who can determine the conditions of work at will.

2. Any degree of participation in the processes of democratic will formation also always presupposes a certain amount of free time outside of work. Becoming a participant in democratic will formation involves a few time-consuming activities.[20] One needs to collect information on particular topics in order to develop reasoned opinions on them; there has to be a discursive processing of this information in dialogue with others; and there has to be a public expression of the position reached, usually in the form of an oral contribution at some meeting (not necessarily a workers' meeting), participation in a political demonstration or active membership in a political association.[21] How much time someone has at their disposal for these activities obviously depends on how much time is taken up by their work and private life. More time being taken up by work means less time for the various activities that constitute the democratic public sphere. However, the time dedicated to work each day is not straightforwardly quantifiable. Depending on how varied, challenging and autonomous the work is, an eight-hour work day can seem much longer to one person than another.[22] As a rule of thumb, we could say that the same amount of time feels 'longer', and is therefore more exhausting, to the extent that more time is required to restore the labour power exerted. According to this formula, someone who, after eight hours of work, needs four hours to restore their labour power such that the same activity can be performed again works 'longer' than someone who, after eight hours of work, needs only two. This is perhaps a slightly odd formula for something that, in the end, cannot be calculated with precision, but it is meant only to convey a fact that is difficult to illustrate: given a particular length of working hours, some kinds of work deprive the workers of more free time than other kinds of work. The obvious implication is that fast-paced, mentally tiring, monotonous and non-autonomous work deprives workers of more energy, and therefore leaves them with less energy for activities in the democratic public sphere. If the remaining energy falls below a certain threshold – which would probably be difficult to quantify – no time remains for

engaging in such activities. What are required, therefore, are working time limits that are sensitive to how tedious and exhausting the work-related activities are, and that in this way ensure that a sufficient amount of time is left for private life and political activities.

3. In addition to economic independence and time, participation in the democratic public sphere also requires a certain amount of self-respect and self-esteem. Without a firm belief that one's political statements are worthy of being publicly heard, citizens lack the courage to participate in democratic discussion. Taking a public stance on some topic of political significance presupposes a conviction that the expression of one's opinion will be seen by other participants as a meaningful and useful contribution to the discussion. However, the sense that one will be taken to be an accepted and recognized discussion partner does not spontaneously arise in a democratic meeting, for to step onto the political stage one must already have sufficient trust in the public worth of one's statements. This epistemic self-confidence has a long prehistory, whose course is determined in no small part by the position someone has in the network of the social division of labour. Someone who receives no social recognition in the workplace, or who is not appreciated as someone with certain socially valuable skills, will not possess the self-esteem that is required to express an opinion in political debate without distress and epistemic self-doubt.[23] Unfortunately, the close connection between position in the social division of labour and self-esteem has been obscured rather than highlighted by John Rawls's emphasis, in itself commendable, on the moral importance of 'self-respect'.[24] Apart from Rousseau and Hegel,[25] no one has pointed out as consistently as Rawls, in his theory of justice, that the feeling of individual worth is a 'primary good' insofar as, without it, citizens will experience their own efforts as meaningless.[26] But when he comes to talk about the necessary social 'conditions' for such trust in one's own abilities, he limits himself to the claim that the necessary public affirmation and recognition of one's activities can be secured through membership in small groups of like-minded people.[27] But this claim is only plausible in the case of the successful pursuit of a personal life plan within a self-chosen reference group. As soon as someone steps onto the public stage to present their beliefs as part of the democratic process, the feeling of self-worth that

they derive from membership in a small group is no longer enough. Potentially, the eyes of the entire political community are fixed on them, so for shame and inhibition to be overcome they require a general social recognition of their abilities and achievements, a recognition that is no longer tied to small groups and that regulates how society values the contributions and efforts of individuals. Its basis is the social division of labour as a system of evaluation. This system determines how the activities that are necessary for social and material reproduction are tailored and distributed, but it also assigns to each activity a 'productive' value for society by way of social typification. This system is the reason why, for instance, housework and childcare – work that is still mostly done by women – enjoys less importance in the social imaginary than activities in businesses and public administrations.[28] The latter activities are, in turn, also hierarchically evaluated according to criteria such as the intellectual effort involved, length of training required or (alleged) economic yield produced.[29] It is fairly obvious that it will be difficult to develop a strong sense of self-esteem if one's work is assigned a low position in this evaluative hierarchy, which operates at a subliminal level. That cannot fail to have negative consequences for one's ability to assert one's own convictions in the democratic public sphere without feelings of distress.

4. So far we have identified economic independence, free time and a feeling of self-esteem based on public recognition of one's work as requirements for participation in the processes of political will formation. We can now add that one must also have some experience of the practices of democratic interaction. I have already mentioned that employees must be able to negotiate their labour contracts so that the design of these contracts is not left to those with greater power – the entrepreneurs. But the practices of democratic interaction go beyond negotiation. Participation in negotiation usually takes the form of membership in an organization that represents the collective interests of employees, and this participation may well create a basic trust that one will not be left helplessly exposed to whatever working conditions are decided by management. But it contributes little to the acquisition of the habits of collective democratic action. Only if employees experience, in their day-to-day work, that their intentions have some influence over decisions about the how and what of their activities will they come to

trust democratic processes and find them meaningful. If employees do not learn that their aims and ideas about their work activities are relevant to the decisions taken within their organization, they will not trust in the efficacy of their convictions in the context of the processes of political will formation. The spirit of cooperation that characterizes democratic deliberation therefore needs to be fostered in the workplace. It is not realistic to expect citizens to engage in dialogue and display an attitude of mutual respect in a political context if, in the workplace, they merely take orders. In the course of an individual life, social cooperation can be learned in various ways: in the family and at school,[30] in sports clubs or in a group of politically like-minded people. But whatever one learns in such contexts is usually put to the test once one enters the workplace. Here, it is often competitiveness, obedience and submissiveness that are expected – even rewarded. If in addition the work is particularly solitary, the result is a lifeworld that is almost the exact opposite of the lifeworld of democratic cooperation: the normatively desired communicative attitudes and habits of the latter are sometimes actively undermined in the former. The less one's voice counts in the workplace, the more limited one's participation in decisions about work processes and the weaker one's attachment to a cooperative group, the less familiarity one will have with procedures of common will formation. If employees do piece work for a distribution company whose processes are ruled by algorithms, if they are constantly surveilled, work entirely on their own and have no right to participation, they will not suddenly be able to see other citizens as partners in a dialogue about political issues, as individuals with whom debate is worthwhile and agreement possible. Declining interest in political procedures and practices – the much-discussed 'disenchantment with politics' – is at least in part the result of a world of work characterized by increasing precarity and isolation, as well as a persistent culture of subordination.

5. Finally, another factor that influences the ability to participate in democratic processes is the volume and mental strain of work. This topic was a major concern of those social philosophy-inclined thinkers who developed the classic accounts of the division of labour, and it continued to be discussed in certain schools of thought even later. We have seen that, at the beginning of the industrial age, Smith, Hegel and Durkheim were

already speculating about a connection between the increasing mechanization of work and decreasing social participation. As Hegel succinctly put it, the increasing *specialization* [*Vereinzelung*] and limitation of particular work' leads to a worrying 'inability to feel and enjoy the wider freedoms, and particularly the spiritual advantages, of civil society'.[31] More recently, a number of psychological and sociological studies have provided clear evidence that this idea was not far-fetched. The more monotonous, intellectually unchallenging, and repetitive the work, the more limited the ability of the workers to take the initiative and change their circumstances and social environment.[32] This is not to say, of course, that employees doing monotonous and simple work are less intelligent or knowledgeable than those doing more complex work. The point is just that the content and volume of their work means that they must endure a significant reduction in autonomous creativity, motivation to demonstrate their inventiveness, and the ability to experience their own efficacy. In other words, after a certain amount of time, the rhythms of rapid, monotonous and unstimulating work begin to mould the intellectual habitus – and the general relation to the social environment as well.

Such rigidity in thought and action significantly impairs one's ability to participate in the practices of political will formation. As Smith, Hegel and Durkheim suspected, the result is that workers will find it hard to keep up with the rest of the population when it comes to collecting and processing politically relevant information. Moreover, they will lack the motivation to take up positions in the democratic public sphere. This lack of flexibility – the inability to play an active role in political life – is the internalized effect, turned second nature, of a form of work that has been reduced to a few basic operations in the interest of cutting costs and thus increasing profits.[33] The principle that all members of a society should, if possible, have an opportunity to participate in the processes of democratic will formation therefore also demands interventions in the form and division of work activities. If these activities are structured in such a way that the work is overly monotonous, repetitive and unstimulating, the workers will find it much harder to make use of their right to actively participate in deliberations in the democratic public sphere.

I have presented the five dimensions of employment under conditions of the social division of labour that, I believe, have a strong influence on people's ability to participate in the processes of democratic will formation. Again, I stress that these dimensions are intended primarily to serve as a heuristic that facilitates the setting of concrete political agendas. Their main purpose is to ensure that, when we come to decisions about which empirical corrections to the existing situation are necessary, our attention remains firmly fixed on the unquestionably close connection between the organization of social labour and the conditions for democratic participation. Each citizen's opportunities and abilities to participate in the processes of opinion and will formation depend crucially on whether and how each citizen is involved in the process of social reproduction under conditions of the division of labour. We can therefore say that there is a relationship of mutual dependency between a functioning democracy and a fair organization of the division of labour. Democracy relies on well-organized and sufficiently cooperative labour relations, and the quality of labour relations relies on citizens' ability to democratically influence the arrangement of the relations of production. This is the reason why the democratic state under the rule of law not only has a duty to create the framework conditions for a functioning political public sphere, but must also ensure sufficiently good and fair labour relations – that is, labour relations that do not fall below the minimum requirements for each of the five dimensions as set out above. Democratic theories that have no place for the mutually conditioning relationship between fair work and a functioning democracy are just as incomplete as sociological analyses of labour relations that do not recognize that their normative vantage point should be the improvement of the conditions for democratic participation. Practitioners of both disciplines should constantly remind themselves that most of the individuals who make up the democratic sovereign are in gainful employment, and are therefore subject to labour relations that determine their ability actively to participate in the processes of political opinion and will formation. If they took this on board, and thus adopted the same normative perspective, they would also see that they would benefit from cooperating with each other, rather than ignoring each other. To paraphrase Kant, a democratic theory without the intuitions of the sociology of labour is empty; a sociology of labour without the concepts of democratic theory is blind.

I have not yet explained in sufficient detail what is meant here by 'social labour' and 'social division of labour'. My discussion of the three competing ideals – estrangement-free, liberated and democracy-promoting – should have made it clear enough that by 'social labour' I do not mean those activities that are pursued for private reasons. How such voluntary activities – often called 'hobbies' – are organized and performed is entirely up to those who pursue them, and they are therefore irrelevant to questions of social morality. It would also be wrong, however, to assume that activities belong to the sphere of social labour only if they can be exploited for profit and only if the individuals performing them are recruited from the labour market. For in that case, all activities that are currently not remunerated but are nevertheless of vital importance – from housework to voluntary social services – would fall out of the picture. My concept of social labour must therefore be narrow enough to exclude purely private activities such as hobbies but broad enough to include work activities that do not form part of the market, are unpaid, and yet are indispensable.[34] The concept of the 'social division of labour' is similarly complex. The definitions in the classic theories of Smith, Marx and the period up to Durkheim typically include activities that serve the purpose of social value creation in some manner. Accordingly, when it comes to questions of how labour was distributed in the past and how it should be distributed in future, only activities whose economic value can easily be calculated are considered. If we want to expand the concept of labour to include unpaid but indispensable activities, whether carried out in private households or in the public realm, we also need to modify the concept of the social division of labour accordingly. That means that the activities to be socially distributed would include not just work that contributes to so-called value creation but all activities that are in some way 'necessary for social reproduction', regardless of the question of remuneration. In the following excursus, I will concentrate exclusively on the question of how we should understand 'social labour' in an analysis that has a normative interest in the democratization of labour relations. Part II, in which I sketch the historical development of labour relations, is followed by a second excursus, which addresses the concept of the social division of labour and asks how our understanding of this concept needs to change to do justice to the normative aim of my analysis.

Excursus I: On the Concept of Social Labour

So often we overlook the work and the significance of those who are not in professional jobs, (Yeah) of those who are not in the so-called big jobs. But let me say to you tonight, that whenever you are engaged in work that serves humanity and is for the building of humanity, it has dignity, and it has worth. (Applause). One day our society must come to see this. One day our society will come to respect the sanitation worker if it is to survive, for the person who picks up our garbage, in the final analysis, is as significant as the physician, for if he doesn't do his job, diseases are rampant. (Applause) All labor (All labor) has dignity. (Yes!)

Martin Luther King, Jr.[1]

As I have mentioned, defining the concept of 'work' is not easy, because today the term is used to describe a variety of activities connected with both private life and employment. We speak of the 'hard work', that is, emotional effort, that couples dedicate to maintaining their relationship, or that people exert psychologically when trying to save face and not lose self-control in difficult situations. Likewise, we call it 'work' when someone is busy cooking food on the barbecue or getting the garden ready for winter. Given all the activities that we now describe as 'work', one could be forgiven for thinking that our lives are a matter of constant physical and mental exertion. Even hiking in the mountains or going to a nightclub are considered work on the body or the soul, as if we wanted to avoid the impression that we simply do some things for fun, relaxation and recreation. This sort of conceptual inflation is not at all useful in the context of a normative theory concerned with a reorganization of social labour that would benefit democracy. In this excursus, I shall therefore try to determine as precisely as possible what 'work' means in the context of my argument, because without this conceptual clarification it would be difficult to see which social operations and activities we need to consider when asking how the world of work could be adapted to the normative requirements of democratic participation.[2]

Early on in the development of modern social theory, the concept of 'labour' was surprisingly narrow. John Locke's *Two Treatises of Government*, for example, justifies the claim to private property by saying that mixing one's labour with a natural object creates additional value, which is the source of one's right to privately own the manufactured product.[3] This value theory of labour, which Marx would adopt 200 years later, is based on a notion of 'labour' that tacitly assumes that work is exclusively a matter of producing or transforming an object. Any activity that does not follow this pattern, that is, that does not have a formed object as its end product, would therefore not fall under this definition. Any kind of service – for instance caring for someone or delivering something – would not count as 'labour' in the proper sense. The inadequacy of Locke's narrow definition becomes evident when we consider the employment relations that prevailed in his era. In seventeenth-century England, most labourers were still working in agriculture and the crafts, and so earned their living through activities to which Locke's definition would have applied. But there were also large parts of the population, both men and women, who did not manufacture products but were servants of some description: cooks, messengers, coachmen, wet nurses, housemaids or gardeners. Moreover, even in agriculture much of the activity was not immediately related to production – goods had to be delivered and supplied; cattle had to be looked after. The implication of Locke's concept of labour is therefore astounding: all these activities, even though they are as important to economic life as the operations of production, are not 'labour'.[4] When the notion of property depends necessarily on transformational activities, the concept of labour is tied to the production of an object, and this tacitly excludes from the definition all those activities that make the transformation possible in the first place. With the Lockean concept, service personnel were cast into the shadows, and as we shall see it took a very long time before some light was thrown on those darkened rooms in which the cooks, cleaners and servants laboured away.

In Adam Smith's economic magnum opus, he picks up on the Lockean idea, although not without expressing some serious misgivings, and not without getting caught up in internal contradictions. Smith initially finds it hard to pin down a meaningful concept of 'labour', because he is operating with two different definitions of the usefulness of social labour. According to one, everything that contributes in some way to the satisfaction of the subjective desire for a pleasant life counts as labour. According to the other, only that which makes a 'productive' contribution to the increase in wealth counts as labour.[5] On the first definition, the innumerable service activities that existed in Smith's time would count as 'labour' in the proper sense, for they provide a 'utility' for the population. On the second, by contrast, only those activities that increase the economic value of an object by forming it, and thus adding something to it, would count. Smith ultimately opts for the second definition:

> The labour of some of the most respectable orders in society is, like that of menial servants, unproductive of any value, and does not fix or realize itself in any permanent subject, or vendible commodity, which endures after that labour is past, and for which an equal quantity of labour could afterwards be procured.[6]

In this passage, Smith apparently forgets his earlier remarks about 'productive' labour being that which provides 'utility' for society. Like Locke before him, he is inclined to consider as genuine labour only those activities that form an object into a 'commodity' to be sold on the market. Unlike Locke, however, he at least acknowledges the fact that a good deal of employment relations involve services, whether rendered in private households or in the public realm. By the time Smith was writing, it was no longer possible to overlook the fact that, just as the wealth of the aristocratic and bourgeois classes was growing, so too was the army of servants, in kitchens, gardens, dressing rooms and stables – so much so that, by the beginning of the nineteenth century, such workers represented almost half of all employed individuals in Europe. Although Smith is not blind to the existence of these 'non-productive' workers, he massively devalues their labour. From his perspective, they are of only secondary importance for social wealth, for instead of producing something, they merely render – more or less useful – services.

Given the enormous growth of the service sector during the nineteenth century – by around 1900, domestic servants represented the largest category of labourers in the English workforce[7] – one would expect the dominant concept of labour to have adapted accordingly. In fact, what happened was almost the opposite. Especially in German social philosophy, the development of the concept of labour after Smith took little note of the expansion of services. Both Hegel and Marx took their cue from Locke, and gave his ideas an anthropological twist that deepened the link between labour and manufacturing even further. Locke's definition of labour is one of the essential elements of Hegel's *Phenomenology of Spirit*, for instance in Hegel's claim that labour has a formative influence on consciousness because, through labour, a subject externalizes its own powers and skills in an object and thus 'comes round to itself'.[8] Hegel's idea of formation through 'objectification' establishes a fundamental connection between labour and the process of production or fabrication of an object, and this means that activities that do not realize themselves in the form of an object must appear empty, lacking consciousness. When Hegel later described the different estates of modern society, the work of the farmer was therefore branded merely passive and unreflective; the farmer simply 'accepts what he receives'.[9] And even though, as we know, Hegel had servants himself, he apparently did not see fit even to mention such household services.[10] Proper 'work', and the 'honour' and 'independence' that come with it, begin only with the productive activities of the crafts and industrial production.

A few decades after Hegel's death – thus during Marx's lifetime – the expansion of trade and banking created large numbers of new service workers in such occupations as accounting, sales and transport. None of these workers was manufacturing anything – they could not recognize themselves in an object that they produced – and yet Marx's 1844 *Economic and Philosophical Manuscripts* follows Hegel in basing the concept of labour exclusively on the production of objects.[11] What distinguishes human species-being from animals, Marx says, is that man 'reproduces himself not only intellectually, in his consciousness, but actively and actually, and he can therefore contemplate himself in a world he himself has created'.[12] Marx adopts from Hegel the idea that proper labour is objectification; unlike Hegel, of course, he argues that under capitalist conditions of commodity production a reflection of the human being's 'essential powers' in the fabricated object is impossible – that labour under capitalism is thus 'alienated' labour. As Marx develops his political-economic approach, however, he increasingly emphasizes that industrial labour, though alienated, is also the source of surplus value, and is thus productive. Like Adam Smith before him, he considers all service activities to be strictly external to the activities he calls 'productive', although he crucially differs from Smith in highlighting the fact that the surplus value created by productive activities is retained by the private capitalist. Marx, too, ignores the fact that services are essential to the production of commodities. To maintain labour power, meals must be cooked; to manufacture products, raw materials must be transported. Trade margins must be calculated, and public institutions must be administered. In short, Marx ignores the infrastructure that must be seen as a necessary part of the production process.

The effect of Locke's and Marx's arguments was that almost all services – with the possible exception of the civil service – came to be seen as doubly deficient. First, services were not labour in the proper sense, because they were not productive, and second they did not contribute to the generation of wealth, because they did not produce any sellable commodities. So influential was this narrow conception of labour that even the dependence of the emerging industrial capitalism on the extraction, processing and transporting of raw materials by slaves, far away from the actual sites of commodity production, was ignored.[13] This eclipse of certain forms of labour and their material content had a paradoxical effect on the social imagination.[14] Throughout the nineteenth century, industrial labourers made up only a fraction of the workforce, but industrial labour occupied such a central place in the cultural imagination that the population at large subscribed to the myth that the production of goods was the dominant activity. Even in places where industrialization had barely begun, the self-image of an 'industrial society' took hold. There was a belief in the progressive, even revolutionary force of the proletariat, even though the workers' movement was initially advanced predominantly by craftsmen who took pride in their estate.[15] The lower social classes forgot that they owed what few daily comforts they enjoyed mostly to agricultural labour, and the upper classes forgot that their lives of luxury and leisure depended mostly on domestic servants and various institutions of business and public administration. That hardly any of the significant thinkers of the period were interested in the specific nature and quality of service occupations is a side effect of the strange perceptual inversions caused by the dominant concept of labour.[16]

Of course, there is hardly a bourgeois novel in the literary realist genre without dozens of cooks, servants, governesses, coachmen and maids silently working away in the background. Émile Zola's portrait of the world of work in nineteenth-century France is a literary monument to saleswomen in department stores and small retailers.[17] But in social philosophy and the budding social sciences, no one had the faintest interest in analysing services in detail.[18] No one sought to distinguish conceptually between personal services and administrative services – namely that the former require one to take the perspective of another person and thus develop communicative skills, and the latter require one to control activities through symbols and tables. Nothing was written about the fact that service occupations do not follow the rhythm of the machine, and therefore sometimes offer more opportunities for autonomous control over one's labour. Around 1900, all these peculiarities had gone unnoticed, for they fell victim to the sole focus on industrial labour, which, against all empirical evidence, was taken to be the standard form of labour done by the bulk of workers.

It would still be decades before services stepped out of the long shadow cast by the dominant concept of labour. The first impulse in this direction did not come from the employees themselves, for they were too large and heterogeneous a group to have shared concerns,[19] but from sociology, although even here attention was paid initially to a relatively small segment of the enormous service sector. In the early twentieth century, the sociology of Max Weber led to the realization that the preceding decades had been a period not just of increasing industrialization but also, and perhaps even more significantly, of progressive bureaucratization.[20] With this the tide turned, and for the first time a wider public became aware that economic activity and social infrastructure depended on an enormous amount of labour in public administrations, private businesses, and banks and insurance companies. These administrative services were not seen in an especially positive light. Weber had already described them as not particularly creative, strangely soulless, and obsessed with rules. But even this uncharitable depiction was enough to finally correct the received wisdom that society's social reproduction and wealth were owed solely to industrial labour. Under the heading 'bureaucracy' or 'bureaucratic administration', services were now seen as a form of labour that was essential to social reproduction. From then on, they were understood in terms of the work typical of the 'employee' or civil servant. The reasons for the choice of the term 'employee' were far from clear even at the time; those who did not work for the state were in fact 'independent' wage labourers who offered their services for contractually agreed remuneration.[21] To the present day, the official – and not particularly plausible – explanation is that the term highlights the difference between their work and the 'real' work of manual labourers.

Further, this somewhat ambivalent acknowledgement of service work did not extend as far as the personal services performed in households or work in health and social care, education or the hospitality sector. At the beginning of the twentieth century, large and growing numbers of employees were working in these sectors, and there was still no awareness of how large a proportion of all labour was made up of such low-paid occupations, which were, and still are, absolutely indispensable for social reproduction. The sociological analysis of the growing importance of bureaucracy and administration, though selective and ambivalent towards its object of study, did succeed in shining a light on forms of service work that had previously been in the shadows. Other kinds of service work, however – those that consist in supporting, educating and caring for other people – carried on below the threshold of public perception. This is perhaps why labour continued to be understood as an activity that involves a subject and an object, whether that object be one that is produced or a typewriter or calculator to be deployed in the course of various bureaucratic or administrative tasks. People-related services and the specific skills they require remained unacknowledged.

This marginalization concerned in large part occupations predominantly carried out by women. Of course, at the beginning of the twentieth century, not all female workers were employed in these areas – widespread deprivation meant that they continued to be active in many sectors of the economy – but it was for the most part women who were employed in the homes of the rich bourgeoisie to cook, clean, shop and look after children.[22] Because the wages of female domestic servants, secretaries or saleswomen were not enough to support a family, a viciously circular logic developed in the political economy of the nineteenth century. According to this logic, 'low wages both caused and demonstrated the "fact" that women were less productive than men': the assumption of their lower productivity justified the low wages, and the low wages indicated that they did not work as hard as men.[23] The labour of women working as domestic servants, in department stores or in restaurants was thus seen as of little economic importance, and it remained unexplored and scarcely noticed by the public. The belittling or authoritarian treatment, the daily sexual harassment and victimization that these spheres of work involved – these may have found their way into pulp novels, but they were not present in the educational or cultural media of the times, let alone the social sciences. The quiet contempt for occupations that did not manufacture objects of economic value but procured, maintained, administered or transported already existing objects had begun with Locke and Smith, had been deepened by Hegel and Marx, and still was deeply influential in the first half of the twentieth century. When, a hundred years after Marx, Hannah Arendt analysed the growing dominance of labour over communicative action in the public sphere, she distinguished between 'labour' that resembles the crafts and machine-based 'production', but she did not even mention services – a conceptual lapse that has so far generated little comment.[24]

The stigma attached to supposedly superfluous and marginal person-related services gradually began to weaken, but this was the result of historical change rather than the efforts of those employed in the sector. For the most part, the young men and women working in healthcare, in private households and in the hospitality sector were the descendants of destitute small farmers, day labourers and craftsmen, and they were humbly resigned to their fate. Thankful for any gainful employment they could find, they were not in a position to seek public recognition for the work they did. It was the Great War and its socioeconomic consequences that put service work – or at least some forms of it – centre stage and ensured that the public came to realize the indispensable nature of such work. Nurses cared for thousands upon thousands of wounded soldiers, showing even the most obdurate members of the ruling classes that these employees played an important role in preventing the death, or at least alleviating the misery, of many of the victims of the war. Where before the services of nursing and care personnel had scarcely been regarded as socially necessary work, as long as the war continued their indispensability could not be overlooked. This increased interest did not last long, however, and it returned only when historical circumstances again made the need for nurses and care workers obvious. It is only relatively recently, following growing concerns about the increasingly ageing populations of Western societies, that we seem to have reached a point at which the social importance of the caring professions can no longer be denied. Even now, however, this acknowledgement is yet to translate into better pay or more public recognition for those working in this area, who mostly come from the poorest parts of the world.

Shortly after the Great War, the work of domestic servants, too, would receive more attention, though for a very different reason. Their work became more visible when the loss of wealth suffered by formerly affluent households across the Western world led to a rapid and dramatic reduction in the number of domestic employees. Suddenly, there was on average just one person employed in each affluent household, and the number of unemployed servants and maids grew accordingly. An awareness of the many household tasks, from cooking and dressing to serving dinner, cleaning and looking after the children, which in the large city apartments and palaces of the upper classes had been done by servants, grew rapidly – as if previously it had been impossible to notice them.[25] Hitherto their importance had escaped public perception – almost inexplicably, since, as mentioned above, in the first decade of the twentieth century domestic servants were still by far the largest group of employees in Great Britain, the motherland of capitalism.[26] It remains a remarkable fact that, to the present day, so little is known about the daily lives and working conditions of this significant group of workers.

The rapid decline in the number of domestic servants during the 1920s marked the beginning of a very slow process that would eventually bring housework into public view. Before it had not been acknowledged, and certainly not as socially necessary work. But now, without domestic servants to help them, women from the affluent social classes were called upon to do the housework – and to do so 'voluntarily'. Gone were the half-dozen 'ministering spirits' (Heidi Müller) who had previously been at their disposal. In the nineteenth century and earlier, women in the lower classes, who would often have also been in some form of employment, would commonly do their own housework, perhaps drawing on the help of relatives and neighbours. Now, the female members of the bourgeois classes had to do the same. Their initial willingness to accept their new role had a lot to do, of course, with internalized ideas about typical female skills and preferences, ideas that reached back into the male-dominated culture of the eighteenth century, which spawned an ideology according to which men's and women's preferences perfectly complemented each other: women's natural inclination was to do whatever had to be done in the household, and men's was to enter the world of public life and gainful employment. As Hegel succinctly put it: '*Estate* of women, – is *housewife*'.[27] From that point on, with the exception of a few early feminists and socialists, the notion that women possess a natural disposition towards housework, born out of caring and loving sentiments, was broadly shared and firmly anchored in social consciousness. The integration of bourgeois women in the intra-familial division of labour did not put pressure on this ideology, but it did challenge its economic foundations and effects. In the 1920s, representatives of the bourgeois women's movement began to demand a social and economic revaluation of housework: men's salaries and wages had to contain a share that accounted for women's household work, the argument ran, because the latter created the necessary conditions for the men's work outside the home.[28] These demands did not get much of a hearing in parliaments or among politically influential circles, but the question of economic remuneration for 'private' household work had nevertheless been put on the agenda. It would take over fifty years before the topic came to more widespread attention in the political public sphere, thus finally sparking a fundamental transformation in the concept of socially necessary labour.

The narrow concept of labour, as denoting simply the production of objects, was not the only reason for the persistent inability to perceive women's necessary, but unpaid, housework as labour. As we have seen, the influence of this narrow concept meant that a capitalism that imagined itself as 'industrial' failed to notice services of whatever kind, let alone judge them in positive terms. But in the case of housework there was another reason, at least as significant, for the total blindness to the efforts of women. This second reason is also connected with an implicit assumption of the classic concept of labour, one that has gone more or less unmentioned in the literature or wider public discourse: in theories of political economy, something counts as socially necessary labour only if there is a quantifiable market demand for it. Despite the clear demand for various services in the nineteenth century, service work did not benefit from this assumption initially, because it had been denigrated as 'non-productive activity', but later it was able to improve its image thanks to this conceptual link between social need and market demand. As a result, the contempt for the serving, cleaning and caring occupations was somewhat tempered. The unpaid work of housewives, however, again found itself excluded from this improvement. Running errands, cooking, cleaning and raising children were still overshadowed by the traditional concept of labour, but now not so much because they did not seem to produce anything of economic value, but because there was no obvious economic demand for them – they were done 'voluntarily'.

In the 1970s, the feminist campaign for the remuneration of housework questioned this link between proper labour and market demand. Its primary aim was not to achieve wages for housework but to expose the scandal of how that work was distributed between men and women, but it nevertheless succeeded in subjecting the second assumption of the traditional view of labour, the necessary link to market demand, to scrutiny. Was market demand really the sole criterion of socially necessary labour, or was such a one-sided approach misguided? This question was the beginning of the end for the concept of labour that had dominated the capitalist imagination since at least the eighteenth century.[29]

As often happens at such critical turning points, old assumptions were suddenly revealed to be obviously specious. It had only ever been possible to assert an essential connection between 'value added' and productive activities because the necessary preconditions of those productive activities, whether material or personal services, had simply been considered external factors, and thus ignored. As the artificiality of this internal–external boundary became ever clearer, the traditional distinction between productive and 'non-productive' – or merely reproductive – labour became untenable. The distinction was plainly not a representation of economic reality. Indeed, there is a case for considering all activities that are necessary for the perpetuation of a given culture 'productive', on the grounds that they are valuable or useful for the social community.[30]

Another assumption that came to be questioned was the idea that real labour involves a relationship between a human being and an object, as the narrow focus on manufacturing had suggested. The caring professions came gradually to be included in the category of socially necessary labour, which it was now accepted could take the form of activities that promote the individual well-being and needs of others. In such activities, the aim of the labour differs fundamentally from the way it is construed under the classic concept of labour. The aim is not to mould an object so that it becomes a useful commodity or an object of daily use. Rather, it aims first to establish the needs of the person cared for by taking their perspective in communication, and only then to determine the means of satisfying them. Neither the old distinction between manual and intellectual labour nor the more recent distinction between material and immaterial labour does justice to the specificities of person-related services, in which communication – taking the perspective of the one who needs care or help – precedes instrumental reasoning about the appropriate means to be employed.[31] If we also add administrative services as a separate category, which I think we should, then what I call socially necessary labour can be divided into three occupational areas: processing natural or man-made objects for the purpose of creating useful goods; caring for others through nursing, advice or education; and manipulating symbols in making calculations, carrying out analyses and handling data in the context of administering social and economic processes.[32] This tripartite classification does away with the traditional understanding of labour as a relationship between humans and nature. It understands a socially necessary activity as any task that is of value to society in general, whether the activity is object-related, symbolic or communicative.

The feminist critique of unpaid housework forced another paradigm shift in our understanding of labour. Because the critique demonstrated that countless household tasks are indispensable yet unpaid, it challenged economists' assumption that the volume of socially necessary labour is determined exclusively by market demand. Severing the link between socially necessary labour and market demand makes even more glaring the fact that there are myriad everyday tasks that are essential for the reproduction of social life and yet are carried out for free: the parent cooking for the family, the grandparents looking after the grandchildren, the individual doing voluntary work in social services or education, and much more besides.[33]

These three modifications – abandoning (a) the distinction between productive and unproductive activities, (b) the connection between the concept of 'genuine' labour and processes of creating or producing useful objects, and (c) the market's role as the sole criterion of socially necessary labour – make the concept of labour much more inclusive. Labour, socially necessary activity, is any regularly performed task that helps to maintain generally desired elements of a society's form of life. But this conceptual liberalization comes at a cost, for it makes it much more difficult – perhaps even impossible – to distinguish between unpaid labour and activities that are undertaken for purely private reasons. It is hard to decide whether, say, collecting vinyl records or making music with friends represents a value to the social community that is important enough to be considered a form of labour. Thus, an overly broad concept of labour risks capturing any activity undertaken purely for personal pleasure or out of subjective inclination. An overly narrow concept, by contrast, may exclude activities that, on closer examination, turn out to be indispensable for the reproduction of a particular form of life.[34] In what remains of this excursus I will therefore attempt to find an appropriate middle ground between these two extremes. Relying on the notion that labour refers to activities that are necessary for the social reproduction of society is less promising than it appears, because what is necessary is not an objective fact but rather something that depends on cultural interpretations of what counts as necessary for the existence of a polity.[35]

I said above that a work activity should be considered socially necessary if it is essential to the reproduction of elements of social life that are considered valuable. If we are to move beyond the problem of the relativity of cultural interpretations, this formulation may serve as a useful starting point. Of course, the phrase 'considered valuable' must not refer to the perspective of an individual person. The aim is not to determine what this or that person considers valuable in social life. Rather, the question is what elements of a social community's form of life that community considers valuable enough to preserve through labour and effort. But we are clearly on thin ice here. For one thing, it is not obvious what constitutes a social community, nor how we are to determine its boundaries. Further, we cannot simply assume that a social community's members share a sufficient number of values to make this approach viable. Let us provisionally assume that we should speak of a social community when a large enough group of individuals share similar educational biographies and historical traditions, with the result that they broadly agree in their normative judgements on situations and issues and behave accordingly.[36] In the case of such a community, whether local, national or transnational, we may assume that its members will also usually agree on which elements of their form of life should be preserved and protected, and it follows that they will agree on the occupations and activities that are required for their preservation and protection. For this kind of social community, it is relatively easy to draw the line between socially necessary activities and merely private, personal activities. Tasks that help to preserve those elements of the lifeworld that are commonly agreed to be valuable are necessary, and they are therefore the responsibility of the political community. Activities that are commonly agreed to be merely personal pursuits, and therefore to reflect individual values, should be considered purely private matters. In his *Elements of the Philosophy of Right*, Hegel draws the same distinction between public and private activities, between work done for social purposes and work done for individual purposes, in a simpler way: in doing socially necessary work, a person must 'determine their knowledge, volition, and action in a universal way', whereas a person undertaking private activity need not follow generally accepted standards.[37]

In what follows, I deploy a concept of socially necessary labour – or, for short, social labour – that combines these two criteria, namely commonly agreed usefulness and generally accepted standards.[38] Thus, any activity that is generally considered to contribute to the well-being of society at large and has to follow general standards qualifies as social labour. It follows that cooking and looking after children in a private home, or voluntary work in the social services, are no less social labour than gainful employment in a factory or office: all these activities have purposes that the community considers valuable and all are subject to informal or legally binding standards. In the case of cooking, there are generally valid nutritional rules; looking after children must be done in a way that promotes children's well-being; and contractually agreed work implies legally binding rules for how the work must be carried out. When we instead consider activities pursued merely out of personal inclination or for personal pleasure, no such normative conditions apply.

Legal rules also apply to do-it-yourself activities – to fishing done as a hobby, or to making music with one's friends – but these activities need not have a general social purpose. Nor must people follow general standards in their execution – anything goes, so to speak. In these cases, the political community has no responsibility to ensure that the activities are compatible with commonly agreed standards or to think about appropriate ways for organizing them. Combining my reconstruction of the past 200 years of social self-enlightenment with Hegel's distinction between public and private activities, we can therefore say that social labour is characterized by the fact that in and through it one determines one's 'knowledge, volition, and action in a universal way' because one is forced to follow the conventionally or legally established rules for what constitutes a proper and adequate performance of the task at hand.

Because this definition is based on whatever a social community currently believes to be a contribution to the general well-being, one might worry that the distinction between public and private activities it implies will be biased towards the status quo. The fact that, only a few decades ago, housework was not understood as contributing to the general well-being reminds us how mutable this distinction is.[39] Indeed, the cultural distinction between necessary labour and private activity is in constant flux, for it depends on ongoing debates about what is socially valuable. An activity that is a mere pastime today may be seen as of general social importance tomorrow, such that the community has a responsibility to organize and pay for it. However, society's moral economy can only shift so far. For most activities that are today pursued out of personal inclination, it is difficult to imagine, however hard one tries, that their purposes could become generally accepted social goods. Paradoxically, the reason for this is our modern cultural pluralism. As the ethical convictions and practices within a society become more varied, it becomes harder for personal pursuits to be considered indispensable for the general well-being. The same pluralism that presumably generates an increase in new kinds of private activity at the same time prevents their ready classification as activities in the common interest. As different cultural lifestyles increasingly diverge, so the bottleneck through which such activities must pass to be recognized as socially indispensable narrows. In modern societies, the scope for radical revaluations of the social character of activities is therefore relatively small. And before it can count as social labour, an activity must first be recognized, from a general perspective, as relevant to the society's continued existence.

The concept of labour I present here does not deny the possibility of future reinterpretations, so there is no reason to suspect it of conventionalism. Changes in cultural attitudes and views must be taken into account, and new interpretations cannot be excluded categorically, but I imagine that society's increasing pluralism will continue to narrow the range of activities that might qualify as social labour. Indeed, it is likely that we will see a development in the opposite direction: that professions will lose their status as socially indispensable and return to the no man's land of private activity. This fate would be a consequence not of these professions no longer being economically viable but of their being devalued by changes in what counts as a task with an essential purpose for society.[40] The theory I propose does not always simply ratify what the majority of a social community considers to be either necessary or dispensable. In fact, it has some modest means of its own for testing such assumptions. First of all, it allows for a conceptual clarification of the general importance and specific tasks of a particular occupational area and the examination of the original functions of societal sub-systems by social theory.[41] We can therefore identify those activities that should be counted as social labour by putting into dialogue the relevant social conventions and theoretical reflection on them, and thus showing whether they in fact help to preserve a cultural form of life and serve a purpose for society. Over the past 200 years, the number of activities that are considered labour in this sense has grown significantly. Accordingly, there has been an expansion of society's responsibility to develop labour policies that will ensure decent and satisfying work conditions and, most importantly, an environment that is conducive to democracy.

PART II

Historical Interlude:
The Reality of Social Labour

In the first part of this book, I discussed three political traditions that question capitalist labour relations on moral grounds and seek fundamental changes to the way they are organized. Each of them justifies its critique in a different way – on the grounds that capitalist labour relations do not allow individuals to realize themselves, prevent them from enjoying their constitutionally guaranteed liberties, or exclude them from the democratic process. All three therefore suggest significant changes to the organization of social labour. These changes are intended to reduce the gap between normative ideal and reality by addressing the deficiency each of them identifies: that is, by making possible non-estranged and meaningful work, working conditions that are compatible with fundamental individual liberties, or conditions that are conducive to democratic participation. I then presented a comparative analysis of these three paradigms for a critique of capitalist working conditions, with the aim of determining which was politically most feasible and most likely to lead to far-reaching change. I dismissed the first paradigm on the grounds that its inherent perfectionism implied an almost limitless flexibility regarding the ability to shape socially necessary work. I criticized the second – republican – paradigm for its one-sided focus on the organizational form of social labour, at the expense of the normative aspects of the quality of the work itself. Chapter 1 thus concluded that the third paradigm was the most promising candidate in the context of this study. Chapter 2 provided a brief sketch of the intellectual roots of this paradigm and its development over the centuries, and Chapter 3 attempted a systematic justification of my thesis that democratic societies depend on, and must provide, fair and participatory labour relations that are conducive to democracy. The fundamental thought was that only individuals whose work is sufficiently complex and autonomous, and who enjoy sufficient social recognition, will have the abilities and resources that are required to participate autonomously – that is, to speak confidently and fearlessly in their own voice – in the processes of democratic will formation.

In Part II, I return from the ideal realm to the reality of social labour. The sketches that follow aim to reveal the chasm between the social reality of capitalist labour and the normative promise that the working population will be included in the processes of public will formation. Taking the concept of labour developed in the first excursus as my basis, I shall present the development of social labour under capitalism, as it were in time lapse, from Hegel's era up to the present. I begin by throwing a spotlight on Western European labour relations in the nineteenth century (Chapter 4), before highlighting some of the changes that labour relations in Europe would later undergo (Chapter 5). Finally, I identify some of the tendencies that pervade the organization and shape of social labour in the present (Chapter 6).

Given the broad concept of labour I employ, any such overview of the transformation of capitalist labour relations in Western Europe will be necessarily incomplete – or, at least, completeness is not something I am able to provide. Even had I the historian's tools at my disposal, which I do not, a truly comprehensive overview would also need to cover the international division of labour and its effects, and the developments in the various organizational forms and professional areas of work. In addition, it would need to pay attention to the way in which unpaid – and mostly unacknowledged – activities in private households have changed. In short, it would be a risky, overly ambitious project. Even the historians most knowledgeable about the detail of the history of work would probably struggle to achieve such a comprehensive overview, although some have made a promising start, whether from a global historical perspective or with a focus on specific geographical regions and epochs.[1] It is not at all my intention to embark on something similar, and so I shall do no more than paint a picture, in broad brushstrokes, of the history of capitalist labour relations up to our own time. The myriad developments in the realm of social labour over the past 200 years in Western Europe, and the numerous phenomena that have accompanied them, will be condensed into three historical miniatures, whose primary aim is to evoke for the reader the social experiences of the body politic, that is, the hard-working population. In each case, the chief focus will be on changes in occupational and employment areas, organizational and business forms, and, to some extent, labour law. Interspersed in the text are a few short vignettes – quotations from literature, research or contemporary witnesses – which aim to throw a revealing light on the harsh reality behind my more academic account.

4

A Spotlight on the Nineteenth Century

One need not contemplate nineteenth-century working conditions for long to reach the sobering conclusion that most workers did not have opportunities for effective participation in the processes of democratic will formation. Most people in employment were preoccupied with the daily struggle to secure their livelihoods, and they had to invest virtually all their energy in staying on top of almost never-ending work duties. Add to this the fact that they would also have been possessed by a deep and abiding feeling of political impotence, and it becomes clear that most workers would not have had the temporal, physical or mental resources required for participation in democratic processes. It was thus not merely a cynical attempt to support the ruling classes when the bourgeois theorists of state law and political theory, from John Locke to Immanuel Kant, wrote that the exercise of political authority required a certain level of wealth; they were simply registering a fact.[1] We today might find it a depressing fact, but the sober, if disdainful, conclusion of those political thinkers was right: those who did not have the necessary means were far too busy struggling to survive to find the time, or to have the knowledge and independence, to participate in political decision-making.[2] The briefest survey of working conditions at the beginning of the capitalist era suffices to prove this thesis – a thesis that, given the era's tendency to simultaneously glorify industriousness, comes across as rather sneering.

However, such a survey initially turns up something surprising, at least for those whose knowledge of the times comes chiefly from Hegel or Marx, whose concept of labour focused strongly on factory work. Throughout the nineteenth century, most employment was not in industry but in agriculture. And household work such as cooking, doing the laundry and raising children – work that was mostly done by women – almost certainly represented the lion's share of all socially necessary activity, even if its importance was not officially recognized.[3] As the process of industrialization gradually took hold, it was still agricultural work that dominated most people's working days. Even England, which was the focus of Hegel's and Marx's analyses – and also of course of Friedrich Engels's *The Condition of the Working Class in England*[4] – remained an economy dominated by the physical labour of peasants and agricultural labourers until the beginning of the twentieth century. Although there were major changes in the legal and socioeconomic organization of agricultural work, the work itself – the effort required and the qualitative aspects of the daily activities – remained pretty much the same.

By the mid-nineteenth century, agricultural reforms had more or less done away with the legal and socioeconomic bases of late feudalism in Europe. Feudal ties persisted here and there, but the vast majority of peasants, if they owned their land, were able to run their farms autonomously.[5] The propertyless, however, worked by far the hardest, on the now private smallholdings and larger farms. And as populations grew and property relations changed, the size of this propertyless group had even increased outside urban areas. Everywhere in Europe, there was therefore an almost inexhaustible supply of rural labourers who could be recruited for seasonal work in agriculture or cattle farming in exchange for payments in kind or meagre wages. And as the management methods of private capitalism exerted their influence, the organization and work patterns of agriculture changed too. The use of labour-saving technologies led to the improvement of older tools or their replacement with new ones. To begin with, this did not really change the substance of agricultural work: its seasonal rhythm, physical character and reliance on nature. The volume and intensity of the work depended on the size of the farm, the number of farmhands, and the efficiency of the tools and equipment, but it always remained tied to the seasonal and weather-dependent activities of cultivating the soil and raising cattle. It was still taken for granted that the whole family was involved in this work – Hegel, somewhat dismissively, said farming required not much 'reflection' but rather a deep trust in what God provides and 'faith and confidence that this goodness will continue'.[6] Despite the increasing influence of the capitalist market, there was also little change in the economic yield of agricultural labour. Smallholdings and large farms continued to be worked by the farmer and his family, the farmhands and additional day labourers. They aimed to make at least some profit above the bare subsistence level, which could be invested in tools or new buildings, or spent on minor non-essentials. The majority of the population possessed little or no land, and they therefore faced doing seasonal work as a day labourer on meagre wages; living as a hired hand on someone else's farm, doing miscellaneous tasks in return for payments in kind or cash; or doing whatever ancillary farm work was needed in return for bed and board.[7] In these conditions, one could hope only to secure the bare essentials for oneself and one's family. Life was a constant battle for survival, and work stretched 'from sunrise to sunset' – the political quarrels of the day would have been far from one's mind.[8]

The poorer the families were the less difference was there between the work roles for men and women. Among day labourers and propertyless farmers, work activities would be shared by men and women, and often also the children, depending on who happened not to be busy. The women, however, would also typically have to look after the household and what few belongings the family had.

'In the case of peasant day labourers and poor cattle farmers, the women do the same as the men. Their intellectual level will also be exactly the same. Both work in the fields, and steer the plough and cart together; sow, harvest, and sell together; or change roles at random. Keeping the house in order is only an occasional addition for the women. Male and female occupations are often like two peas in a pod. Thus, we may find the male shepherd knitting socks when watching over his sheep, while his wife steers the plough.'[9]

What the members of these social strata received was often below subsistence level, so they were forced to look for new sources of income. This desperate search for employment beyond farm and field was perhaps the most significant historical experience for peasants in the nineteenth century. There were only a few options for agricultural workers seeking alternative employment. First, there was the so-called putting-out or domestic system: workers produced commodities in their own home, and at their own expense, for a profit-seeking employer, and received a low piece rate in return. Second, there was the option of moving to richer provinces or cities and finding employment as a domestic servant among the aristocracy or well-heeled bourgeoisie. Third, they could seek an apprenticeship at one of the ubiquitous craft workshops, which still faced little competition. Fourth, they could try to find employment, whether nearby or further afield, in one of the factories that were sprouting up everywhere as the process of industrialization gradually gathered pace. Apart from household and agricultural work, most members of the working population earned their living in one of these four occupational areas.

The putting-out system was dominated by female workers, and its history stretches back to the Middle Ages. In the nineteenth century, it was the link between village and city – between the staid world of agriculture and the increasingly dynamic world of industry. In rural areas such as Silesia or Brittany, as well as in proto-industrial centres such as Lyon or Nuremberg, many destitute workers had little choice but to produce commodities in their own homes. Their tools were either lent to them or, more frequently, acquired on credit. The commodities were sold at a low piece rate to an entrepreneur, a so-called 'Verleger', who kept all the profit from their distribution and sale. Most of the goods were textiles – the raw material was therefore cotton or silk, and the tools spinning wheels or weaving looms.[10] This arrangement allowed for work to be performed between one's other obligations,[11] but the price to be paid for this 'advantage' was destitution and extreme exploitation. The number of pieces to be produced was dictated by the entrepreneur, the 'Verleger'; the piece rates were in most cases regulated by law, but were usually so low that there was enormous pressure to produce as many goods as possible in the shortest possible time. The revolt of the Silesian weavers in 1844 – portrayed, a half century later, in Gerhart Hauptmann's best-known drama, *The Weavers* – and the repeated revolts in the 1830s of the 'canuts', the silk workers of Lyon, were reactions to the working conditions of the putting-out system, which were characterized by unacceptable wages, insecurity and, as a result, abject misery.[12] In addition, cottage industry, which is today mostly seen as a form of 'proto-industrialization', increasingly came under pressure from expanding factory production.[13] It was almost impossible to compete with cheaper, mechanically produced goods, and thus cottage industry could not keep up with the economic possibilities created by techno-logical development in England, France and even Germany, where the process of industrialization lagged behind.

> 'With the introduction of machinery all this changed. Prices were now determined by the machine-made product, and the wage of the domestic industrial worker fell with these prices. However, the worker had to accept it or look for other work, and he could not do that without becoming a proletarian, that is, without giving up his little house, garden and field, whether his own or rented. Only in the rarest cases was he ready to do this. And thus the horticulture and agriculture practiced by the old rural hand weavers became the reason why the struggle of the hand loom against the mechanical loom was so protracted everywhere, and in Germany has not yet been fought to a conclusion. This struggle showed for the first time, especially in England, that the same circumstance which formerly served as a basis of comparative prosperity for the worker – the fact that he owned his means of production – had now become a hindrance and a misfortune for him. ... The possession of house and garden was now of much less advantage than the possession of complete freedom of movement.'[14]

The fate of the many young women who left the countryside to seek employment in the homes of affluent families was, in fact, not much better. During the nineteenth century, the number of servants in Europe rose continuously, and by the end of the century, the profession formed the largest sector of the workforce in some European countries – slightly ahead of agriculture, and far ahead of industrial work. Jürgen Kocka's description of the nineteenth century as the 'century of the maidservant' is therefore not far from the mark.[15] The steadily rising incomes of the middle and upper bourgeoisie meant they could delegate household chores to servants, and employing large numbers of servants became a status symbol. Servants, mostly young women, were employed in a wide range of activities, including cooking, serving, valeting, doing the laundry, sewing and cleaning. The children of the well-to-do were looked after by female servants: they were breastfed by wet nurses, and cared for and put to bed by nursemaids. There were, of course, male servants too; following the near extinction of the private tutor in the wake of the introduction of public schools, they were mainly coachmen or chauffeurs, gardeners, less frequently butlers, and very often factotums who did any odd job that needed doing.

'Get up at 6 o'clock, clean the saloon until 6:45.

From 6:45–7 light the fire and clean two pairs of boots.

From 7 to 7:15 clean clothes.

From 7:15 to 7:30 serve coffee for the sub-maid.

From 7:30 to 8:15 clean the dining room.

From 8:15 to 8:30 clean two lamps.

From 8:30 to 9 take care of the corridor and the sub-maid's beddings.

At 9 clean vegetables and put them on the hob for lunch.

From 9:30 to 10 tidy up the lady's bedroom.

From 10 to 12:30 cook lunch, do the dishes, and lay the table. Lunch must be ready promptly at 12:30. The gentleman, lady, and the sub-maid take time for their lunch until 13:30.

From 13:30 to 15:30 do the dishes and tidy up the kitchen.

From 15:30 to 16:00 the sub-maid must wash and get dressed for the second time, and on Mondays and Tuesdays do needlework for me. Wednesday afternoons the sub-maid has time off.

Thursdays, the furniture and carpets are dusted, in the afternoon the silver doorknobs and oven doors are cleaned.

Fridays, the windows are cleaned and the washtubs are soaped, in the afternoon thoroughly cleaned the kitchen.

Saturdays: cooking meals and cleaning lamps thoroughly.

Washing the clothes of the sub-maid and myself every fortnight in my kitchen takes half a day.'[16]

Domestic servants' duties were varied, as were their legal statuses, remuneration and working times. The regulations for servants that were introduced in many countries at the beginning of the nineteenth century, following the abolition of hereditary serfdom and servitude, were a first step in the liberation of servants from their masters' rule, but they were still subject to the legal and economic power of the head of house. Depending on their rank and position in the household, in the worst case this could mean up to sixteen hours of work per day[17] in return for board and lodging and no wage.[18] In the best case, a governess for example, it meant sufficient remuneration and inclusion in family activities. For female domestic servants especially, more attractive options only emerged when the expansion of capitalism and trade led to the creation of large department stores in the big cities and increasing demand for office workers in public institutions and insurance companies. The continuously expanding demand for cheap labour in these sectors created entirely new employment opportunities for young unmarried women.[19] And even though the remuneration in these new professions – the saleswoman, secretary or switchboard operator – was in most cases poor, at least the employees were no longer personally dependent on the family in whose home they worked or exposed to the whims of the head of the household.

Émile Zola's *The Ladies' Paradise* conveys well the awful working conditions in department stores.[20] Denise, the protagonist, flees poverty in rural France and comes to Paris. Her fate, working in the fictional department store 'Ladies' Paradise', is not unlike that of thousands of real young women who went to the new centres of trade to escape desti-tution. On their own and without any economic or social resources, they were forced into fierce competition with each other for these highly sought-after jobs. Success in this struggle often depended on their behaviour towards male supervisors looking for sexual favours.

Surprisingly, small craft businesses are almost absent from Zola's survey of French working conditions circa 1850, despite the fact that in 1870, the year he embarked on his literary career, about two thirds of industrial production took place in small craft shops.[21] Small craft shops catered for every daily need. Masters and apprentices worked closely together to make and repair shoes, furniture and tools. During the nineteenth century, increasing competition from industrial mass production meant that these workshops, which had been of central importance since the Middle Ages, gradually decreased in number.[22] Nevertheless, the crafts continued to offer relatively secure employment, especially for young men, in cities as well as in rural areas. The crafts also promised a collegial atmosphere, a fairly good social reputation, and varied work. The working conditions in craft shops differed significantly from those in cottage industry or in the factories that would soon spread everywhere. Although the guilds declined as economies liberalized, vestiges of the old comradeliness and pride in one's trade remained. A good was produced in close cooperation, from the first to the last step, so that one could see the result of one's activity. As long as it was difficult to create artificial light, for instance by using candles or petroleum lamps, the working day typically ended when dusk fell. Because of these advantages, craftsmen were much more likely than other workers to pass on their profession to the next generation. Their strong sense of togetherness, their professional pride (which meant they were unimpressed by industrial progress) and their greater control over their working conditions – all this created a scepticism towards the new economic conditions. This scepticism led craftsmen to play a leading role in the formation of the early workers' movement and to continue to have a formative influence on its culture right into the twentieth century – contrary to the Marxist history.[23] To take just one example, the tailor's apprentice and early socialist Wilhelm Weitling, born in Magdeburg – incidentally, as the illegitimate child of a domestic maid – is for many the first German theorist of communism.[24] In sum, the small crafts remained a fairly stable refuge, well beyond 1850, for the growing number of people seeking employment. Despite economic fluctuations and increasing competition from industrial mass production, they generally offered bearable working conditions and an income that covered the cost of living.[25]

Finally, those driven out of agriculture had one other way of earning a living, namely the factories, which, after the invention of the steam engine, spread quickly in England, and then in France and Germany. Factories were an entirely new form of enterprise, both with regard to work processes and production methods and with regard to the profits to be had. They were powered by technologically advanced machinery – now made of cast or wrought iron, rather than wood – that allowed for the creation of large plants. With gas lighting, they could operate day and night. With the division of labour and flow production, they could produce large quantities of goods, and as a result the economic yield derived by private entrepreneurs shot up. From our vantage point, it is difficult to appreciate the full extent of the changes to which employees had to adapt in every aspect of their work and life. Gone were the days of agricultural labour and the crafts, when people's activity had still mostly been autonomous and had closely followed the rhythms of the natural world or had been in direct physical contact with the materials that were used. Even in cottage industry it had at least still been possible to take breaks when necessary. Now, workers followed the monotonous rhythm of the machine and repeated the same movements over and over again. The noise in the factory halls was ear-splitting, and work continued long into the night. It was a transformation of everyday experience so deep and comprehensive that later generations would have described it as a 'culture shock'.[26]

'The lights in the great factories, which looked, when they were illuminated, like Fairy palaces – or the travellers by express-train said so – were all extinguished; and the bells had rung for knocking off for the night, and had ceased again; and the Hands, men and women, boy and girl, were clattering home. Old Stephen was standing in the street, with the old sensation upon him which the stoppage of the machinery always produced – the sensation of its having worked and stopped in his own head.'[27]

'Meanwhile, at Milton the chimneys smoked, the ceaseless roar and mighty beat, and dizzying whirl of machinery, struggled and strove perpetually. Senseless and purposeless were wood and iron and steam in their endless labours; but the persistence of their monotonous work was rivalled in tireless endurance by the strong crowds, who, with sense and with purpose, were busy and restless in seeking after – What?'[28]

Of course, this transition did not happen overnight – it was a process that stretched over decades – but factory conditions appeared so novel, threw life so off balance, that people soon came to imagine that factory work, despite making up only a small proportion of all work, was the universal fate of modern society, and moreover would produce an entirely new class: the proletariat. When Marx later added the claim that this new class was the 'revolutionary subject' of history, the mythical illusion was complete.[29] The idea bore little resemblance to social reality: industrial labour would remain only a small sector of the workforce throughout the nineteenth century. Moreover, the suggestion that the proletariat would be immediately united and powerful was made even less plausible by the fact that the industrial workforce was made up of groups from very heterogeneous backgrounds, cultural orientations and work histories. Despite the economic uncertainty, torturous working hours and humiliating strict discipline of factory work, people sought this employment because, as beggars, tramps, rural day labourers, impoverished farmers, wives or daughters without means of their own, seasonal migrant workers or unemployed apprentices in one of the crafts, they saw no other way of securing a livelihood.[30] The employment conditions in mechanically operated manufacture and factories were also highly diverse in terms of recruitment and remuneration. The raw material to be processed had often been extracted and transported by slaves in Europe's peripheral regions or overseas colonies.[31] Some of the smaller jobs around the factory halls were done by underlings who were hired on a short-term basis, without a contract, in return for the smallest of wages. Many production workers employed in low-skilled work within the division of labour were recruited by local contractors, who, in return for a flat fee, '"procured" the necessary numbers to work for a fixed wage over a specified period of time'[32] – often labourers from far afield. In short, a great many factory workers could not rely on conditions that they had contractually agreed with the factory owners, and even those who had 'freely' entered into a contract had no real alternative.

So far this account of labour relations in nineteenth-century Western Europe has not really mentioned any broader transformational processes, and thus appears to have painted a rather static picture. Indeed, I have simply described the typical activities by which the working population secured its subsistence. In addition to the hard work in agriculture, cottage industry, trade and the crafts, and factories, there were also, especially for women, the unpaid daily activities in the household, which could not be avoided. It is clear, then, that the body politic would have had neither the necessary time, nor the independence and mental energy, to be politically active and fulfil the role of political sovereign. Although the promise of political participation had by this point been established in the form of certain citizens' rights, and been insisted upon by democratically minded theorists of the state, the people had no real right to have a say in government affairs. Even had there been universal suffrage it would hardly have helped the mass of people who were mostly concerned with keeping a roof over their head and finding enough to eat.

As we shall see, the gulf between ideal and reality, between the promise of political participation and the actuality of nineteenth-century working conditions, did, however, at least bring about some change in labour relations. As technology transformed economies and whole professions disappeared, new fields of employment emerged, and the size of others markedly changed. In the main, though, the era was marked by the symptoms of an unbridled capitalism, in particular mass poverty, which became more and more pronounced and obvious towards the mid-nineteenth century. In rural areas, the structural changes brought about by capitalism were evident in the increasing transformation of farms into agrarian capitalist enterprises, which, however, differed significantly with regard to size and yield. Millions of rural workers across Europe were at the disposal of this relatively small group of independent farmers, and with the gradual erosion of traditional patrimonial loyalties, rural workers' labour rights increasingly began to resemble those of industrial wage labourers. However, one difference remained: the farmer often still exercised a kind of patriarchal authority over his workers. Combined with the miserable lot of the rural worker, the enormous physical strain of summertime work and the remote location of the farms, this explains why agricultural labourers failed to mount any real organized resistance.[33] The crafts were in a much better position. The steady growth of the population and rapid urbanization created huge demand for essential goods, repair shops and housing construction, and thus for carpenters, pavers, locksmiths and bricklayers, and so the crafts experienced another upturn, despite growing competition from industrial production. With technological transformation, some crafts disappeared – Wehler mentions, among others, sword cutlers, rifle makers and needle makers in Germany[34] – but population growth and urbanization meant that others did fairly well.

It was therefore craftsmen who were the first to collectively rebel against capitalist working conditions in Europe. When these revolts began to spread to the industrial workforce, the first worker associations were founded, and strikes took place.[35] The bourgeoisie's reaction, of course, was a growing restlessness, even panic.

'Each resident lives in his workshop like planters living in colonies amidst their slaves; the sedition in Lyon is of a similar kind to the insurrection of Santo Domingo. ... Barbarians threatening society are not all to be found in Caucasus, nor in the steppes of Tartary. Rather, they are in the suburbs of our manufacturing cities. It is necessary that the middle classes know where things stand.'[36]

In the first half of the nineteenth century, the suffering of the working population was dismissed as self-inflicted, even as the result of moral depravation, but the tone changed significantly after 1850. As the might of the workers' movement grew, talk of 'pauperism' or of the threat to law and order from the 'dangerous classes' became increasingly rare.[37] The plight of the workers was now discussed under the heading of 'the social question', a term that would come to dominate debates about the fate of the working classes.[38] To begin with, however, the spotlight was on the misery of industrial labourers, while the social conditions of agricultural labourers and domestic servants, who made up a much larger part of the workforce, were more or less ignored – and housework, of course, was still not seen as work at all. Nevertheless, various reforms were gradually introduced, more or less rapidly in different countries, to solve the 'social question' of industrial labour, just as working conditions in other sectors would eventually be improved in the twentieth century.

The moral principles underlying these early reform initiatives are more relevant to our topic than they may initially appear. Of course, the various efforts at improving the working and living conditions of industrial workers were often motivated by purely economic considerations, for instance concern that excessive exploitation would reduce the productivity of labour. Or else it was political calculation: the workers' movement had become 'dangerous' and needed to be kept in check through careful concessions, for instance along the lines of Bismarck's social reforms.[39] For all that, these strategies were accompanied by a vague presentiment that the measures merely delayed something that was ultimately inevitable. The gap between the rights that citizens had by this point been granted in almost every country and the everyday reality faced by the working population was simply too large, and it forced those in positions of power to recognize the normative urgency of reform. Whatever their ulterior motive and whatever their form, the reform measures were thus also partly brought about by the moral force of generally accepted norms. Thomas H. Marshall convincingly described the role that the peculiar power of legal-moral imperatives played in bringing about early improvements to labour relations in England. Once it had been conceded, as it had in England and many other Western countries, that liberal civil rights had to include the right to political participation, it was inevitable that eventually people would conclude that the social conditions for the realization of these rights had also to be created.[40] The detail of how these conditions would be provided for resulted from tough negotiations with representatives of the workers' movement, and of course it varied from country to country – often even from region to region. But in general the reforms included a public education system; factory laws that limited working hours, prescribed breaks and prohibited the employment of children; regulations regarding safety at work to reduce the risk of harm; a legally binding minimum wage; and finally welfare state measures that guaranteed financial compensation in case of illness or unemployment. These improvements in labour law and social policy differed in detail, but together they mark the dawn, within the history of capitalism, of the normative idea on which this book is based: if a democracy is to flourish and do justice to its own standards, it must be committed to a social organization of labour relations that enables employees to participate in the political debates of the democratic public sphere.

It would be a long road, not without conflict, from these first reforms of industrial labour relations to the turn of the century, past two world wars, and into the 1970s, and further improvements, technological innovations and shifts in the workforce lay along the way. Only in a handful of European countries, including Great Britain and Germany, did industry become the leading employment sector during this time. In all other countries, there were still more people working in agriculture and the service industry. Around 1970, what was, for some countries at least, a short industrial interlude came to an end, and services became by far the largest employment sector.[41] The putting-out system, one of the central elements of nineteenth-century relations of production, disappeared almost completely, outcompeted by factory-based mechanical production. As we will see, it has recently resurfaced in a very different guise. From the beginning of the twentieth century, agricultural labour relations changed dramatically, not only because of new machines and increasing mechanization but because the production processes, 'from the original farming to processing stages to final marketing', increasingly came to be included in global capitalist trade, leading to an 'internationally active agro-industry'.[42] The reforms to the industrial sector that began around 1870 soon set the pace for the improvement of working conditions in general – with the exception of agriculture. The most enduring breakthrough was the introduction of compulsory insurance – the culmination of the systematization of social welfare measures – which, Castel says, brought with it a 'silent revolution in the condition of wage-earners'.[43] This significantly raised the social status of all wage-earners, whether manual workers or white-collar employees, who were now legally entitled to compensation payments, in most cases from the state, when they lost their job or fell ill through no fault of their own. This breakthrough, won by the trade unions as the institutional arm of the workers' movement, created what Castel describes as normalized salarial relations.[44] As the next chapter will show, however, this contractual protection was in fact a fragile, easily penetrable façade. Behind it, the old working conditions, so inimical to democracy, continued to exist.

5

From 1900 to the Threshold of the Present

Capitalist labour relations from the turn of the century to around 1970 present both continuities and discontinuities. Housework had never enjoyed much public recognition, and around 1900 it underwent a further feminization, as the traditional bourgeois juxtaposition of 'female' caring and supportive activities and 'male' gainful professional activities made deep inroads into the social understanding of the lower social strata. This development was aided by the 'ideological state apparatuses' (Louis Althusser), namely schools and the church.[1] It was helped, too, by pay scales and by ideas about typically male or female professions, which further segregated the labour market. There was also a belief that women were less economically 'productive'. All this led to the view that housework was women's natural occupation.[2] After the Great War, large parts of the upper bourgeoisie lost a great deal of wealth and with it the ability to employ armies of domestic servants to perform household tasks. This meant that poor young women lost an important employment opportunity and were therefore forced to accept the typical nuclear family division of labour: a husband going out to work and a wife looking after the home. But bourgeois women had to take on more household chores too. In this way, social reality seemed to confirm the image – by this point widely held – of the cooking, cleaning, child-rearing wife. However, housework no longer demanded the same level of physical exertion as it had in the nineteenth century. A number of technological innovations had made it a lot easier, even if the introduction of home electrification, which took off in the 1920s, modern appliances and ergonomically designed kitchens was delayed for some because of a lack of income.[3] However, such modernization came at a price: where before women's work had been carried out in spaces where there were opportunities for regular communication with other women, housework now increasingly became the technologically mediated domain of the solitary housewife.[4]

Women returned to the labour market in significant numbers only long after the end of the Second World War, with the economic boom of the 1960s, when the affordability of modern technological innovations enabled them to go out into the workplace. Women's growing feeling of social isolation and expendability were complemented by a desire for greater independence.[5] In addition, the economic upturn created a strong demand for labour, which in turn changed the way housework was perceived: although modern appliances meant there was now less of it, housework was finally beginning to emerge from the shadow cast by an understanding of work based on industrial labour. It was coming to be acknowledged as a form of social labour in its own right. This was the beginning of the most recent phase in the development of capitalist labour relations, to which I shall return in more detail in Chapter 6.

Despite growing migration from rural to urban areas, agriculture remained the largest employment sector, in terms of the number of workers, throughout the nineteenth century. In the twentieth century, agricultural labour relations were thoroughly restructured. With the expansion of international agricultural trade and industrialization, agriculture became increasingly dependent on state protection, and it was forced into constant technological innovation, higher capital investment and, accordingly, a progressive reduction in expenditure on labour power. In this brief historical sketch, I do not have space to go into great detail about the endlessly increasing insecurity and isolation of agricultural work.[6] The reality of farm work had always been almost eerily invisible to consumers in the city, unless they had relatives in rural areas, and this remained the case. City dwellers ate and enjoyed the products of farm workers' innumerable labours (which now depended to a much greater extent on machines), and they acknowledged the importance of such work in general terms, but as a rule they lacked detailed knowledge of the employment relations and working conditions on farms and rural estates. Nor did they register the rural population's growing anxiety about the rapid technological transformation of farming and cattle-raising, or smallholders' fears that their traditionally produced goods would no longer find buyers.

'Who knows? Maybe one day all this will be done by machines. On many farms this is already the case. They have milk pipes leading right up to the truck. And then you will no longer need a foreman either; all you will need is an accountant and engineers. And the calves will be brought out using pulleys.'[7]

The globalization of agriculture, which began at the end of the nineteenth century, saw whole branches of the sector moved to parts of the world where production costs were lower – often territories that were still held as colonies – and, in turn, the development of monocultures at home. If anything, these changes reinforced the invisibility of agricultural work. Who today still understands all the stages of manual labour – from sowing to harvesting, or from raising cattle to slaughter and transportation – that are needed before agricultural produce ends up on the delicatessen counter or the supermarket shelf? This obscurity is the result of the temporal separation, dislocation and division of work that once was done by family businesses. In the industrial and service sectors, labour relations improved significantly in the twentieth century through social welfare measures, greater financial security and consistently rising wages. Agricultural work, however, was much too tied to the seasons, its workforce needs far too changeable and its need to make savings too urgent for welfare state measures to be effective. Early in the twentieth century, agriculture profited from the beginning internationalization of trade, the mechanization of agricultural work and the development of artificial fertilizers.[8] But these advantages soon turned into disadvantages: small-scale and medium-sized farms came under pressure from a growing number of large farms, a slump in the prices of agricultural goods and an almost hopeless struggle to find labourers, who could usually secure wages 15 per cent higher by going into industry. From the end of the nineteenth century onwards – interrupted only by the two world wars – agricultural businesses became dependent on seasonal workers, who came mostly from Eastern Europe or the Mediterranean. They were badly housed, badly provided for and miserably paid. Under such conditions, developing professional pride or a spirit of cooperation was out of the question, as was acquiring bargaining power by founding a trade union.

'It was consistently the case that – to a rapidly growing extent – labourers from abroad whose sustenance was cheaper were preferred to domestic labourers, despite the latter's superior performance. Where this difference in performance is not accepted, this is the result of a simple law: a worker with German nutritional needs, when provided with three quarters of his needs, does not retain three quarters of his potential performance. He retains less, and therefore does not achieve what a Polish labourer, who needs less nutrition but is fully provided for, can. When his nutrition is fully provided for, a German worker achieves not only more than the Polish worker in proportion to the excess of his consumption, but far more. The reason why migrant workers are hired even where domestic workers are available is partly – but only partly – that they are paid lower wages in absolute terms. In general, however, leaving aside the greater obedience of foreign workers who come from a precarious background, the reason is that their labour power can be used in the summer without the need to provide for them during the winter as well, and in particular without having the same legal and other commitments that would apply in the case of domestic workers. In *this* sense foreign labour is *always* cheaper for the employer.'[9]

The emergence of a proletariat of rural migrant workers without any protection or unified voice – in many ways the exact opposite of the 'steady farmer' of the early nineteenth-century imagination – was also accelerated by the path that agriculture was forced to take, despite the protectionist measures in place in almost all Western European countries. Agriculture was under constant pressure to make expensive capital investments, which, given the lack of financial resources, necessitated an extensive employment of cheap seasonal labour. Villages were also becoming increasingly modernized and less and less agricultural, which eroded local networks with autonomous economic identities. Further, the production process was gradually bureaucratized, creating a need for farmers to familiarize themselves with the constantly developing methods of rational management. Finally, value creation came to depend on state subsidy, which led to a general sense of a loss of economic control and a dependence on processes that could scarcely be understood. There emerged as a result a group of farmers that was neither an estate nor a class, and that, in the absence of permanent employees, had no stable base beyond each farmer's responsibility as an independent entrepreneur. Where once the predominant attitude in agriculture had been a humble trust in sufficient yields – although even that did not rule out the occasional rebellion against falling prices and profiteering – agriculture became a deeply divided sector of production: on one side were farmers under constant pressure to rationalize their production, on the other were the growing number of large-scale agricultural enterprises. The mass of seasonal migrant workers from poorer neighbouring countries, no longer tied to a particular region, shifted back and forth between these two sides. The fact that consumers and urban dwellers were less and less aware of the reality of the tough, sometimes undignified, work that was done (and still is done) in this sector almost certainly also had something to do with the steep decline in the number of employees in agriculture: in the early 1950s, about 24 per cent of all employees worked in agriculture and forestry; around the year 2000, this figure had dropped to roughly 2 per cent.[10]

A similar fate befell domestic servants in the early decades of the twentieth century. Even before the turn of the century, an excess supply of domestic servants, and the strong personal dependence on employers that the work entailed, had made their economic and social circumstances unenviable. Servants often had to be available day and night, and there were few regulations governing working times and conditions. They were trapped in their positions, without any hope of social advancement, and their employment continued only until the head of house ended it for whatever reason. For all that, because of the sheer number of fellow sufferers who worked, usually long term, in the same household, they had something approaching a collective awareness of their social significance, professional identity and shared dependence. This sense of being a group with a shared fate ended when, following the Great War, the number of servants employed in wealthy households sank rapidly, reaching an average of just one person per household by the end of the 1920s. At this point, a servant was suddenly responsible for everything, and had to deal with the head of house alone. Whatever solidarity – and thus collective bargaining power – there had been was gone. When domestic servant wages eventually began to approach those in industry and services, other employment opportunities were opening up, for instance those in the growing trade sector, and so bourgeois households began to look for cheaper labour. Given the prevailing xenophobic attitudes and racial prejudice, it seemed natural to draw on the huge masses of unemployed people in the poor regions of neighbouring countries or, where they still existed, the colonies. The process that took place in agriculture was thus now repeated in domestic service, albeit this time interrupted only by the Second World War. There was an influx of foreign domestic workers, who were taken on for considerably less pay, were offered hardly any contractual protection and, it was assumed, could be bossed around and disposed of at will, given their allegedly inferior background. Today, little has changed in this continuation of colonialism by other means. In fact, it has accelerated: there is now a global market for domestic servants who can be hired for next to nothing, who have little social protection and who do whatever domestic jobs need to be done.[11] This market is another symptom of the immeasurable damage wreaked by colonialism, which still affects relationships between rich Western countries and the Global South whose countries the West exploited, and in some cases still exploits.

This development resulted in a specific and very pronounced social distribution of qualifications that was to last for the rest of the twentieth century. Within rich European countries, female domestic servants who could not compete with cheaper foreign labour were often forced to acquire further qualifications, and they therefore sought employment in new and better-paid professions, for instance as a commercial clerk, switchboard operator, doctor's receptionist or primary school teacher. The qualifications of the cheaper domestic servants from poor foreign regions, by contrast, remained stuck at the level they had reached at the beginning of the century.

'The tendency is here, born of slavery and quickened to renewed life by the crazy imperialism of the day, to regard human beings as among the material resources of a land to be trained with an eye single to future dividends. Race-prejudices, which keep brown and black men in their "places," we are coming to regard as useful allies

86

with such a theory, no matter how much they may dull the ambition and sicken the hearts of struggling human beings. And above all, we daily hear that an education that encourages aspiration, that sets the loftiest of ideals and seeks as an end culture and character rather than breadwinning, is the privilege of white men and the danger and delusion of black.'[12]

The nineteenth century's armies of 'ministering spirits' (Heidi Müller) never profited from the increased wages and improved social policies that came with industrialization, but they retained a modest degree of pride in their indispensable work and represented a social group that was surprisingly self-reliant. Today, they are a dispersed mass of individuals from the world's poorest regions. Constantly on the move, they are in most cases paid wages that fall below the social security insurance threshold.

In Germany, domestic servants forced to find alternative employment often moved into rapidly expanding industry and the increasingly differentiated service sector. Female servants were driven out of private households and into new employment opportunities in offices, department stores or, if they were less qualified, factories. Siegfried Kracauer's 1930 study *The Salaried Masses* is still a useful reference point if we want to understand the hopes that such women would have had.[13] The heady dreams, often bordering on delusion, that Kracauer describes rarely came true for them, although the new forms of employment offered better working conditions and higher pay, as well as more leisure time, independence and social security. As in industry, the purchasing power of wages in the service sector had continuously risen since the last third of the nineteenth century, and often even permitted the purchase of minor luxuries. From 1918, working hours across Europe were legally limited to eight hours per day and a six-day working week. Without a family to look after, unmarried individuals had some leisure time on their hands, and there was a legal entitlement to financial support in case of illness. Without a doubt, this was a massive improvement on the previous century, but whereas the domestic servants of the nineteenth century were largely insulated from economic downturn, at least if they had sufficient financial resources, the employees, secretaries and factory workers of the twentieth century were much more exposed to the ups and downs of the capitalist economy. The threat of redundancy following business bankruptcies, banking crises or slumps in the industrial sector was a permanent presence in everyday consciousness, and the worker's day therefore often began with an anxious look at the paper and the job listings. The competitiveness of the labour market sometimes even strained relationships with colleagues. The humiliating and all-embracing dependence on the head of a household was gone, but often it was simply replaced by a formal, depersonalized but equally strict subordination to the manager or business owner. The suggestion that workers might have a right to participate in discussions about working conditions, or even procurement or investment decisions, was absurd. Moreover, workers confronted an entirely new reality: the constant evaluation of their work in the name of efficiency. In the households of the aristocracy and the bourgeois upper class, such measures had been prevented by a deep-seated trust in the traditional way of doing things. Now, one's employer, even in offices and in the trade sector, was always looking to increase profitability through streamlining or accelerating processes. These were the first signs of Taylorism in a sector that Taylor probably did not have in mind when he applied his revolutionary method for the organization of work to industrial mass production.

'Music at least has not entirely vanished from a process that the National Board for Economic Viability has defined as follows: "Rationalization is the application of all means offered by technology and systematic organization to the raising of economic viability, and therewith to increasing the production of goods, reducing their cost and also improving them." No, it has not quite gone. I know of one industrial plant that hires girls straight from high school with a salary and lets them be trained at the typewriter by a teacher of their own. The wily teacher winds up a gramophone and the pupils have to type in time with its tunes. When merry military marches ring out, they all march ahead twice as lightly. The rotation speed of the record is gradually increased, and without the girls really noticing it they tap faster and faster. In their training years they turn into speed typists – music has wrought the cheaply purchased miracle.'[14]

The realization that the transition from domestic work to a more secure, better-paid position in services or industry was no guarantee of a secure livelihood came, at the latest, with the global economic crisis at the end of the 1920s. Employees in trade and banking were the first victims of what soon became mass unemployment, and millions of factory workers and saleswomen in the newly prosperous department stores also found that their promised job security was not all it was cracked up to be – that in fact their livelihoods hung by the thread of capitalist growth. The crisis took a slightly different course in each country, but it created mass unemployment everywhere, and caused a long-lasting trauma among the salariat as well as the industrial proletariat.[15] In the decades that followed, the fear of mass unemployment and its psychological and social consequences coloured lower-skilled wage labourers' perceptions of contemporary events, just as the anxious expectation of poor weather or crop failure influenced farmers' perceptions, and even periods of economic boom could not shift the fear.

Despite technological innovation and significant improvements in social policy, the material conditions and psychological experience of many people's work changed little until the 1920s. By then, there were tractors on farms, electric typewriters in offices, cash registers in department stores and steam irons at home. But in one sector, almost revolutionary changes were about to take place – namely industry. Until the turn of the century, no more than around 30 per cent of workers were employed in industry in Western Europe, and factories often still resembled a 'conglomerate of craft workshops'.[16] To be sure, work followed the monotonous rhythm of the machine, but there was still scope for individuals to influence the temporal dynamic and physical organization of the production processes: there was still a good deal of manual labour, and command came by way of oral communication. Bullying by foremen or managers who abused their positions may have been quite frequent, but at the same time it was often possible to agree special arrangements, for instance a period of lower-intensity work on account of exceptional circumstances. What remained of such autonomous control over work processes and individual interpersonal communication began to disappear once technological innovation and increasing bureaucratization led to a further division and specification of work processes on the factory floor. Most importantly, this streamlining of work processes made it possible to decouple them from linguistic communication. It was only at this point – shortly after the Great War – that capitalist countries underwent the comprehensive rationalization of industrial production that from then on was labelled 'Taylorism'.[17] Adam Smith and Hegel had feared that mechanization in the first factories – almost idylls from today's perspective – would lead to mental torpor, the loss of social skills and the decline of social integration, so it is hard to imagine how they would have reacted to assembly line work as presented in Charlie Chaplin's *Modern Times*. In any case, as Taylorist principles spread, the organization and nature of industrial work changed dramatically and enduringly. The production process of the small-scale factory was often still relatively unfragmented, not strictly regulated, and work was coordinated by employees speaking to one other, but this was now replaced by the hierarchical organization typical of middle and large-scale enterprise: standardized goods mostly produced on assembly lines according to a strict temporal regime that allowed for the precise measurement of individual performance.

> 'The great automotive boom was on. At Ford's production was improving all the time; less waste, more spotters, straw-bosses, stoolpigeons (fifteen minutes for lunch, three minutes to go to the toilet, the Taylorized speedup everywhere, reach under, adjust washer, screw down bolt, shove in cotterpin, reachunder adjustwasher, screwdown bolt, reachunderadjustscrewdownreachunder adjust until every ounce of life was sucked off into production and at night the workmen went home grey shaking husks).'[18]

Of course, this new way of organizing industrial labour was not pushed through in the space of a few years, nor without resistance from labour organizations. Disputes over time measurement, work intervals, breaks and framework agreements on wages, and also over the general moral justifiability of the rationalization process, intensified dramatically throughout the 1920s. Sometimes the agreed mechanisms for negotiation between capital and labour broke down. But protest and debate could only delay, not stop, the march of Taylorism. Soon the system was present in all larger industrial enterprises.[19] At the same time as these radical changes to production were bringing about a further deepening, fragmentation and acceleration of the division of labour on the factory floor,[20] industrial labour became the dominant form of employment in Western capitalist countries. Only then did these societies become what in their cultural self-understanding they had been since the mid-nineteenth century: industrial societies whose social order, institutional structures and forms of work were aligned to the industrial production of goods.

It still took several decades of conflict and compromise between capital and labour before the seed of Taylorist mass production had finally developed into 'industrialism' – the apposite term coined by Martin Baethge for the social labour and employment model that emerged after the Second World War.[21] At the heart of industrialism were 'medium and large-scale enterprises with strong hierarchies and vertical integration' that distinguished clearly 'between productive and non-productive functions'.[22] What counted as 'productive' was the work of the qualified male worker who, in the best-case scenario, acquired his skills on the job and could expect to gradually rise up the business's hierarchy if he met expectations. Further institutional elements were arranged around this core employment model – all of them a reflection of the priority of industrial work over other professional sectors in the social division of labour. The most important such element was statutory social security insurance, which was financed on a solidaristic basis through contributions from the working population and which offered social protection in the case of sickness or unemployment and old-age pensions. The second most important element was a corporatist bargaining system in which trade unions and employers' associations were encouraged to reach agreement on questions of social policy. A third element was a 'family model based on the man as the main breadwinner and with clear roles for men and women'.[23]

After 1950, the industrialist institutional structure, with industrial labour at its centre, drove a period of economic growth in almost all European countries. However, after only a couple of decades, it began to show the first signs of deterioration. The service industry soon came to account for most employment – or, rather, it again came to account for most employment, resuming the status it had had during the time in which domestic and personal services dominated. After a period in which they had mostly been banished to the home, women gradually returned to the labour market in search of independence. But most importantly, the legal regulation of the labour market, and the social policies in which it was embedded, began to break down. Together, these three developments threatened the entire social fabric of industrialism. In the final part of my historical interlude, I deal with the circumstances under which, about forty years ago, this labour and social policy model finally collapsed, before sketching the employment relations that are now beginning to emerge from the rubble of the old order. I conclude the leap to the present with a survey of recent developments in the world of work, which, like vanishing lines, point to an as yet unspecified point in our future.

6

The Capitalist World of Work Today

In the preceding chapters, 200 years of changes in Western European forms of work and labour conditions were condensed into two brief sketches. The sketches approached the subject as a matter of ideal types, highlighting central points, rather than providing comprehensive descriptions, but they at least brought us, if in rather large steps, to the threshold of today's capitalist world of work. I will not at this point present the quantitative empirical data that would demonstrate one important result of these historical developments – namely that as far as wages, working hours and social security are concerned, labour relations have clearly improved. Notwithstanding these quantitative improvements, my main interest is the qualitative aspect of labour relations, which continues to be characterized by daily toil, dependency and the ever-present possibility of unemployment. As we saw, barring times of economic downturn or war, pressure from trade unions helped to secure rising real wages throughout the period we have considered. Likewise, average hours worked continuously fell across various sectors of employment, while workers' social security protections improved significantly. Nevertheless, the workers' experience essentially remained the same. For those who had to work to earn a living, employment almost always meant dependence on individual superiors or anonymous authorities. They had no influence over decisions that affected how their work was organized, and they rarely felt that what they did was acknowledged by society at large – that it was something that made an essential contribution to the preservation of a shared culture. Subordination, dependence, the experience of dispensability, few participatory rights regarding working conditions, the fear of unemployment and, finally, a lack of recognition – these were the main features of large areas of social labour over the decades. These characteristics created an opposition between the world of work and the world of political democracy: in the world of work, the abilities and faculties that are normatively demanded by democracy were systematically undermined. Before turning in Part III to the question of how this situation might actually be changed, we first need to sketch the most recent trends in the capitalist world of work, for they contain so many uneven developments and upheavals, and so much unpredictability, that democratic labour policies might seem incapable of dealing with them – so much so that there are growing calls to completely uncouple employment from one's ability to secure a livelihood. Part III will therefore also have to address whether, in fact, democratic labour policies can still be effective.

Today's capitalist labour relations differ from those of fifty or sixty years ago, when the social structure of 'industrialism' was establishing itself. That judgement may sound as though it makes too much of something that is in fact rather trivial – after all, the world of work has always been characterized by more or less rapid transformations, and we have already got to know quite a few of them. Such transformations are usually precipitated by technological innovations that lead to the disappearance of whole branches of work,[1] by reforms in labour law that change the powers of the parties involved,[2] or by the influence of the economic cycle on the labour market.[3] However, in the relatively short period since the mid-1970s, there seem to have been significant changes with regard to more than just one of these three variables. In fact, new developments in all three seem to have set in train processes that are now fundamentally reshaping labour conditions. I shall examine whether, and to what extent, this impression is correct by tracing the history of the most recent developments. I begin with the massive wave of deregulation that began about forty years ago – the effects of which are today rather sweepingly referred to as 'neoliberal' – for no other reason than that I have had to pick some reasonably identifiable point of departure within a constant stream of change. Some changes in relation to these three variables began earlier, others later, so the manner of presentation here is something of an idealization – one that is, however, methodically unavoidable.

There is a surprising level of agreement about the economic and social consequences of the rapid changes to the organization of the capitalist economy that set in around 1980. Experts disagree, however, about what caused these changes. Everyone agrees that the pressures of growing international competition over profits and rising social security costs led

Western countries to follow the US's lead in gradually abandoning various regulations that had been imposed on markets. Doing so was supposed both to reduce government spending and to spur investment. Among political economists, there also seems to be a certain degree of consensus regarding the political and legal means by which states hoped to achieve these two aims.[4] Drawing on the dominant doctrines of economic liberalism, policy makers freed key industries, including financial institutions, from burdensome regulation; reduced the number of government contracts; substantially watered down many environmental, consumer and labour protections; revoked a number of anti-trust laws; outsourced services to private enterprises; and introduced tax relief for businesses and wealthy private individuals. Of course, these measures were implemented in different combinations and to varying degrees from country to country, but their overall effect was the creation, at breakneck speed, of a new capitalist regime of accumulation – that is, a new production system. This new system left the social structure of industrialism behind, cast off the fetters of the old 'organized' capitalism and – under the aegis of financial capital – set out to find opportunities to make profit around the world. At this point, opinions begin to diverge, and commentators offer differing views on causes, present various normative evaluations and adopt different terminology. Some speak of 'neoliberalism', others of the 'financialization' of capitalism; a third group, following Foucault, uses the term 'ordoliberalism', emphasizing that these new measures were orchestrated by the state.[5] For my purposes, these theoretical differences are not particularly relevant. The important point is that the various measures to increase the flexibility of capital flows played a major role in undermining legal protections for wage labourers. Rules governing dismissal were severely weakened in almost all European countries, and temporary employment was made much easier. It was also made much simpler to create temporary employment agencies. In Great Britain, Germany and Austria, the payment of unemployment benefits was increasingly made conditional upon recipients' willingness to accept jobs that they were neither qualified for nor interested in, and that were highly unlikely to lead to permanent employment.[6] We must acknowledge, however, that these regressive steps were also accompanied by some clear improvements. In almost all of Europe, anti-discrimination legislation expanded rights to paid maternity leave and counteracted structural discrimination against women, people with disabilities, and ethnic and sexual minorities. Overall, then, 'there has been a decline in the enriched quality of standard employment' over the past forty years,[7] while at the same time the demands of disadvantaged groups in the context of 'identity politics' have increasingly been incorporated into law. I have previously criticized contemporary theories of justice for their one-sidedness, and we might say that in recent decades labour law has in fact tended to adopt the one-sided suggestions of such thinkers as Rawls and Habermas: legal equality has been reinforced, but little has been done to address the lack of participation in the workplace, the poor quality of much work, and the barriers to democratic participation created by labour relations.

This structural transformation of labour law would not have brought about such significant changes to the world of work if it had not been complemented by another innovative shift, which began even earlier. Information technology created a new productive force that, from early on, fitted well with a more or less unbridled finance capital that was looking for quick profits. Without the internet – and the temporal acceleration and spatial independence it brought with it – new instruments for short-term speculation, such as high-frequency trading and day trading, would have been technically impossible. But the new medium was also a very promising area of investment for speculative capital seeking short-term profits.[8] Practically overnight, this partnership between the internet and speculative capital gave birth to three new types of business that would fundamentally reshape social labour over the coming decades. First, the growing demand for speculative financial investments with large returns quickly led to the emergence of listed companies in which the interests of shareholders – usually organized in the form of holding companies – were primary, and the interests of employees and suppliers secondary. Shareholder value thus became the crucial factor in the decision-making process, which compounded the deterioration of workers' legally guaranteed rights: now, employees' representatives had less internal influence over decisions regarding production sites, production targets and the recruitment of senior managers.[9] Second, the use of online platforms created a business model in which individuals, as self-employed clients, could be connected to customers looking for transport, food or parcel deliveries, or accommodation – a major part of the so-called 'gig economy'. Legally, those who work in the gig economy are not the employees of the companies running the platforms. They are independent actors who take on the risk themselves, without being protected by any labour laws, and have to hand over most of what they earn to the companies as a commission.[10] Third, as unfettered finance capital looked for profitable investment and technological development enabled increasingly rapid data transfer, there emerged large – indeed, globe-bestriding – internet companies such as Amazon, Google and Facebook. These companies soon realized that by making access to digital entertainment, information and communication conditional on payments and/or the provision of personal information, they could use their vast amounts of data to achieve a significant additional income from advertising and ultimately become monopolies. Thanks to internet connectivity, these companies could outsource a major part of the necessary labour – software maintenance, data control, personnel support, delivery – to hugely underpaid remote workers all over the globe. In addition, the use of in-house software allowed the companies to create new methods of control: employees were forced to constantly monitor their own performance against the goals set by the companies – a wholly new regime of domination.[11]

How have these recent developments changed today's world of work? The contemporary world of work presents a rugged landscape in which old and new, familiar and unfamiliar, are joined together in a variety of temporally uneven combinations. The organization of work has changed so dramatically and so rapidly that it is difficult to know where to begin this short survey. Agriculture has probably changed the least: it has merely seen a continuation of a tendency that developed after the Second World War. Despite moves towards more ecological animal husbandry and farming, the sector is still dominated by large-scale, almost industrial businesses, or capital-intensive private farms in which feeding, fertilization, milking and work on the fields are now guided by computer-controlled machines. Depending on what the farm produces, and how much of it, any additional workers required during labour-intensive phases of production are still recruited from so-called 'low-wage countries', because it is too expensive to train employees in-house. Today, a typical farmer is a manager who runs the farm more or less on their own, spends more time in front of a computer than in the field and, because of rising production costs and falling producer prices, cannot persuade the next generation to take over the business.

'The biggest difference between now and 100 years ago is life on a farm as such. Back then, the whole family was working in the household. There were farmhands, maids, temporary workers came to help with the harvest, and so on. Today, I am a solo entertainer in my business. I live, like everyone else, with my family on the farm and have become more like a manager. Our father and his whole generation often have bad hips, bad backs. Our generation suffers heart attacks, nervous breakdowns, burnout, and so on. These things have really changed a lot. Whereas back then half the village rallied together and helped with the calving, today I stand there alone. I need to employ technical help, or if necessary call the vet, in order to get the calf out. And it is the same during the peak-time of hay-making. You met on the moor, people appeared from out of every corner. If I have a problem on the moor today, I have to rely on my mobile. I am the only person far and wide. This has changed a lot.'[12]

Even when farmers get creative – generating side income by directly selling special high-quality products or letting out holiday apartments on working farms – they must always fear being unable to make enough for their family to live on, even if they concentrate exclusively on one branch of agriculture (arable farming, vegetables or fruits, animal husbandry).

As we saw, housework was long ignored. Here, too, little seems to have changed in recent decades. But this impression is deceptive: below the surface, there have been massive transformations in the way household work is organized. The social and cultural developments that we touched on briefly above led to yet another large increase in the percentage of women in the workforce. In Germany, the figure is about 47 per cent. However, of these women, 45 per cent work part-time – a large percentage compared with many other European countries, yet not an altogether unusual one. As this fact clearly indicates, there has been no fundamental transformation in the division of labour – by now almost a century old – in which men work full-time and women earn an additional income. This model flourished during the era of industrialism, and despite all the calls for a fairer distribution of housework it is still going strong. For the most part, it is still the female partner or wife who cooks, cleans and raises the children, regardless of how much additional employed work she has taken on.[13] The entrepreneurial spirit of capitalism has proven creative enough to exploit this dual burden, too: more and more areas of housework have been turned into goods and services that are offered to private households on the free market at the highest possible price. In this way, the dilemmas faced by women who have to combine professional life and housework have been addressed through a commodification of housework.[14] Today, the most significant trend in the economic dimension of private and family life is the substitution of work that was previously done in one's own home by products that are delivered to the door or services provided by others. There is a flourishing market that covers nearly every traditional household activity, from the preparation of meals, ironing, cleaning and dog walking to evening entertainment, watering flowers and sewing and knitting – all can now be bought in the form of goods and services. Of course, this tendency towards the commodification of housework is not an entirely novel phenomenon – it probably began, at least in a rudimentary form, as early as the nineteenth century[15] – but it must be clearly distinguished from the employment of servants. Servants were 'traded' on an informal and locally circumscribed market. They received a personally agreed wage, usually directly from the head of the house, were remunerated in the form of bed and board, and provided their services on private premises. Today, the goods and services that promise to reduce the burden of housework are 'commodities' in the sense that they are provided or produced by private capitalist enterprises and made available in an anonymous form, whether they are services rendered by workers or products delivered to the home.

The marketization of housework has transformed the character of the double burden faced by women in employment. Housework has become less a matter of physical labour and more a matter of advance planning and calculation – ordering the goods and services needed for the running of the household. Further, rationalization in those jobs that are still seen as typically 'female' – in health and social services, education, retail and catering – has meant that employers increasingly expect employees to be flexible in combining their professional and family commitments. It is not surprising, then, that the main stress factor – one could even say curse

– for women who work is the constant need to be flexible in their time management. An impressive empirical study by Tanja Carstensen shows that housewives in employment increasingly have to use digital means to organize, arrange and order things if they want to stand a chance of coordinating their private and professional lives.[16] This applies mainly to the middle class, but it is probably also true of those in lower income strata. The almost daily transactions needed to keep the household going require mobile phones, email and messenger services, making these electronic technologies a permanent feature of life. Such digital intrusion into daily life does not even spare those employed women who earn enough, together with their partners, to employ someone to help with the housework. Even where some relief from the burden of housework is possible, the internet still permeates the material reproduction of life: the few tasks left, such as preparing meals and shopping, are carried out with the help of digital service providers. The group that stands to lose out in this process of the commodification of housework is without a doubt the vast and constantly growing reserve army of poorer women, be they native to the country or living abroad, who hope to find employment as a servant, caregiver, cleaner or babysitter in a well-to-do family. Because of the proliferation of internet companies offering all kinds of household services, the situation of these women has deteriorated even further over recent years. Often from poorer parts of the world, they have no bargaining power and usually provide their services without the security of a contract. They are seen as disposable at will, and they must send a large part of their meagre wage to families back home.[17] To quote Max Weber, 'the term "exploitation" is too mild' for this form of social labour.[18] The wages are so low that these women are unable to afford anything beyond the bare essentials, and there is no state oversight.

> 'I lived in a small bedroom – it was like a servant's room fifty years ago! There was no radio, no television, no internet. No private space, no free day – nothing. During the night, I regularly had to get up five times. Ah, yes, once every day, the lady watched a fifty-minute programme. During that time, I could leave the house, do the shopping, visit the post office to send letters home.'[19]

Turning from housework to the 'typically female' professions, it becomes clear why it is women in particular who have been forced to so carefully manage their time. In recent decades, the service industry, and especially those service jobs with a disproportionate number of female workers, has undergone a process of rationalization resembling that which took place in industry following the Great War – a development we discussed in Chapter 5 under the heading of 'Taylorism'. In the case of services, this rationalization was the effect of a synergy between the privatization of the public sector and an unfettered striving for the greatest possible returns. The guiding principle behind these changes, then and now, is the aim of increasing the yield from each individual task – the only difference is that today the means for achieving this aim are specifically tailored for the areas of care work, cleaning and administration. A short survey of these changes provides an insight into a significant part of the world of work for many employees today. In commercial and administrative office work, retail, customer-facing elements of the insurance and finance industry, and health and social care, economic yield from workers has increased while labour costs have stagnated or even fallen, meaning bigger profits for employers. This was achieved through a reduction in services, the standardization of products, a deepening of the division of labour and more detailed performance evaluation.[20] How this concentration, streamlining and intensification of services changes the worker's experience has been well documented by sociologists and in literature.[21] One's work constantly threatens to intrude into one's private life: even outside of working hours, one frequently gives advice, deals with enquiries and confers with others. Specific work activities are even less meaningfully related to other activities in the business. Further, performance evaluation has become more intense and individualized through the use of digital tools: the gaze of management, interested only in profit, seems to scrutinize every action of the office worker, bank clerk, cleaner and carer.

'So today we are going to be trained to do the *sanis* in the passenger cabins. Mauricette hands us a plastic basket with two sprays and a score of cleaning cloths, then we follow her at the double down the first of the ferry's endless corridors – this one is so narrow that you have to flatten yourself against the wall when someone else comes past. The cabins are all on the one side, about every six feet or so. Mauricette opens the door to the first one and dashes into the tiny space where four bunks are fitted over each other and there's a boxroom toilet which itself includes a washbasin, a shower, and the toilets. She drops down to the ground, so suddenly that I initially think she's stumbled over something. I go forward to help her up but, without even glancing behind her, she shakes herself to push me away and, on her knees on the tiles, starts to aim her spray at everything in sight, from the floor to the ceiling. Then, still squatting down, she crumples, dries, disinfects, polishes, changes the toilet paper and the bins, arranges the bar of soap and the tumblers in an immaculate row over the washbasin, and checks the shower curtain. It's all taken less than three minutes: that's the time allowed for this task.'[22]

The strain on female workers in the ever-growing field of care work – most of them from Eastern Europe, Asia or Latin America – has increased dramatically. Whether employed by private or public institutions, they are paid scandalously low wages, or, if they work for well-to-do families, it is almost always without a contract, and they are exposed to the whims of the family members. At least in these booming areas of service work employees do not have to use their own possessions to perform their work – a small privilege, but one that is not enjoyed by workers in the lower strata of the growing service industry: the level of internet companies and their 'independent' workers. Here, the world of work gets even tougher; in fact, the working conditions amount to nothing less than a resurrection of the old putting-out system of the nineteenth century. Colin Crouch, in his recent study on the so-called gig economy – that is, tech companies who use independent workers to deliver their services – expresses his frustration over the fact that many of these new forms of employment recall practices we thought were gone for good. In the early days of industrialization, workers – mostly women – produced pieces of clothing from raw material delivered to their houses, using weaving looms or other tools that they were responsible for maintaining

– just as they were responsible for their own safety and well-being.[23] Similarly, 'independent' workers now provide tech platforms' services at their own risk, but the volume of services rendered, the level of pay and the way the services are delivered are determined solely by the internet companies.[24] When we see workers racing through our cities, on their own bikes, electric scooters, or in their own vans, to deliver parcels or food, it is not difficult to appreciate that we are seeing a return of the old in the guise of the new. To cover as many customers as possible, they rarely take breaks. In most cases, these self-employed workers have to pay for their productive forces – the bikes, scooters and vans – out of their own pockets. As a rule, they are similarly responsible for their own health insurance and unemployment protection – a responsibility that, given how much of the profit the workers generate goes to the company that offers their 'private' services, is difficult to meet.[25] The main difference from the old putting-out system is that today's self-employed workers are no longer connected by neighbourhood relations or local networks. Thus – and given that they also rarely meet those for whom they work in person – the kind of organized resistance mounted by the Silesian weavers or the canuts in Lyon is much more difficult to initiate.[26] The growing isolation of the worker characterizes the new world of work more broadly – a result on the one hand of the use of computers and telephones, technologies that cut workers off from their surroundings, and on the other of the rapid growth of systems for individualized performance evaluation.

'The equipment – delivery box, jacket, T-shirt, and helmet – was sent to her by post after she had transferred a refundable deposit. Every two weeks, she used the app to register her upcoming shifts, and every Monday she received an email with her weekly performance data. In the categories *Time at Customer*, *Reaction Time*, and *Speed*, Marcela had lately managed to be consistently among the *Top 10 Riders of the week*, and all in all she liked her job. Since cycling hundreds of kilometres across the city every month, she had lost seven kilos; her parents had hardly recognized their *Gordita* [little chubby one]. And then there were all the people to whom she had

> delivered: politicians at the party's central headquarters; American tourists queuing in front of a sneaker shop, and a fellow student from her *Linguistics II module*. She had never spoken to a flesh-and-blood person at the company, something that was agreeable to her. However, to be called by a machine and be given orders? What the fuck!'[27]

While the working conditions of the gig economy are spreading fast, some branches of industrial labour have disappeared from our world almost completely. The architectural remnants of this type of work, which only a few decades ago represented the prototypical form of industrial labour, are the colliery towers or blast furnaces of the coal and steel industries, which, even where such infrastructure has now been put to a different use, are poignant testaments to the suffering and pride of many generations of industrial workers.[28] Other traditional – and not always duly acknowledged – jobs seem fairly immune to change: for instance, the work of the refuse collector who has the tough, and 'dirty', task of removing our rubbish; the hairdressers who dexterously bring their customers' hair into good order; and the chimney sweeps who move from house to house throughout cities and rural communities, cleaning and certifying the good working order of the flues.

There also seems to be little change in the productive industries, which now employ only a quarter of all workers. For instance, in construction, although larger building components are prefabricated using computer-aided processes and building plans are electronically produced, the actual casing, assembly and concrete filling still depend on the use of human labour power. The situation is somewhat different in the key industries of Western Europe, that is, the automotive, metal and chemical industries. Here, Fordist assembly line production underwent a serious crisis in the 1970s, as if in a kind of counter-movement to the expansion of Taylorism in the service industry: during these times of severe sales and production crises, trade unions sought an end to the degrading assembly line work that reduced the worker's input to a few repetitive movements. Their aim was a 'humanization of the world of work'. At least in parts of these industries, the disputes led to the establishment of working groups 'who elected their own representatives and had a say in their work processes and organization'.[29] These developments were enthusiastically welcomed in industrial sociology, but although the trend would certainly have advanced workers' interests, it did not last long. Soon, companies faced with growing competition and cost pressures began to outsource whole branches of production to suppliers and subcontractors. Eventually, this led to the situation with which we are only too familiar today: the final assembly is carried out on well-organized shop floors by highly qualified workers who are integrated into the company's quasi-paternalistic culture, perform their tasks using assistance systems and robots, and receive a solid wage; among the medium-sized subcontractors and suppliers, meanwhile, 'time pressures, extortion, a constant struggle for survival and social coldness' still prevail.[30] It is as if the development towards 'human resource management', which represents at least a symbolic appreciation of work, had silently passed these companies by. However, behind the façade of what is apparently old and familiar in these peripheral areas of industrial work, in particular in building and construction, the abyss of the new, precarious employment relations of financialized, or neoliberal, capitalism often opens up too. Many of the workers doing the physical labour are migrant workers from more or less distant countries, and are hired only for a particular building project, meaning they do not qualify for social security. Domestic workers frequently work on an on-call basis, as agency workers, on a self-employed basis, or they hold jobs that are paid below the social security threshold.

In sectors that require more qualifications, it seems that despite increasing digitalization many things have stayed the same. Every doctor's surgery now has digital patient files, and all bills are settled with the health insurer electronically. But the conversation between doctor and patient, even if it may increasingly take place via video link, is still indispensable, and many types of physical examination have survived the march of medical technology.[31] By contrast, the changes wrought by digitalization seem more pronounced, possibly the most pronounced, in the areas of banking and insurance. Personal conversations with clients are of only marginal importance, and creditworthiness is checked against a file that is constantly digitally updated. Stock market trading and investment banking take place electronically and, of course, at a vastly accelerated pace, and insurance is brokered globally via the internet.

As practices in the finance industry become increasingly digitalized, employees in these sectors become ever more isolated in their work. Even where social cooperation and agreement are still required, they are undermined by the competitiveness fostered by the promise of performance-related bonuses. Any sense that these employees should adhere to a professional ethos that is committed to the well-being of society more broadly has been lost along the way.[32] Parts of the finance and insurance industry have become so detached from the rest of society that they have lost any awareness that, behind the risk analyses, share prices and profit margins, there are real people with financial worries and needs. The attempt to bridge the gap between number crunching and flesh-and-blood human beings through well-advertised charity events does little to buck this trend.

> 'Then there is Social Day. Quite frankly, it makes me want to vomit. Goldman Sachs has one every year. All employees get a day off, and the company showcases its social commitment. They all descend on some kindergarten, wearing white overalls, and begin to paint anything they can get their hands on. And at the end of the day, the Frankfurter Rundschau or the Neue Presse turns up and takes photos of the Goldman guys, and the next day they can look at themselves in the papers. Maybe they also bring along one of those oversized cheques with 10,000 euros written on it. That's great, isn't it? It really makes me angry, as I'm sure you can tell. And these events are the *only contact points* [with the real world] that these businesses still have.'[33]

The banking and insurance sector – the 'bourgeoisie of the service industry' as it were – exemplifies a key change in the work of highly qualified employees in the service industry: the essential steps in the work process are increasingly separated from one another and are carried out by isolated individuals working at computers, possibly even from home. Because there is little need for employees to coordinate their work, there is less and less communication and cooperation. In turn, the collective professional ethos that once ensured individual commitment to social benefit and societal well-being is lost. As computer-based data manipulation replaces traditional values such as customer-orientation and trust-building personal communication, tried-and-tested practices and established knowledge become less relevant. Instead of adopting 'good practice' that has emerged in the past, there is a constant need to adapt to the latest software update. Anyone who is quick on the uptake and reasonably knowledgeable in mathematics or information technology can enter these new fields of administrative and financial services – a development that threatens to rapidly de-professionalize whole areas of work that were once socially important. It is difficult to predict what effect this might have on social cohesion, which is possible only if the social division of labour allows different groups of workers to develop a mutual understanding of each other's concerns and existential needs.

My sketch of today's world of work is far from comprehensive, but let me attempt at this point to draw some tentative conclusions. We can make out five general developments in the physical character, organization and form of employment. None of these tendencies is yet sufficiently pronounced for us to make reliable long-term predictions about structural change, but each indicates a possible direction in which the world of work might develop.

1. Overall, the social division of labour seems to be creating increasingly isolated working conditions. There is less of a need for direct communication with those who do the same or related jobs, and workers increasingly have to rely on themselves. This tendency towards fragmentation and isolation has been accelerated by digitalization and individualized control and performance evaluation.[34] Another factor may be the ascendant cultural ideology of 'individual responsibility' and 'self-optimization', which leads employees to believe that they should take on more and more and thus increase their productivity.[35] Many socially necessary areas of work are abandoning communicative practices of deliberation, personal exchange and cooperation in favour of independent acting, calculating, planning and monitoring, as though the preferred model of employment was the solitary desk job that has long characterized many professions in the service sector. Even the more intersubjective nature of occupations in the expanding areas of

elderly care, education and customer services has done little to arrest this tendency towards solipsistic modes of work. These areas may require more empathy and communicative openness than the production-based understanding of work would have suggested, but this requirement does not say anything about how the work will be institutionally organized or remunerated. The manner of its organization will instead be determined by whether it is seen as individual work, done by individual people, or cooperative work, done in exchange with others – and here we find that even this 'communicative' work is increasingly performed in social isolation.

2. This tendency towards social isolation is intensified by far-reaching and ongoing changes to the organizational form of businesses in the secondary and tertiary sectors. If they are to survive on the global market, these businesses must keep up with the latest developments in knowledge, information and innovation, which leads them to focus their resources on departments responsible for the improvement and marketability of products. Even middle-sized universities now seem to feel the need to found innovation centres, sitting above the academic departments, to attract hotly contested grants and external funds. Responsibility within businesses is no longer distributed vertically, as in the old model of industrialism, but is more and more decentralized and network-like. Some elements of production or service provision are outsourced, others become independent elements inside the business and still others are subordinated to the innovation centres – all so that business can react faster, more flexibly and more innovatively to accelerating global market processes.[36] These fundamental changes to business structures do not leave the forms of work untouched, of course. Instead of forms of employment that permit a continuous process of further training in the core areas of production or service provision, sequences of shorter, project-like stints in the many subdivisions or outsourced areas of a company, each of which requires different skills, are fast becoming the norm, making an organic accumulation of experience-based knowledge almost impossible.[37] This creeping de-professionalization of work is the opposite of what was once promised by the industrialist ideal of lifelong employment in one place and in the same trade, with guaranteed career opportunities: that employees would have the opportunity to become

familiar with a particular area of work and gain specialist knowledge in a process of lifelong learning, finally achieving a substantial degree of expertise in a particular field. Instead, we are beginning to see individual professional biographies that comprise sequences of different jobs. The requisite knowledge for a particular project must be acquired quickly, and loses its significance just as soon as the project is complete; the fast-changing nature of technological challenges is such that the next job will require very different knowledge – to be acquired with the same speed. If the reduction in the need for face-to-face contact with colleagues increases social isolation at a given time, this second trend, towards project-style work patterns, increases it over time: because colleagues change from project to project, employees have fewer lifelong or long-term ties to colleagues in the workplace. The social network that holds the division of labour together becomes looser, and relationships become more short-lived, and thus potentially more superficial.

3. My brief sketch of today's world of work has also identified a shift from manual labour to activities that require a higher level of analytic skill, formal knowledge and mental ability – a development that is often referred to as the dematerialization of socially necessary labour, or disembodied labour.[38] The jobs that are necessary to maintain all aspects of social life that are generally considered valuable are increasingly purely intellectual in character. One might speak of a silent transition from hand–eye-coordinated work to cognitive-symbolic work.[39] Of course, physical labour done by hand has always relied on the eye, which mediates its intellectual aspect – no physical task could ever be accomplished without visual coordination – but the digitalization of communication and information appears to change the relative importance attributed to the two organs. The importance of symbolic activity gradually overtakes that of physical activity. Workers still use their hands – at the computer, at control terminals, at the supermarket checkout, or when tiling a roof, delivering mail or applying beauty treatments – but the activities that make up the new world of work increasingly require the hand merely as a trigger, rather than as an active, grasping or installing organ. We might expect, then, that work activities will increasingly be dominated by the mental and symbolic understanding of the eye, which will replace the hand as the foundational organ of work. For example, where before

many hands were involved in the painstaking work of manufacturing a car, today the final assembly requires just a few pair of eyes to check the work performed by computer-aided robots. With this epochal shift in the mode of work, the specific strains caused by work have also changed. The place of 'industrial fatigue' (Georges Friedmann) has been taken by psychological and mental exhaustion.[40] Likewise, the nature of work-related illness has also changed.[41]

4. The fourth trend is the increasing commodification of public services and household services. This process has distinct causes and follows different patterns in each of the two spheres, but in both cases leads to a similar reconfiguration of social labour, with more or less the same results. Services that were previously provided by public institutions controlled by the state, or 'voluntarily' carried out in private households, are increasingly transformed into work that is 'procured' by capitalist enterprises and sold for the purpose of maximizing profit, and consequently subordinated to the goal of increased productivity.[42] The commodification of services results from the process of market deregulation undertaken by states, which I briefly described at the beginning of this chapter. Among the measures that Western countries adopted in the late 1970s and 1980s to strengthen domestic capital and reduce government debt were wide-ranging privatizations of services that had previously been run by the state. Precisely which services were privatized depended on each state's specific institutional architecture, but many were handed over to private – often international – companies that competed for profit on the 'free market'. This rush to privatize services seemed to have no limits, not least because the public purse was often empty. Public transport, energy firms, prisons, health services and telecommunications only remained in state hands where electorates made it plain that they would not vote for parties pushing privatization. The work done in private households came to be commodified as capitalist firms responded to a situation in which women in employment who had previously done the cooking, cleaning and child-rearing for free were keen to be relieved of some of their burdens. There was thus a market for services that could be bought in, and businesses seized this opportunity to make a profit. The past three or four decades have seen a proliferation of companies offering a variety of goods and services that replace household work with market-based

commodities. These two process of commodification – of public services and household-related services – have the same result: work that previously came with secure professional prospects and reliable remuneration, or work that one previously did at one's own pace and without external pressure, becomes fragmented into measurable, standardized units and subjected to personal performance management – all with the aim of raising productivity. Thus another two areas of work are left to the seemingly unavoidable fate of marketization.

5. Finally, there is a clear trend towards more precarious working conditions. At the zenith of social democracy, under capitalist industrialism, the vast majority of employees enjoyed the socially protected and legally recognized status of 'wage labourer' (Robert Castel), which opened up, at least to some degree, the possibility of democratic participation. All this now seems a distant memory. The old wage labour relations seem to have unravelled, not only at the margins but at the core of every employment sector, from agriculture and manufacturing to services. In their stead are atypical forms of employment, such as temp and agency work, temporary employment, or the new precarious forms of self-employment. Workers thus no longer have the certainty of legally guaranteed rights to collective bargaining, trade union representation, protection against redundancy, social security benefits or paid holidays – the ensemble of benefits that Thomas H. Marshall called 'industrial citizenship', which he took to be an intermediary stage in the battle for the democratization of labour relations.[43] The growing precarity of work reveals a reality that had been cloaked by the status of wage labourer for about half a century: subordination, an absence of worker influence over working conditions, dependence on anonymous market processes and a lack of recognition.[44] This is not to say that capitalist labour relations are now showing their 'true' face, for there is no such thing as the authentic face of capitalist labour relations: their contours depend on ever-changing power relations, political and institutional frameworks, and forms of economic management. Nevertheless, what has been revealed is that the capitalist world of work has for the most part remained the opposite of the world of democracy. For those employed under such precarious conditions, acquiring the resources and capacities necessary for free participation in the democratic process will be extremely difficult.[45]

We can certainly make out other trends beyond these five, although they are less pronounced and distinctive. These days, professional skills and qualifications quickly become outdated, mainly because of technological developments. The boundaries between once clearly defined professional fields are becoming increasingly hazy – and along with them standards of good practice and commitment to social usefulness. In one way or another, most of these trends run counter to the conditions required for an organization of social labour that is conducive to democracy. Rather than working subjects being brought closer together and social labour's function of social integration being strengthened, workers are increasingly isolated and reliant on themselves. Rather than economic independence, freedom from want, and the possibility of democratic participation, jobs that scarcely pay enough to live on are growing in tandem with atypical forms of employment. Rather than a social division of labour that is intelligible to individuals, the anonymization of ownership structures and power relations makes it even more difficult to identify relations of dependence and lines of command. And rather than extending those areas of social labour, whether publicly or privately controlled, that are not subject to the pressures of the capitalist labour market, the commodification of labour has only intensified. Of course, there are also employee-friendly trends in the social division of labour that increase the likelihood of democratic participation, most notably laws that ban discrimination in the labour market and that provide for more flexible working hours. Both measures are very much in the justified interests of a part of the working population, even if the broader scope for individual decisions about working patterns also tends to blur the line between work and private life.

Overall, however, the picture I have painted points in a negative direction: the gap between the aspiration and the reality of democratic participation is widening. Before turning, in Part III, to the question of policy measures that could reduce this gap, I must first clarify which categories we should use when thinking about social labour if we are to identify how it might promote democratic participation. I approach this question in the second excursus, which explicates the concept of the social division of labour.

Excursus II: On the Concept of the Social Division of Labour

We have discussed the concept of labour, but we have yet to define another concept that plays an important role in my argument: the social division of labour. Defining it will continue the train of thought begun in the first excursus. There, I said that my proposed extension of the concept of labour would have significant consequences for our ideas about the social division of labour. This concept must now also be revised – not only regarding the activities that fall under it, but also regarding the way in which these activities relate to each other. We are pursuing a normative perspective according to which the possibilities for democratic participation should be improved by introducing a more transparent, more flexible, and fairer social division of labour, and to do so we must fundamentally rethink our ideas about how the different activities within the division of labour are integrated.

A political understanding of the world of work as a place of daily struggle and contestation does not depend, at least not exclusively, on understanding individual activities and their remuneration. It also depends on an understanding of the way in which such activities are connected within the social division of labour. In our search for principles that promote democracy – that is, democratic labour policies – our point of departure should therefore not be the work of the individual. Rather, this normative perspective requires an examination of the complicated network of interdependent contributions that make up social labour.[1] Ever since Adam Smith tentatively asked whether the mechanization of work might hinder the formation of opinions about public affairs (see Chapter 2 above), thinkers who were committed to the political inclusion of the working population through improved working conditions, among them Hegel, Marx, Durkheim and Cole, have looked not to the work of the individual but to the social organization and integration of work. Any proposal for an organization of labour that better suits the requirements of democratic will formation must therefore also include an account of how the social division of labour should be altered.

The social division of labour is a complex concept that denotes various levels of interacting activities and processes. In the social sciences, it is therefore now considered of little theoretical value. Currently, none of the major social theories uses it to explain mechanisms of social integration or, as Durkheim did, the formation of social morality.[2] For my purposes, it is crucial that the concept is used solely to refer to the constitution of social relations, and not to broader contexts beyond potential social interactions. In what follows, I use 'social division of labour' to refer to the society-wide differentiation of whole sectors of work and professional roles and to the fragmentation of work processes within businesses and administrations. Members of a society directly experience both types of division, as well as the necessary interlocking of the resulting elements. My definition follows Marx, who also distinguished between the society-wide division of different activities and the division between different steps in the work process within individual businesses.[3] Hegel, too, although not drawing on as much detailed evidence as Marx, assumed that the differentiation between various trades in society and the division of labour within 'factories' represented two different types of division of labour.[4] To determine the scope of the concept, we also need to ask what kinds of activity – both at the sectoral level and at the individual level – should be included in the social division of labour. The common response (not common to Durkheim, however) is that the concept includes only those activities for which there is a market demand and which therefore provide gainful employment in the widest possible sense.[5] I have already pointed out that this response has a disadvantage, or perhaps is even simply mistaken, in that it does not capture all those activities that are clearly necessary for the social reproduction of a given form of life but are not remunerated through market-based transactions. The concept must therefore be expanded such that it includes *all* activities that serve a general social purpose, whether remunerated or not – for example unpaid housework – but not so expanded that it begins to unravel, as is the danger with Durkheim's notion of labour, which leads him to speak of a 'sexual division of labor'.[6] Thus, my proposal is to count an activity as labour only if it makes an indispensable contribution to the repro-duction of a form of life, is therefore subject to normative rules, and can be divided into sub-elements that allow for the distribution of specialized sub-tasks to different groups of people.

The limitations of the thesis that the division of labour includes only activities performed for remuneration also highlight a number of further problems with the classical theories that could hinder my project. Many assume, for instance, that a given division of labour results from freely taken decisions, or that the degree of differentiation is determined by technological necessities that drive attempts at raising productivity, and that, once the social division of labour has taken a particular shape, there is something unavoidable about it – there are no alternatives. If that were correct – that is, if a particular division of labour had come about under conditions of free choice, was determined by technological develop-ments and did not permit of any alternative – then the social division of labour could not serve as a point of departure for a project that sought the democratization of labour. It would not be possible to change the network of interconnected activities, so we would need to limit our search for improvements to the level of individual activities. It probably comes as no surprise that I wish to avoid this negative conclusion, so I must examine the claims just mentioned, in order, I hope, to invalidate them. I shall focus on two of these common assumptions in particular – chosen because of their importance in debates about the degree to which a given division of labour can be modified or improved. Helpful to my argument in this context is the fact that there are some concrete examples, past and present, of possible rearrangements of the division of labour, at both the societal level and the level of the individual business, even if these new arrangements have not always been implemented.

I begin with the claim that a given division of labour is the result of freely made decisions: that the legally enshrined principle of the free choice of profession and equal opportunities means that all employees are pursuing their preferred professions. If this were empirically true, a project that aims to transform the division of labour in the interests of democracy could be accused of being anti-democratic, for it would be seeking to impose change on a structure that emerged without compulsion. I then turn to the assumption that productivity-enhancing technological change determines the degree and the depth of the division of labour, from which it follows that any changes to the latter would be highly impractical. My argument against the first claim is that it is guilty of what I label the voluntaristic fallacy (1). I shall spend more time on my argument against the second claim, for it plays a more significant role in public consciousness. Here I argue that the claim commits what I label the deterministic fallacy (2).

(1) Adam Smith's example of the shoemaker and tailor who depend on each other for their shoes and cloths[7] doubtless captures the sound intuition that specialization relieves individuals of the need to acquire superfluous skills and thus gives them more time to hone their own valuable talents. Overall, specialization therefore is in everyone's interest.[8] However, Smith appears to apply this idea not just to the case of individual talents in different professions but to the fragmentation of activities into separate steps within a single business. He assumes, somewhat naively, that it was often the workers themselves who pushed for mechanization, and so specialization, on the grounds that it would make their work easier.[9] Despite his reservations about excessive mechanization, he still seems to have believed that as a rule any intensification of the division of labour was welcomed, even longed for, by workers who thought it would make their lives easier.

Durkheim's analysis of the social division of labour still has something of Smith's optimism. Unlike Smith, of course, Durkheim is convinced that only a highly regulated, fair and transparent labour market will allow employees to freely choose professions that suit their capacities and qualifications. But his discussion of the socioeconomic conditions that would guarantee such a free choice of profession reveals that he did not properly account for the underlying mechanisms that compel individuals to accept a given division of labour. Peculiarly, his discussion of decisions to pursue particular professions initially focuses on the issue of genetic inheritance: a full three chapters of his book on the 'division of labor in society' are dedicated to showing that the influence of biological endowment on an individual's capacities and talents has diminished. New cultural technologies and working methods, his argument runs, have developed at such speed that they can no longer be 'fixed in the organism',[10] with the result that one's choice of profession no longer depends on one's biological inheritance. Durkheim treats the far more important factor that might constrain someone's choice – social background and status – only very indirectly, namely by way of an analysis of 'abnormal' forms of the division of labour, a term he uses for all socioeconomic conditions that prevent the modern division of labour from exerting the benevolent effects it normally has as the source of solidarity among the members of society. Durkheim sees the greatest obstacle to the free choice of profession in what he calls the 'forced division of labor'. Here he has in mind extreme inequalities of income and wealth that make it impossible for less privileged employees to reject certain contractual conditions, as the better off are able to. Durkheim convincingly argues that a lack of resources will force the less privileged to accept any contract, regardless of its contents, because they simply cannot afford not to.[11] Once income and wealth inequalities are removed through such measures as progressive income taxation and regulations limiting inheritance rights, Durkheim seems to suggest, all obstacles to the free choice of profession will have been removed. Once everyone is on the same economic footing, each person will heed the moral imperative of modern individualism: specialize in a single profession and do your best for the well-being of society through that profession. However, this optimistic outlook overlooks the fact that other mechanisms, apart from economic dependence and hardship, can also limit individuals' choice of profession and force them to take up particular occupations. And these mechanisms are no less effective.

In Part II, we came across one such factor, which seems to have passed Durkheim by: during the nineteenth century, women were forced to accept a household division of labour that was based on a male-dominated ideology's biased understanding of allegedly natural female characteristics. Women were expected to do all the housework, except where servants could be afforded.[12] However, ideologies that promote ideas about the allegedly natural capacities of particular social groups are far more widespread than this example might suggest. Other social strata or ethnic groups can also be subjected to forms of ideological typecasting that ascribe a range of natural properties to them, such that they seem predestined to take on particular kinds of activity – usually activities that are disdained. We need only remind ourselves of the antisemitic prejudice of the commercially talented Jew or the racist stereotype of the cotton-picking African American. Such ideologies have a particularly vicious effect on the choice of profession; the subtle violence of these illusions of 'natural talents' can even compel the members of these groups to specialize in the professions that the ideology ascribes to them. And if they reject the stereotypes and try to choose some other occupation, they soon confront social barriers that guard their chosen profession against outsiders.[13]

Durkheim also overlooked another mechanism that severely constrains workers' freedom to choose their professions and thus indirectly forces them into certain positions within the division of labour. Unlike the first, this mechanism involves a kind of unconscious selection by the workers themselves: they assume that they only possess the skills or qualifications for professions that are mainly practised by people from their social environment. In this case, collective typecasting is not even necessary – a generational narrative of the impossibility of social advancement suffices. Young people who imbibe this narrative underperform at school in order not to suffer disappointment when they eventually look for a job. The English sociologist Paul Willis was the first to provide empirical evidence for this disheartening but probably very common phenomenon of self-deselection. In the 1970s, he followed a group of young working-class pupils over several years, finding that they did whatever they could – getting low marks and engaging in inappropriate behaviour – to ensure that they would only be considered for the less demanding jobs and occasional work that, because of inherited doubts about their skills, they felt they could do.[14] In this social environment, the desire to avoid disappointment wins out over the courage to consider professional paths that differ from those of parents and relatives. Any kind of exploration of talents that might later become the basis for one's professional life is undermined from the very start.[15]

These are just two examples among many that underline the fact that people may be compelled to specialize in roles that may not be in their best interests – even if, legally speaking, they have a perfectly 'free' choice of profession. If we add to that the plausible assumptions that the number of jobs in certain professions is often limited (even under conditions of full employment), and that even when there is strong interest in a particular kind of labour, the low remuneration and lack of social esteem associated with it often make it so unattractive that people look for work elsewhere, it becomes obvious that Durkheim's belief in a mostly voluntary distribution of workers among the various professional fields is misguided. Indeed, it seems highly unlikely, even given a legally guaranteed right to the free choice of profession, that everyone will find a job that suits their preferences. There are too many obstacles that stand in the way of a purely voluntary allocation of workers to workplaces: socialization in school, self-doubt imparted over generations by the social environment, and subliminal effects of ideologies concerning the allegedly 'natural' talents of certain groups of people. There is therefore little reason to suppose that the contemporary division of labour is the result of free decisions taken by workers in the past. Nor is there any reason not to examine the given form of the division of labour to see whether and how it could be improved with a view to strengthening workers' capacity for democratic participation. However, the voluntaristic fallacy is only one of the objections against questioning the existing division of labour's compatibility with democracy. I now turn to another, far more substantial objection, which I call the deterministic fallacy.

(2) The second objection claims that the division of labour emerges as a result of technological developments that aim to raise productivity, and that therefore there is little point in criticizing the existing division of labour, much less seeking to change it. There are two different versions of this technological determinism: one focusing on the higher level of whole sectors of production, the other focusing on the lower level of activities within individual professions. The first version claims that the division of labour between whole sectors and professions is the result of technological imperatives: its form is inescapable because current levels of productivity and efficiency could not have been achieved in any other way. The second version claims that the ways in which various activities are aggregated into different professional profiles or job descriptions is similarly unavoidable: there is no other way of organizing these activities with the same degree of purposive rationality and efficiency. Because the two claims are based on different arguments, I shall discuss each separately.

As Michael Piore and Charles Sabel have shown in their influential book *The Second Industrial Divide*, the first version of technological determinism can already be found in Adam Smith and Karl Marx.[16] Both believed that industrial productivity could be raised only through the increased use of specialized machinery in the production of standardized goods and through the deployment of workers who could be quickly trained in its operation. For both Smith and Marx, there is no alternative to mechanized mass production in large-scale factories, nor to the resultant down-skilling of the workforce: any production technology that involves a less advanced division of labour will be less productive, and thus reduce levels of consumption and satisfy fewer needs. This argument is deterministic in the sense that it assumes that a set goal, in this case greater productivity, can be reached only in one way, in this case mechanized mass production. Piore and Sabel's rejection of this technological determinism uses the image of the 'industrial divide': moments in history when there are several technological and organizational options for successfully continuing the current path of industrial production. They argue that the option that wins out is chosen not on account of its 'intrinsic superiority' but because of the economic and political resources at the disposal of its advocates.[17] The authors present two examples of such historical junctures as evidence for their claim that industrial divides are decided politically. One is taken from the second half of the nineteenth century, when in some regions of Western Europe the crafts and small trades became an alternative to mass production. The crafts had the advantage of flexible work processes and could produce a wide range of specialized goods; moreover, because of their close ties with local markets and political administrations, they had every chance of economic success.[18] The other example is from the late 1970s, where the authors locate a similar industrial divide that could have allowed for the return to more flexible specialization in small-scale craft trades.[19] Here I provide a very brief account of the first example and ask what it means for the first version of technological determinism, which still exerts a strong influence over our ideas about the social division of labour.

Piore and Sabel hope to demonstrate that in some regions of Western Europe – they mention in particular the area around Lyon, the Siegerland and the area around Sheffield – an economically promising alternative to industrial mass production existed in the second half of the nineteenth century. These were small traditional craft businesses with highly flexible work processes and only a small degree of separation between individual activities, and they produced a whole range of specialized goods for local markets. The secret of their success, according to the authors, lay in several factors: there were agreements between neighbouring businesses that considerably reduced competitive pressures; the workers were highly motivated because of the flexible organization of the work; the businesses could easily find out which goods were in demand because of their local integration; and the production sites were often owned by cooperatives, a further motivation for the employees. All this made these businesses a viable alternative to the model of mass production that was spreading at the time. If there was consistent demand, these small businesses could also produce specialized goods for more distant markets, and in general there were few concerns about slumping sales or a dwindling customer base.[20] For Piore and Sabel, the obvious question is why such an 'astonishingly viable economic system'[21] soon gave way to mechanized mass production and thus became no more than a supply industry. As I have mentioned, the reason cannot be sought in the 'intrinsic superiority' of the victorious model's productivity or profitability, for both organizational options were level on that score: both were innovative and economically successful, and each satisfied a growing demand. Yet the craft-based mode of production was quickly sidelined, and soon came to occupy a merely peripheral position within the industrial sector. How was such a rapid reversal of fortunes possible? Piore and Sabel's answer is complicated, but it can nevertheless be reduced to a central thesis: with support from state institutions, 'those who control the resources and the returns from investment choose from among the available technologies the one most favourable to *their* interests'.[22] With this explanation, our focus shifts from the factors typically invoked in this context – productivity and efficiency – to the dimension of social struggle and political conflict. In other words, it is not the economic superiority of one method of production over another but political conflict between the advocates of the two models – with each side having different resources and degrees of influence at its disposal – that ultimately decides which will prevail. In the competition between craft-based small-scale production and mechanized factory-based production in the second half of the nineteenth century, mass production was victorious, and quickly became the 'technological paradigm' of subsequent decades, simply because its advocates were more powerful: with the help of the institutions of the state, they succeeded in economically draining their opponents of various subsidies and credits, thus bringing them to their knees.[23]

What implications does this have for the first version of the deterministic argument? Following Piore and Sabel, we need first to abandon the idea that a certain level of economic development can be achieved only through a particular organization of the social division of labour.

There are branching points in the history of technological development that offer different options for the organization of work, all of which would allow for the same level of efficiency to be maintained, but with different forms of interaction between machines and workers. As a rule, the competition between these alternatives is decided by a political struggle between the advocates of the different models; the model that wins out is the one that has more powerful advocates who can bring state decision-makers on side. Once one model has been implemented as the sole form of production, it soon acquires an aura of indispensability – a sense that it is the only productive and efficient solution – and the alternatives are forgotten. The first version of the deterministic argument thus wrongly concludes that there was only ever one feasible option for maintaining industrial growth, when in reality there have been several, equally promising options. If we resist this deterministic fallacy, any given division of labour appears far less set in stone. Whatever path of economic development is chosen, there are always technological alternatives; every path contains hints at other ways of combining machines and labour power, technological processes and human activities. The first version of technological determinism thus rests on a fallacy, and therefore cannot preclude our thinking about new ways of organizing the sectoral division of labour in the interests of democracy.

The second version of technological determinism claims that there is no alternative to the way in which individual activities are grouped into job profiles and professions, because only the existing groupings satisfy the technological demands that are intrinsic to the tasks in question. In other words, the second version of the deterministic argument applies to individual activities the claim that the first version applies to whole sectors of employment: the existing way in which labour is organized is necessarily the most efficient and conducive to economic growth. It is more straightforward to show that the claim is erroneous as it relates to this second version, for the history of capitalism provides ample evidence that the boundaries between neighbouring professions are fluid, and thus in part arbitrary.

To understand the second deterministic argument, we must first understand what it means to group different activities into professions. First and foremost, a profession is simply a name for a set of activities that has been singled out from the totality of work that needs to be done in a particular sector. Singling out a particular set of activities marks this set as a purposive unit alongside other such units, and allows for its enduring institutionalization by way of administrative stipulations regarding the qualifications required to work in this profession. An elementary example from the sociology of work is the loading of hay onto a trailer. This work process can be simplified by dividing it into the forking of the hay onto the trailer and the distribution of hay on the trailer. Those involved then have to specialize in one of the two steps.[24] Once we conceive of professions as institutionalized sets of activities and their associated skills, we may ask the same question we asked of whole sectors of employment: are these professions the result of technological and functional necessities, or are they rather the result of social and political struggles, and thus open to revision? If the latter, it is at least possible – and it is perhaps even necessary – for us to cast a critical eye over the given delineations between professions, with a view to democratizing the world of work.

We may approach this question by again looking to historical cases, for example the professional institutionalization of skilled work at the beginning of the twentieth century, which has been exhaustively researched by Ulrich Beck, Michael Brater and Hansjürgen Daheim. At the beginning of the twentieth century, the standard practice in industry of recruiting qualified workers from the traditional crafts was proving to be no longer feasible, because the development of mechanical production required novel skills that were entirely different from those required in the crafts.[25] The craftsmen recruited into the factories had specific specializations, but these were closely related to manual production processes, and so these workers lacked the expertise required to operate the ever more complicated machinery. The initial response from industrial companies was to remedy this skills shortage by creating their own training facilities, where workers could acquire the necessary qualifications as quickly as possible – with the aim of keeping to a minimum the amount of time workers spent away from productive labour on the factory floor. But this soon created new problems. Each training facility was designed very specifically to serve the interests of a particular company, so the skills acquired were often useless in other companies – a situation that was in the interests of neither industry nor the industrial workforce. This impasse posed a severe threat to the functioning of the labour market and, following the Great War, there appeared to be only one solution to it: the state had to be persuaded to create vocational training schools where the required qualifications could be gained in a legally regulated way. This 'improvement, regulation and standardization of training at a level above individual businesses' was considered to be in everyone's interest.[26] With the foundation of these schools in the 1920s – a development welcomed by all parties – the hour of the institutionalization of skilled labour had come. For our purposes, this moment is of particular significance, for it allows us to ask whether this restructuring of industrial professions was precipitated by technical and functional factors or, instead, by social and political ones.

Beck, Brater and Daheim's study provides a succinct description of how the move towards uniform professional training altered the qualifications and activities of skilled workers. The state was tasked with introducing vocational training courses that would impart both the virtues of the crafts – that is, technical skill in high-precision work – and the new, more abstract skills required to work with advanced machinery and materials. Fulfilling both requirements in a time-limited training course meant having to drop some elements of instruction in traditional craft skills, and the elements that ended up not making the cut were precisely those involved in workers' autonomous and independent control of the production process. The activities of overall control and supervision – once the basis of craftsmen's pride in their work – were now increasingly approached through scientific methods, and responsibility for these activities was handed over to professions that were the domain of the academic elite.[27] However, this removal of cognitive and supervisory activities from skilled labourers' work was by no means a consequence of technological and functional necessity. If there had been a willingness to provide more time to train these skilled labourers, such activities could well have remained a part of their job portfolio. Beck, Brater and Daheim are unequivocal: the decision not to do so was a strategic political calculation. It was based on the intention to include in the various professional profiles only those skills that, 'with regard to training resources, motivation to learn, and basic qualifications, could be developed within *one* social background'.[28] This fixation on social background reveals the political, rather than deterministic, consideration at play in this calculation: if many of the cultural, motivational and cognitive preconditions for the training had already been established during socialization at home, less money and time would have to be invested in it. The delineation of the professions in terms of sets of capacities and skills therefore often closely mirrored common assumptions about the knowledge, attitudes and expectations that were informally acquired in specific social environments prior to formal training. Thus the 1920s saw a 'new clear-cut separation of professions according to the amount of training required, and in this context a homogenization and one-sidedness of the sets of skills grouped together to form the profile of a profession'.[29] This development came about not because of technological necessity but because of considerations of economic policy.

Today, little has changed. The social construction of professional fields is still driven by an economic interest in keeping training as short and cheap as possible, and the boundaries between professional areas still run roughly between sets of skills that are assumed to be acquired in an elementary form when growing up with a particular social background. This is not to say that the fairly stable hierarchical division of professional activities into 'unskilled', 'semi-skilled', 'skilled' and 'academic' precludes any major transformations of boundaries and specializations within these categories. The rough division of professions according to the amount of training and basic qualifications required may be fairly stable, but within the broad professional fields, the boundaries between sets of skills are highly fluid and contested. There is hardly a private business or public institution in which the delineations between areas of activity are not subject to ongoing – sometimes almost imperceptible – disputes between employees and management. Should the train conductor also serve food and drinks? Should a nurse have the authority to issue prescriptions? Should a clerk have to bring the boss's morning coffee? Should teachers be responsible for maintaining the computers they use in lessons, or should the school hire a technician? All these are typical examples from the last couple of years that concern the delineations between various sets of activities, and the list could easily be extended. I mention them only to illustrate a fundamental truth about all divisions of labour within individual businesses: namely that they do not follow necessarily from the 'subject matter' or from requirements that are intrinsic to the activities in question. Rather, they result from negotiation among the individuals involved, and always remain open to revision. There is therefore no iron law that determines the differentiation between specialized activities. Employees may have a variety of motivations in this context: first, the desire to expand one's professional field by incorporating neighbouring activities, thus making one's work more interesting, less monotonous and, potentially, better paid; second, the aim of avoiding one's profession becoming devalued through the addition of extrinsic activities that are not held in high esteem and that would therefore make work in this area less qualified; and third, the desire to retain as many activities as possible within one's competency, as a protection against a potential loss of income or prestige. The resulting conflicts among employees over their areas of activity take place in the context of the management's interest in fragmenting individual activities into ever smaller elements so as to increase control over them – by way of computer-based mechanisms – and make savings. Today, the constant pressure to divide and subdivide activities in the interests of measurability and controllability characterizes work not only on shop floors but in public administrations and the service industry.[30] The way a given professional field is configured reflects an institutional crystallization of a temporary compromise between the various interests at play. If the power relations between the interests shift, the compromise will break down, and the delineation between professional fields may again begin to shift. If the set of tasks that characterizes a profession or specialism is contingent and open to revision, the division of labour within individual organizations permits of correction and improvement. It is not an integrated system, born of technological or functional necessity, to which there is no economically viable alternative. Political intervention thus need not be categorically ruled out.

The fact of the fluidity of the demarcations between specialized sets of activities deprives the second version of technological determinism of its rationale. The notion that the differentiation of professional fields reflects objective requirements, namely the technological requirements for performing particular tasks, has proven to be false. In other words, this deterministic argument depends on a fallacy because the elements of each set of tasks could also be differently distributed.

With this, we reach the end of my discussion of the concept of the social division of labour. Let us recapitulate. The first step in my argument aimed to show that the fragmentation of work processes into ever smaller units is unlikely to be met with universal approval if it is nothing but the upshot of inescapable technological change and the pursuit of efficiency gains. The inference from the absence of explicit criticism of a given division of labour to the conclusion that workers in fact freely endorse it is also not valid. The second step in my argument examined the cogency of various versions of technological determinism, and here I reached a similar conclusion. Technological determinism claims that there is no alternative to the given division of labour, whether at a sectoral level or at the level of individual professions, because a given division of labour is determined by technological and functional necessities. In countering this widely held thesis, I drew on historical examples that show that the division of labour at both levels results in fact from social and political decisions. Talk of our being compelled by inescapable technological or functional demands is therefore a deterministic fallacy. Neither the voluntaristic nor the deterministic argument need hinder my project of identifying political interventions that could create a more flexible, less monotonous and more cooperative world of work – in short, a more democratic division of labour. I embark on this project in the third and final part of my book.

PART III

The Political Struggle for the Future of Social Labour

In the concluding part of this book, I return to the normative perspective set out at the beginning. Part I discussed three ideals for a fair and appropriate organization of labour, and argued that any project for the improvement of social labour relations would be well advised to choose the third of these ideals, which I labelled 'democratic'. The democratic ideal holds that such improvement is morally necessary because democratic societies must create labour conditions that allow all labourers, whether they do paid or unpaid work, to play an active role in public will formation. If they are to have regard to their own principles – and if they are to preserve themselves – democratic societies therefore have a normative obligation to guarantee such conditions. In providing a justification for this perspective, I identified five aspects with reference to which someone's position in the social division of labour may hinder, or even prevent, their participation in democratic deliberation. Part II highlighted particular moments in the history of the world of work over the past two centuries with the aim of demonstrating that, even if there have been certain temporary improvements, we are still far from the democratic ideal. While welfare measures gradually became a standard feature of employment relations, they are being rolled back, and for most labourers the essence of their working conditions has more or less stayed the same. Most forms of employment are still characterized by a degrading dependence, lack of participation and absence of recognition, which creates a stark contrast between the world of work and the world of the democratic public sphere. The task of democratic labour policy is to change this – that is, to reduce, or even eliminate, the distance between how people experience the world of work and how they experience the world of politics. The goal must be to reorganize the existing social division of labour so that everyone, independent of their position within it, is able to participate in the processes of political will formation without external pressure or internal anxiety.

In the development of democratic labour policies, we will confront a number of serious obstacles, some political and some conceptual. At the political level, a sober analysis reveals that over the past 100 years societal attitudes were rarely as unpropitious as they are now for a project that aims to improve labour relations. For quite some time, the political public sphere has turned its attention away from the world of work and has instead focused on remedying social and cultural ills. Politicians and the media pay more attention to the protests of social minority groups that feel their issues and vulnerabilities are going unnoticed than to the labour conflicts that flare up every now and again. This shift in public attention is not in itself a problem. It reflects the fact that we live in increasingly heterogeneous modern societies, where the recognition of underrepresented – even discriminated against – groups, their identities and goals is an urgent political task. However, these conflicts – sometimes referred to as 'identity politics' – now absorb so much public attention that the capitalist world of work's deficiencies, disadvantages and hardships risk being sidelined.[1] The tendency to downplay work-related issues is exacerbated by a crisis whose severity and social impact overshadow all else. The impending climate catastrophe rightly captivates the public to such an extent that the ills of social labour relations seem more or less irrelevant by comparison. Any attempt to bring about a lasting improvement to working conditions is immediately met with the question of whether the proposals might conflict with the far more important requirements of climate protection. However we propose to democratize social labour, then, we must do so in a way that is compatible with the aim of protecting the earth's threatened ecosystem and reducing emissions.

Compounding these difficulties are the vast differences of opinion, even among those who are interested in the topic, about which reforms would be best. One – apparently growing – faction is convinced that any attempt to improve working conditions would be in vain: that they are at the mercy of the uncontrollable whims of the international labour market, and that worker solidarity has been utterly eroded by processes of work fragmentation. This group therefore suggests the introduction of a universal basic income, which would, it is said, reduce the pressure to seek employment and open up new spaces for democratic activity. This position is diametrically opposed to a project that aims to democratize existing working conditions. Each aims to create more opportunities for democratic participation, but one by improving labour relations and the other by reducing their influence on democratic participation as far as possible. As far as I can see, there is no middle way between these two options: one turns its political efforts towards the conditions of the present world of work and the other away from them. The idea of a universal basic income is therefore a fundamental alternative to the project proposed in this book, so I begin my discussion of a new politics of labour with a critical account of it. The conceptual problems I adverted to earlier will also be discussed in this context. They concern the questions of what should count as resistance and whether the world of work still contains any such forms of resistance that a politics of labour could use as social anchor points in pursuing its aims.

7

The Politics of Labour

Should we stop seeing labour as the frontline of our battle for a better future? There is a striking argument that suggests it would be a political mistake if we failed to make labour a strategic question: the presence, today and in future, of the market and the fundamental problem that the rule of the market represents for society's solidarity.

Robert Castel[1]

About forty years ago, André Gorz's *Farewell to the Working Class* laid the foundations for the project of a universal basic income. Gorz argued that it was time to bid farewell to the Marxist idea of a working class that would necessarily become the revolutionary force of history, and that instead it was time to look for ways of revitalizing democratic processes beyond the world of work. One appropriate means of effecting such a revitalization, he suggested, was the regular payment of a basic income to all adult members of society. This payment was to be unconditional, and it had to be generous enough to permit everyone to participate in the public sphere without economic anxiety.[2] Eight years later, he radicalized this idea, setting out a comprehensive theory of society according to which the technological autonomy of the industrial system had developed to such an extent that the old Marxist motto of 'liberation *within* work' had been rendered hopelessly outdated. For Gorz, the aim was now people's 'liberation *from* work' – to be achieved through a citizens' income.[3] His central thought was that this innovation would allow employees to lead a life in the community under conditions of democratic freedom. When this project was picked up a few years later by Yannick Vanderborght and Philippe Van Parijs, they expunged any trace of the influence that Hannah Arendt's thought had very clearly had on it, extracting a number of less speculative principles for a socioeconomic theory of a universal basic income.[4] Van Parijs's philosophically leaner but ethically well-justified approach helped to found a global network of activists who advocate a form of democratic politics that is independent of social labour. I will present some objections to this political programme, focusing on the core of the social theory that informs it and leaving aside the economic issues – the level at which a basic income should be set and the means of financing it. I thus also ignore the much-discussed question of whether a monthly or annual basic income could be set at a high enough level to entice people to actively participate in democratic processes. My doubts about a universal basic income provided by the state have nothing to do with the debate among different commentators over the level at which it could or should be set.[5]

Quite apart from these economic considerations,[6] the programme's core idea is that people who have sufficient income and are not compelled to work will develop a keen interest in democratic discussions about matters of public concern. This thesis contains two premises, which are not always explicitly mentioned or clearly distinguished from one another. The first assumption is that, regardless of the specific qualities of a job or workplace, people – or at least the majority of people – no longer identify with their employment as an organizational centre of their lives. André Gorz justifies this assumption by claiming that the growing importance of technology means that employment has lost its unifying and meaningful character. Claus Offe claims that the increasing 'de-professionalization' of work means that employees feel very little moral commitment to their jobs.[7] For both, this assumption justifies a decision to look beyond the sphere of work for possible factors leading to political emancipation or democratic rejuvenation. Because the sphere of work has become a normativity-free space of compulsion to which workers must adapt themselves, the authors argue, there is little reason to believe that it can foster the forms of civic behaviour that citizenship requires. From this, the advocates of a universal basic income derive the programme's second premise: that eliminating the need to find gainful employment will bring about the democratic commitment that today's forms of work can no longer provide. In effect, a basic income is seen as a surrogate for a sphere of work that still fostered community, political awareness and participation in public debate. However, as I shall try to show, this line of argument throws out the baby with the bathwater.

The baby – to continue the metaphor – is a certain function of the social division of labour, namely its role in creating an awareness of common responsibility among the members of society. Without this awareness, an understanding of the activities involved in democratic will formation cannot emerge. If citizens do not appreciate that the burdens and liabilities involved in the economic reproduction of a polity are borne by all in common, they will not recognize the need to care about the concerns of others in the exchange of political arguments and opinions. Despite its many grave deficiencies, the social division of labour remains one of the few sources from which this awareness of social community flows. When it dries up, or is cut off, any interest in engaging with the needs and concerns of others will disappear too, for individuals will no longer have any necessary links with their fellow citizens. Without a basis in an organized division of labour, democratic will formation would be a private event: whether to take part would be left to each individual. Because there would no longer be any objective need to coordinate people's individual interests, each person would be left to their own devices, and anyone who preferred not to work could live 'parasitically' off the taxes paid by those in work.[8]

It is only by being included in the social division of labour that one comes to appreciate the division of labour's role in integrating the activities of all in society – and the fact that one owes one's livelihood to this integration. Apart from state schools, there is no other sphere where almost everyone comes into contact with – and solves problems alongside – individuals from other social backgrounds.[9] Employment is unique in forcing us to step outside the narrow circle of family, neighbourhood and voluntary association, and it still possesses the potential to shape our social experience. Despite every criticism levelled against it, work is the only context in which we encounter attitudes and interests that would otherwise remain alien to us. This property of social labour – that it is a kind of melting pot that brings together culturally divergent groups and thus fosters, as a kind of by-product, elements of a communal spirit – remains its indispensable function. It establishes social 'ligatures' (Ralf Dahrendorf), even among those with stark cultural differences, and sparks an interest in social connections that would otherwise wither. In this way, social labour contributes to a broad network of communication that includes all members of society. Ever since the Marienthal study, empirical research has repeatedly confirmed that socially organized labour, even under the most miserable working conditions, still has one advantage over unemployment: that it provides a sense of social inclusion and thus secures the individual's position in society.[10] Recent studies during the Covid pandemic also seem to confirm the deleterious psychological consequences of working from home: a lack of social contact with colleagues, customers and clients reduces workers' sense of belonging.[11] Interactions in the democratic public sphere therefore require a functioning system of social cooperation.[12] To reiterate, only those who are included in such a system will be able to develop an awareness of communal responsibility that motivates them to participate in processes of public will formation. Those, by contrast, who feel that they are superfluous, that they are not contributing any socially recognized labour, will fail to develop a sense of what it means to be a member of a community, and will therefore lack an impulse to participate in such deliberation.

Because it denies this link between social cooperation and civil commitment, the political idea behind a guaranteed basic income fails. The suggestion that eliminating the need to find gainful employment will strengthen people's willingness to participate in democratic processes overlooks the fact that democratic citizenship presupposes a sense of shared responsibility and shared burdens. Today, inclusion in the social division of labour is the sole source of this attitude – at least if we seek to avoid the dangerous path of nationalism.[13] A basic income, however generous, could never replace this pre-political sense of community that employment cultivates. How could any sum of money foster social exchange, when the payment allows individuals to opt out of processes of social integration? Social labour acts as a mediator between diverse interests, and its shared responsibilities and activities compel individuals to engage in social community. But a basic income leaves individuals' interests unchanged: they remain oriented towards the satisfaction of subjective preferences, because there is no need to shape them in a social direction. In short, a universal basic income would produce private consumers, not citizens who are willing to enter into dialogue and compromise. The advocates of such a programme seem to believe, mysteriously, that the recipients of a basic income would develop an autochthonous interest, as it were, in participating in the public sphere. Perhaps they are influenced in their optimism by Hannah Arendt, who, following Aristotle, assumed that human beings are political animals by nature, or perhaps their view is an altogether unfounded result of a vivid imagination. In any case, the advocates of a basic income do not propose a functional equivalent for the sphere of work – something that would provide the social ligatures that are a necessary condition for processes of democratic deliberation. Of course, a potential objection to my argument is that communities can also form outside the social division of labour. But private associations, religious communities or sports clubs will simply strengthen existing private interests and individual preferences, rather than preparing the ground for a public space in which political activity can take place.[14] Gainful employment is one of the few pre-political spheres that support the formation of political interests and the inclination to engage in politics. Freeing people from the need to find gainful employment, without putting anything else in its place, would not only destroy that sphere but, most likely, would intensify social isolation. Sooner or later, one of the few sources of civil commitment and political participation would dry up for good.

The universal basic income project appears in a rather different light when these potentially disintegrative effects are acknowledged, and when the proposed financial support is accordingly reduced to a level that would simply strengthen the bargaining power of employees.[15] In this version, a universal basic income is not a means of democratization but rather an instrument of economic policy that provides employees with more exit options. The only significant political hope associated with this approach is that in the long term this would put pressure on employers to improve working conditions for fear that failing to do so would harm recruitment.[16] However, this attenuated version of the programme would need to confront a potential unintended side effect: that over time it might undermine the collective bargaining power of trade unions by strengthening the bargaining power of individuals. Individuals could reject disadvantageous contracts, but at the same time they would come to believe that the collective representation of their interests was unnecessary. This could lead to a vicious circle that would do employees more harm than good: the bargaining power of the individual would be increased, but at the expense of the capacity of employees' collective representatives to bring about improved working conditions and wages across the board. Therefore, *pace* the advocates of a universal basic income, the only way of making it easier for employees to access processes of democratic will formation is to identify labour policies that will bring about a democratization of labour relations.[17]

This brings us to the question of how the division of labour must be reorganized if it is to be more conducive to employees' inclusion in democratic will formation. The answer must be sought in a socio-logically imaginative democratic politics of labour that is not afraid of unconventional solutions. At this point, however, a further problem arises. Whether a policy programme can be successfully implemented always depends on the degree of support it enjoys among the members of the affected group. So if the currently dominant public impression was correct and there is hardly any resistance to contemporary labour relations, then a democratic politics of labour would be unable to rely on any solid backing on the ground, and the project of democratizing social labour would stand no chance of success. If employees express no hope or desire for working conditions that are more conducive to democracy, all our efforts will be in vain.[18]

However, there is no straightforward empirical answer to the question of whether the working population endorse the social conditions of their labour. Before undertaking any investigation into this question, we would need to define what types of behaviour would count as empirical indicators of endorsement or rejection. A widespread opinion has it that there is currently little public support for radical labour reform, because in general employees are quiescent, and there are no public demonstrations of large-scale discontent. In the hope of invalidating this assumption, I will briefly address the question of what should count as endorsement or rejection. In doing so, my intention is to broaden our ideas about forms of resistance, rejection and conflict in employment and labour relations.[19]

A common assumption is that one can speak of resistance among employees only if large groups of workers withdraw their labour or publicly express their discontent – exit or voice, as Albert O. Hirschman famously summed it up about half a century ago.[20] The notion that these alternatives exhaust the options for the expression of discontent has since become so engrained in the social sciences, as well as in wider public opinion, that the absence of these two patterns of behaviour is commonly interpreted as tacit acceptance of the status quo. If there is no public protest or mass exodus from the labour market, it is assumed that the current regulations and regimes of social labour must be broadly accepted. In fact, the bar can be raised even higher, such that to count as 'protest' or 'objection' these behaviours must be 'principled', that is, must be justified with reference to normative principles.[21] On this view, unless there are mass protests or large numbers of workers exiting employment *and* these actions are justified in normative terms, we can assume that people endorse the current working conditions.

My impression is that these assumptions bolster the widespread belief that discontent with the world of work is limited and that in general most tacitly accept the current conditions. Of course, many will concede that such passive acceptance can also result from employees' feeling that they have no alternative or are politically powerless, but this concession does little to alter the conclusion that the status quo is accepted rather than rejected. There is, of course, good reason to be cautious when drawing conclusions: not every strike or intra-office dispute is a symptom of collective dissatisfaction with working conditions. It is also true that, certainly when compared with the mass demonstrations over climate policies or the treatment of sexual minorities, there is little protest against the current organization of social labour. Yet, to draw a conclusion from the absence of visible resistance to acquiescence, even tacit acceptance, risks mistaking a façade for reality.[22] The increasing disorganization, informality and isolation of work means that resistance to the status quo has taken on new forms, which can easily be overlooked and escape public notice. Here I draw on sociological research that looks behind the scenes of today's world of work in order to give a brief sketch of these new forms of labour dispute.[23]

The most striking feature of expressions of discontent with the current world of work is their individualistic, often defeatist and mostly purely negative character. Most likely, this reflects the fact that labour disputes unravel and fragment once their motivations are not formulated by political organizations in moral terms that describe collective experiences.[24] Compared with the situation two or three decades ago, practices of resistance have clearly shifted more towards small-scale, sporadic acts of civil disobedience, defiant sabotage, mockery of superiors, and time-wasting.[25] In sum, these isolated expressions of discontent, although not an assertion of a collective will, nevertheless raise serious doubts about whether labour relations really enjoy the level of acceptance that many often suppose they do. However, caution is necessary here too: we should not be too hasty in interpreting individual expressions of dissatisfaction as genuine criticism. The obvious rise in micro-political practices of resistance – ridiculing incompetent superiors, exposing the absurdity of instructions from managers, sabotaging work processes, routinely pilfering goods or tools, and time-wasting – may have a variety of causes.[26] Perhaps workers desire some relief from the daily grind, feel bitter about being devalued or not receiving enough recognition, or need to express their anger about the volume of work or the poor pay. None of this would amount to a form of rejection that could count as morally grounded criticism. In none of these cases is there a need to reflect on and normatively justify one's behaviour, for others do not come into the picture at all. Most of these practices, however, do seem to have a characteristic that we might very cautiously describe as proto-moral: the sometimes truculent, sometimes defiant, sometimes desperate wish to gain some measure of control over the labour relations into which one has been thrown and not to have them decided exclusively by one's superiors. Whether we interpret such desperate efforts at self-empowerment as genuine resistance to the status quo, or as a search for personal meaning in a situation forced on the worker, they reveal a degree of aversion and reluctance. In other words, these phenomena should lead us to reject the assumption that contemporary working conditions are broadly endorsed. Today's labour disputes rarely play out on the national stage. Instead, like many struggles over the validity of normative rules, they take place in the backrooms of social life, unnoticed by the public, because the issues seem too unimportant, or the disputes too small-scale. The project of developing democratic labour policies can draw on these hidden moral upheavals in the world of work – the 'mole' that 'forces its way on',[27] as Hegel so nicely put it – and in this way give the project political weight and a basis in social reality. In other words, this project is not as detached from society as sceptics might claim, for it can point to the many employees whose small, silent and invisible struggles show that they want something more, something different, from their labours.

What exactly this 'more' and 'different' is, however, cannot be inferred from these extremely individualized labour struggles, despite their hidden commonalities. When the labour movement was strong, it gave a shared language, a common moral orientation, to vague feelings of injustice, but today's struggles appear mostly reactive and negativistic by comparison. People know what they do not want, but they have no clear idea of what they want in its place. In what follows, I try to provide the outlines of a democratic politics of labour that might help to fill this vacuum. To achieve this, we must first identify the common denominator of these isolated, micro-political acts of resistance, so that they might be interpreted as expressions of a desire for an as yet unknown goal – a goal that will become clear only as democratic labour policies are implemented. Any labour politics that is meant to be more than a public expression and political representation of interests that have already taken on a clear form must lay claim to a kind of transformative performativity. The dispersed, silent acts of resistance must be interpreted in a way that clarifies their as yet unarticulated aims. In suggesting such interpretations, we have no choice but to trust that they will initiate a process of reflection and emerging consciousness that will result in an explicit and shared understanding of the previously unarticulated interests, an understanding that is compatible with the interpretive framework offered.

A performative approach to policy formation creates the conditions of its own application and success. To work, it has to avoid two pitfalls. First, it must resist the temptations of an idealist or normative exuberance that would offer interpretations that are out of touch with the micropolitical acts of resistance. Otherwise, the interpretations run the risk of not being seen as reflecting the concerns of the workers. Second, the approach must not simply restate the demands expressed by individual acts of resistance as general aims, for in this case these interpretations would fail to give the acts a new meaning that could create a community with shared goals. The first mistake is to provide normative demands that are not recognized as the workers' own. The second is to fail to use the subjective expressions of resistance to draw out generalizable interpretations that transcend the personal and the individual.

What is needed, therefore, is a middle path that, on the one hand, cleaves as closely as possible to the aspiration present in subversive acts of resistance – namely to gain more control over one's workplace and become more autonomous in one's work – and on the other generalizes from workers' subjective desires by integrating them into an interpretive moral framework that can be normatively justified. Within such a framework, these desires should become intelligible as demands for labour relations that are more supportive of democratic participation.[28] Whether such a transformative reinterpretation is justified – that is, whether all these inconspicuous acts of resistance really imply a shared interest in bringing about a world of work that bridges the gap to political democracy – must, of course, remain an open question. As I have mentioned, the validity of the interpretation would be revealed only if the relevant workers take it up in a productive way, discover commonalities between their previously personal concerns and, in hindsight, recognize the interpretation as an appropriate articulation of once vague aspirations. To me, a 'politics of labour' is an anticipatory practice that becomes an effective political force only once its most important ideas meet the collective approval of those in whose name it was begun. Such a politics can be called 'democratic' because it is guided by the normative belief that labour relations should be improved such that those people it seeks to represent can participate in democratic will formation unhindered, more actively and with more self-confidence.

For obvious reasons, a politics that has to create its own preconditions cannot insist from the start that free and democratic labour relations imply the abolition of capitalism.[29] We cannot simply bring about a world without capitalism with the wave of a magic wand; we would first need to know what a future economic order that lacks a labour market, and that nevertheless maintains fundamental civil liberties, might look like. As far as I can see, no convincing account of such an order has yet been provided. Moreover, the insistence on the need to abolish capitalism is particularly unhelpful in the context of a politics that seeks moral acceptance: the people this project aims to win over are unlikely to agree that their discontent with existing labour relations requires the revolutionary abolition of wage labour. Such glib slogans point towards goals that go far beyond what today workers consider possible, so they cannot hope to unlock, or transform, workers' quiet aspirations. A democratic politics of labour must instead set out from the status quo. It must offer a sober assessment of the possibilities for improvement and reorganization, and should consider only those political measures that might allow us, under present conditions, to take the first steps towards the democratization of labour relations. This premise in fact implies that there are only two such kinds of measure. The first is institutional arrangements that could serve as alternatives to the allocation of labour via the labour market and could integrate employees into the processes of democratic will formation better and more efficiently. There are many ways of convincing people to take on socially necessary work even without special financial incentives: for instance, self-administered cooperatives, voluntary social service and public service. Of course, for our purposes, such institutions would need to bring work into a closer and more stable relationship with the democratic practice of public deliberation. If we are to avoid Durkheim's grave mistake of focusing exclusively on improving the social conditions of workers in the labour market, we must look for such institutional alternatives.[30]

This brings us to the second kind of measure that can realistically be deployed in the interests of a democratic politics of labour. We need bolder, more focused and perhaps more creative efforts at identifying improvements to working conditions that could bring wage labour closer to the world of democratic action. Here, recent efforts by trade unions have fallen short. The range of potential interventions in this area is broader than a focus simply on remuneration and working hours might lead one to suspect. As I shall show, when it comes to these broader reforms, we can still learn a lot from Durkheim, although we should be more clear-eyed than he was about the fact that such reforms may imply far-reaching limitations on private enterprise. This interference in economic decision-making will likely require the successful mobilization of political power.

The difference between the two types of measure, or two strategies, may also be described as follows: the first strategy aims to improve the conditions for participation in democratic will formation through ways of organizing social labour outside the realm of market-based wage labour (I discuss this strategy in Chapter 8); the second seeks the same aim by democratizing the conditions of wage labour from within the framework of the labour market (I discuss this strategy in Chapter 9). It should be obvious that a democratic politics of labour would be far more likely to succeed if both strategies could be pursued in parallel, or if they could even be connected so that they reinforce one another.

8

Alternatives to the Labour Market

The history of capitalism contains examples of labour-allocating mechanisms other than the 'free' labour market, and such mechanisms still exist today. These mechanisms past and present include slavery, independent businesses (e.g. craftsmen running their own craft shops or doctors running their own surgeries), forced labour (e.g. forced prostitution), cooperatives (in the heyday of the workers' movement) or mandatory public service (e.g. military service). Housework is a special case. Once it was no longer done collectively by the 'whole house', a mixture of naturalistic and patriarchal ideology ensured that it was handed to women. Whether reluctantly, defiantly or obediently, they took on the role and fulfilled its duties 'voluntarily'.[1] In the case of slavery, socially necessary work is given to labourers who are owned by slaveholders.[2] Work in independent businesses is done autonomously and remunerated with whatever residual income the business generates. Forced labour involves workers being ruthlessly coerced under the threat of physical violence. In self-administered businesses, or cooperatives, the work is done by a group of morally highly motivated individuals who operate at their own risk and on a cooperative basis. Finally, in the case of public services, the state officially allocates work to a group of people deemed suitable for it, on the grounds that such allocation is fair, advantageous or necessary.[3] Of these five possibilities, the final two are best suited for the purposes of organizing the sphere of work more democratically, albeit for very different reasons, but we should also keep the example of housework in mind. It goes without saying that we will disregard slavery and forced labour, which brutally violate the right to a free choice of profession – a necessary condition for participation in democratic processes of public will formation. The compatibility of independent businesses with democratic principles depends entirely on the political attitudes of the individuals involved – that is, doctors, craftsmen or lawyers – although the norms and regulations of their respective professional associations might help to foster a commitment to the common good and thus their integration into the democratic polity. However, in what follows I concentrate first on public service and then on cooperatives, and in doing so aim to show that, suitably modified, these models could strengthen the inclusion of the working population in the democratic process.

If it is relatively easy to see how cooperatives might be a suitable means of democratically empowering employees, the case of mandatory public service – by which I mean labour that those of a certain age are legally bound to provide for a period of time – is rather harder. Public service seems to be an authoritarian method of recruiting labour. Before we can ask whether it could promote the democratic participation of the working sovereign, we must first accept the idea that it is sometimes legitimate to suspend certain civil liberties for a limited period of time. However, here we must first distinguish more clearly two non-market allocation mechanisms for social tasks which so far I have usually mentioned without specifying their difference. Public service, as I have said, is labour that a certain group is bound to provide for a period of time. This labour must be in the interests of the common good and fulfil further criteria that I will set out below. But there are also publicly financed services, that is, labour that serves the purpose of protecting and maintaining public goods, which could be offered to the involuntarily unemployed in return for a level of pay that is not determined by the market. Both these forms of non-market-based recruitment may serve to foster the inclusion of the working population in democratic processes, albeit in different ways.

The best-known example of a public service is military service. As Michael Walzer points out, the 'moral purpose' of legally mandated military service is to 'universalize or randomize the risks of war over a given generation of young men' – and today, we may add, young women.[4] However, in almost all parts of the world, the work of soldiers has been so morally discredited that states are now forced to attract new recruits on the labour market – that is, we are increasingly seeing the return of professional armies and mercenary troops. That said, other kinds of socially necessary labour could perhaps be provided in the form of legally mandated public service as a way of promoting democratic participation. Such labour would have to clearly contribute to the common good, not require too much training and bring together people from diverse social backgrounds. Supposing that these conditions are met, two arguments speak in favour of providing labour for certain areas of work – for instance education, care for the elderly and sick, and perhaps even refuse collection – on the basis of public service rather than through recruitment on the labour market.[5]

First, given the increasing distance between cultural sub-groups and disparities between individuals' social backgrounds, compelling every fit and able member of society to spend a short period of their life – one or two years – working in a job that benefits individuals from different social backgrounds would give them an opportunity to acquire the cardinal democratic virtue of empathy for people from other social groups. Without this experience, the priorities of other groups remain alien and unintelligible, and it is difficult to take account of their concerns in the process of democratic opinion formation. Following Debra Satz, we might say that one positive effect of mandatory public service is that it gently guides individuals towards solidarity.[6] If people in a certain age group are obliged to complete public service in a variety of social environments, they will perforce extend the range of people with whose needs they are able to sympathize. Public service can thus be justified on the grounds not only that it strengthens democratic solidarity within civil life, but that, by broadening citizens' social understanding, it facilitates democratic participation – and this second point in particular makes it relevant to the normative interest of this book. Mandatory public service leads to a redistribution of the burdens of social labour, and those who were previously responsible for the relevant labour – geriatric nurses, hospital staff or social workers – will profit from this redistribution. Their work, which is often poorly paid, physically and mentally draining, and little acknowledged, will be made easier by the support of the conscripts. Because many more people will become familiar with this work, and its associated strains and burdens, it will also come to enjoy more recognition. In addition, the professional employees will be tasked with training the new recruits, which will expand and enrich their professional roles. Overall, therefore, the redistribution of social labour effected by mandatory public service will promote democratic participation by increasing the likelihood that employees in particularly stressful, poorly paid and little acknowledged professions will have more time and energy to become active in the democratic process. Employees in healthcare and the social welfare sector in particular will find that their work becomes more versatile and more publicly recognized, as well as entailing a richer range of social relations.

The legal arguments against the introduction of mandatory public service are weighty, of course. It means suspending the right to freely choose one's profession, if only for a short period of time, and the economic advantages and opportunities alone are certainly not enough to justify such a significant restriction of individual freedom. On balance, however, I believe that the positive effects of mandatory public service on democratic life make this time-limited restriction a price worth paying. These positive effects can be illustrated by looking at communities on the east coast of the US that, for several generations, have had a rule that obliges every adult, depending on their abilities, to work for an essential community service at certain regular intervals. If we are to believe the reports, this form of collective self-obligation not only strengthens community spirit and creates mutual trust in the cooperative attitude of its members, but means that the workers employed in these services are better integrated in the community and perform their roles with greater self-confidence. But it is obvious that such a community-based model of public service cannot easily be transposed onto a larger polity: the requisite personal contact, mutual trust and solidarity would be absent, so people would be unwilling to render services voluntarily. In smaller, more intimate communities, this willingness is based on an immediate understanding of joint responsibility, but in larger polities it must be replaced with legal coercion by the democratically legitimized state, which in this way would bolster citizens' more attenuated sense of community through a short-term obligation to do socially useful work. This legal obligation would be the functional equivalent of the collective self-obligation that smaller communities use to maintain a general sense of common responsibility for their achievements.

The intention and function of state-financed services differ significantly from those of a mandatory public service, and the beneficial effects of such services on the inclusion of individuals in democratic will formation are therefore also of a very different kind.[7] A state-supported service also offers an alternative to the labour market, but like the labour market it rests on the legal principle of voluntariness. Like mandatory public service, only activities that are clearly in the common interest count – that is, work in areas such as healthcare, education, public transport or municipal services. In the first instance, such work would be offered to individuals who are long-term unemployed but who are willing and able to work, in return for relatively modest pay that would be fixed independently of the market. For this group, working in a state-financed service – preferably organized by public institutions such as welfare organizations, churches or trade unions – would allow them to regain self-confidence, receive social support and reintegrate into the system of social cooperation. This should not be confused with any sort of forced labour introduced in the name of whatever political ideology: the schemes would be based on voluntary participation and require the explicit agreement of those taking part. To have the desired effect, the services rendered would need to have an obvious social purpose, so that the participants gain public recognition and thus develop confidence in their own abilities.

Strictly speaking, mandatory public service and state-financed services complement the labour market rather than replacing it entirely. Public service aims to foster democratic attitudes and ease the burdens on those working in strenuous professions; state-financed services aim to offer the unemployed an opportunity to regain a sense of social belonging. Mandatory public service of one or two years would complement the labour market by removing a structural deficiency of modern democracy, and could thus be permanent. State-financed services schemes, by contrast, would probably be introduced only during periods of high unemployment. Even then, a well-funded programme of continuing education or training is probably a better tool for bringing the long-term unemployed back into the system of social cooperation.

Self-administered businesses differ from these two models in that they offer a genuine alternative to the capitalist labour market, even while remaining subject to the laws of economic competition. In my view, a gradual transformation of private and state-owned businesses into autonomous cooperatives is a direct path to a world of work that is compatible with democracy, but progress along the way will probably involve surmounting a large number of obstacles.

We speak of producer cooperatives – as opposed to consumer cooperatives – when the workers control all decision-making, including in relation to the appointment of managers, because they own the means of production and capital. There are, of course, many hybrid forms of cooperative, involving different combinations of ownership rights (profit sharing, shareholding) and rights to make particular kinds of decision (on business goals, profit distribution, composition of the management, etc.).[8] As early as the nineteenth century, many observed that the capacity of producer cooperatives, of whatever form, to increase workers' self-esteem, solidarity and ability to act politically could be useful in the political emancipation of the working class. This belief was held not just by figures in the workers' movement but by some philanthropic entrepreneurs and liberal thinkers, who promoted the idea through policy initiatives or public advocacy.[9] The most prominent liberal proponent of the model was John Stuart Mill. In his *Principles of Political Economy*, he explains at length that producer cooperatives could bring about a more active exercise of workers' and employees' political rights – that the experience of working in self-administered businesses would promote 'a new sense of security and independence in the labouring class; and the conversion of each human being's daily occupation into a school of the social sympathies and the practical intelligence'.[10]

Numerous authors have adopted Mill's argument, albeit with varying political intentions. One group, taking a position we might call 'market socialism', sees state support for producer cooperatives as a means of transforming capitalism towards a system of market-based competition among self-administered businesses.[11] A rather more liberal group takes producer cooperatives to be a helpful complement to capitalist enterprises: cooperatives' more satisfying working conditions, higher levels of motivation and thus greater productivity would create an economic incentive for capitalist enterprises to follow suit and give their employees more participatory rights. In addition to such pleas for cooperatives in the name of social reform, there have also been concrete economic policy initiatives aiming to transform private businesses into self-administered businesses, despite the predictable difficulties arising from competitive pressures in the process. In some cases, cooperatives were founded by philanthropic entrepreneurs who wanted their employees to receive a higher proportion of the profits and have a greater say in decision-making. In other cases, employees of a business threatened with insolvency took it upon themselves to save it by transforming it into a cooperative. A French law, passed in 2014 under a socialist government and still in force today, is worth mentioning in this context. It aims to promote the creation of cooperatives through significant tax breaks and to strengthen solidarity between businesses. It has since led to the foundation of numerous cooperatives.

When a business is based on a belief in the idea of democratic self-administration, it confronts all the problems that typically arise from the tension between moral intentions and the capitalist profit motive.[12] In particular, these problems relate to the need to recruit suitably skilled workers, maintain a stable and highly specialized management, and avoid free riding.[13] One common aim behind the foundation of cooperatives is to narrow the gap between the wages of skilled and unskilled labourers and thereby to promote egalitarian attitudes and solidarity, but this often means that the skilled workers the cooperative urgently needs may be enticed by offers of better pay from capitalist companies. Likewise, subjecting recruitment decisions to a majority vote of all workers often proves impractical: crucial decisions regarding sales markets, the purchase of materials and intelligent risk analysis require an experienced management whose composition cannot be left to the unpredictability of voting outcomes. Finally, the cooperative ethos of the majority always runs the risk of attracting free riders who seek to enjoy the benefits of membership without making much of a contribution themselves.

These structural problems have affected cooperatives operating within a capitalist framework from the very beginning. Today, they face the additional problem posed by intensified competition in a global market for labour and goods. Once they have reached a certain size, traditional capitalist companies have no difficulty in moving parts of their services or production processes to low-wage countries. For logistical as well as moral reasons, self-administered businesses find this much harder: as a rule, they do not have the international connections or expertise to make such moves, nor does their ethos permit them to cut costs by using labourers in low-wage countries.[14] A large body of evidence demonstrates the positive effects that democratic organization has on workers' collective self-confidence and ability to be politically active,[15] but the economic prospects of cooperative enterprises are not hugely promising, at least within the current economic system. Under capitalism, the typical fate of the producer cooperative is either economic ruin or a dilution of its original aims. Changing this would require generous state subsidies and provision of qualified and morally motivated managers for as long as it takes for cooperatives to operate successfully in the market and thus become a testing ground for this alternative labour regime. If the cooperatives could survive after the state support ends, without compromising on their principles of democratic self-control, this would be some indication of their viability as an alternative to the conventional labour market. Such an experiment would no doubt require an enormous amount of public money, but this could be justified on the grounds that there is a constitutional obligation to facilitate democratic participation, and that this investment would do more to cleave a way for the hard-working population to join the democratic process than most other subsidies. As we have seen, cooperative control over work processes and business aims are ideal means for creating the necessary conditions – at least the psychological and social conditions – for participation in democratic will formation.

In this context, it is worth mentioning cooperative initiatives in the area of housework, which was traditionally seen as solitary work. I have frequently touched on the situation faced by women who are forced to do housework, sometimes in addition to their paid employment. For them, it was, and still is, difficult to participate in the democratic arena. In addition to the burdens of cooking, cleaning and childcare – which were particularly exhausting after servants disappeared but before labour-saving devices were present in the home – the work was done in isolation, away from social networks.[16] Feminists of various political persuasions frequently sought a fairer distribution of housework between the sexes, but they also asked how housework could be socially integrated in such a way as to reduce this isolation. Perhaps the most radical proposals were put forward by female activists in Red Vienna – the city between 1919 and 1934.[17] Working with the social democratic city council, they helped to create communal spaces for housework in the new council-built apartment blocks. In a considerable number of the new buildings, cooking and washing were done not in individual households but in large kitchens and washhouses that were easily accessible for all tenants. Thus, these tasks could be performed cooperatively, rather than in isolation. In some cases, the cleaning of the flats – which, despite the best efforts of the feminists, was still primarily the task of women – was also handed over to cooperatively organized cleaning services.[18]

However, this historical example of the socialization of housework had no significant effects in the long term. The model ended with the end of Red Vienna, when the Fatherland Front took control of the municipal council in 1934, and as far as I can see it has not been taken up again since. Indeed, today we see the opposite trend: the commercialization of housework (see Chapter 6 above). Food preparation, cleaning and doing the laundry are now market-based services that are provided for profit. They belong to the sphere of private consumption, and their quality thus depends on the family's income.[19]

At present, neither producer cooperatives nor Red Vienna-style cooperative models of housework enjoy a particularly good reputation among the general public. Over decades, the idea that work is something done by individuals to secure their own livelihood has become deeply rooted in the cultural understanding of Western capitalist societies, so any suggestion that we might move towards more cooperative forms of communal action is unlikely to arouse significant interest. If we never-theless want to keep hold of the idea – because, as I have mentioned, it is a direct path towards the establishment of a connection between political democracy and the social division of labour – we might more realistically look to introduce self-administered businesses in more peripheral areas of the economy. This suggestion fits with a thesis proposed forty years ago by Johannes Berger and Claus Offe, who argued that the niche economy of alternative, small-scale, self-organizing businesses could be the seed for a new generation of cooperatives.[20] Since then, the number of such initiatives in large Western cities – offering neighbourhood services such as bicycle repair or homework support for pupils, or selling books or organic food – has most likely risen. Because these community-based businesses are under no pressure to generate large returns, those running them can organize their work with a fair degree of autonomy. Nor does pay have to be performance-related: the businesses are characterized by a general spirit of mutual support that tends to lead to an equitable distri-bution of profits. Because of the local nature of the businesses, they have good relationships with customers, who are often personal acquaintances or regulars, and knowing their customers' preferences makes it easier to anticipate what merchandise needs to be bought in. These alternative businesses in fact seem to represent small-scale producer cooperatives. The employees control the business – sometimes as trustees, but often as full owners – and are therefore free to decide on the organization of work and the goals of the business. However, two factors mean that community-based alternative businesses might be unable to serve as trailblazers in a rejuvenation of the cooperative model. First, their economic success is closely tied to a narrow local consumer base whose foreseeable needs allow the businesses to plan their work. Second, they therefore rely heavily on a particular social environment, and thus rarely attempt to forge connections with other organizations in their sectors. All in all, the combination of economic necessity and voluntary self-limitation means that this alternative economic model cannot spread far beyond the niche in which it originally blossomed. Autonomous small-scale businesses are characterized by an insularity and an unwillingness to become part of the social division of labour, which limits their usefulness in the context of a democratic politics of labour. Their culture and attitudes are far removed from those of the majority of workers, so they are unlikely to be seen as a model for a transformation of the world of work more broadly.[21] If the alternative economy cannot be lured out of its niche existence and integrated into a democratic labour reform initiative, whether by means of substantial subsidy or political persuasion, it will continue to be a small remote island of successful cooperation, far off from the precarious mainland of gainful employment. There is no connection or social exchange between the two, so there is no mutual support in the battle against the capitalist economic compulsion towards ever increasing profits. To bridge the gap to the world of gainful employment, small-scale community-based businesses would need to opt to join existing rudimentary networks of cooperatives. Failing that, the only hope for cooperative alternatives to wage labour is that various isolated experiments with cooperative business models – such as those listed by Erik Olin Wright under the heading of 'worker-owned cooperatives' – will be replicated more widely.[22] This will only happen if there is public pressure on social democratic-leaning governments to offer cooperatives generous tax relief and help in the recruitment of suitable management personnel.

9

Improvements to the Labour Market

In the previous chapter, we discussed alternatives to the labour market. The second strategy for democratizing labour relations is to improve the conditions of wage labour so that the workplace allows employees to experience themselves as fully fledged members of a democratic polity. Given the account of contemporary capitalist working conditions provided in Chapter 6, we might think that a comprehensive transformation of wage labour is a pipe dream. As Johannes Berger and Claus Offe warned long ago, any social theory that attempts to project future social developments on the basis of a philosophical belief in the correctness of some normative principle is fatally flawed.[1] We must therefore first understand what steps we would actually have to take to improve wage labour, for without this account of the necessary reforms we would have only an imaginary leap from the status quo to the bright future.[2]

To begin with the obvious, without a return to 'standard employment' conditions and adequate legal protections for wage labourers, the democratization of the labour market will be impossible. There must first be a 'constitutionalization' (Johannes Berger and Claus Offe) of employment relations for all workers who are recruited on the labour market. There must be legally guaranteed bargaining powers and fundamental statutory rights for economically active citizens. Only then can we begin to think about measures that aim to improve the division of labour in terms of the quality of the work, its distribution and how the various tasks can be cooperatively coordinated. The 'end in view', as John Dewey put it in his reflections on progressive action,[3] is therefore to reduce and eventually eliminate the low-wage sector and to institutionalize rights for wage labourers, thus handing them back the protections and entitlements they once enjoyed under the welfare systems of the past. Only when these protections have been clawed back – when we have recovered a past that, today, looks like a utopia – can we turn to the issue of what further measures are necessary to democratize the world of market-based labour.

At this point, we need to return to the five dimensions of a person's position within the social division of labour, which I identified in Chapter 3: the economic, temporal, psychological, social and intellectual dimensions. Each of these, I said, can have a strong and lasting negative impact on workers' ability to participate in democratic processes. Each dimension can throw up particular obstacles. A lack of economic independence will make it difficult to form political opinions without taking the expectations and views of third parties into account. If work is time-consuming and strenuous, there will be no time left to become politically informed and politically active. If one's work is not socially recognized or appreciated, one will lack confidence in the validity and value of one's political convictions. If workplaces do not allow workers to become acquainted with processes of cooperative will formation – a kind of 'pre-political' democratic practice – then this will have negative consequences at the social level. Finally, if work is unstimulating, overly repetitive and monotonous, workers will not develop a sense for their own creative abilities or a sense that their ideas are relevant; at best, they will participate in public will formation in a spirit of resignation, rather than as courageous advocates of their own ideas and opinions.

I put forward the following thesis: the less a workplace positively supports workers along one or more of these dimensions, the less the workforce will be able to participate in public deliberation in a way that satisfies the normative promise of political participation. For a labour politics that seeks to reorganize the labour market so as to make it more compatible with democracy, these five dimensions are levers that can be used to bring about improvements. I shall therefore go through each in turn to identify possible reforms that might reduce – or perhaps remove altogether – any negative impact on democratic participation. It quickly becomes clear that such interventions imply substantial limitations on entrepreneurial freedom. We will also see that some of these levers influence each other. Further, it is worth bearing in mind that I present only a procedural outline for my proposed interventions. I merely sketch some normative vantage points: more detailed proposals cannot be formulated without taking concrete historical conditions into account.

The first of our levers illustrates this difficulty. As I have demonstrated, economic independence is clearly an indispensable requirement for free participation in democratic will formation. But what does this requirement mean in the context of an actual labour market? What would a workplace that guaranteed such independence actually look like? It is difficult to provide a list of necessary and sufficient conditions here.[4] Two conditions are intuitively plausible, even if they are in themselves not sufficient. First, wages must be high enough to guarantee the subsistence of the workers and those who are dependent on them. The calculation of the necessary level of income must take into account culturally specific standards and the number of dependants who, for whatever reason, are incapable of generating their own income. Second, it is also obvious that wage labourers must not be pressured by the threat of sanctions, such as redundancy or reductions in income, to adopt views, whether on private or public matters, that suit their superiors or employers. We must not forget that under conditions of wage labour, economic independence also means that one must be able to form an opinion on the basis of one's own, freely chosen principles, despite being dependent on an employer.[5] But these two conditions – the guaranteed right to a minimum wage (including sickness pay) and the guaranteed right to freedom of opinion in the workplace – are clearly not sufficient to ensure economic independence. To be genuinely free from economic influence in the formation of one's will and opinions, one cannot be forced to do work that one finds repellent, or that requires skills one feels one lacks, over longer periods of time. Today, some social security systems make the payment of unemployment benefits conditional on a commitment to accept any job that is offered. This not only contradicts the formal legal right to a free choice of profession, but forces people into acquiescent and conformist behaviour that is incompatible with what an autonomous citizen is entitled to expect in a democracy. Finally, employees' economic independence will be guaranteed in part by having some participatory rights regarding the formulation of the conditions of the labour contract. Without such rights, and thus without any control over their living and working conditions, employees will not be able to develop a sense of self that allows them to make full use of their democratic rights. Taken together, these factors define 'economic independence' under conditions of wage labour. They amount to what Robert Castel describes as normalized salarial relations – the result, as Castel writes, of the workers' movement's struggle, over at least the last 100 years, for better working conditions. In other words, we are talking not about achieving something new but about regaining what had already been won.[6]

The situation is slightly different in the case of the second factor. Since Karl Marx wrote his famous chapter on 'The Struggle for a Normal Working Day' 150 years ago, it has become clear that the length of the working day is not the only influence on economic growth and social prosperity.[7] Technological innovation, workplace reorganization and the colonial exploitation of natural resources and labour in the Global South played equally important roles.[8] As a result of all these factors, working hours in Western countries almost halved during the period from the mid-nineteenth century to the peak of industrial capitalism around 1965. During the same period, and at the expense of the world's poorest regions, economic productivity rose sharply. Four decades ago, European trade unions were still fighting for a further reduction of working hours in the interests of full employment. Since then, however, astonishingly this trend seems to have gone into reverse, as a precarious and underpaid stratum of working poor has developed in the West. To secure a livelihood, people in this group have no choice but to take on several precarious jobs.[9] One reason for this reversal is digitalization, especially in the service sector. In many areas, digitalization has led to fluid boundaries between work and leisure time,[10] meaning that some are now working longer than people did in the 1980s.[11] For workers, of course, this means less time for private, social or political activities. But it is not just the quantitative reduction in leisure time that narrows the scope for political participation: the intense mental strain of working several jobs or of having work intrude into the private sphere also takes its toll. In Chapter 6, I spoke in this context of 'mental exhaustion' as a new symptom of work-related illness. Recall the basic formula with which I attempted to capture the way the quality of the work influences levels of political participation: the more intense the mental or physical strain of the work, the longer and more tiring the time spent at work will appear to the workers, and the more time they will require to restore the capacity to work.[12] This means that a politics of labour faces a difficult task: finding a way to significantly reduce working time in fast-paced occupations that are mentally and physically particularly exhausting while avoiding compensating for these reductions by drawing on cheap labour from poorer regions of the world. The traditional idea that all forms of social labour should have roughly the same working day has, in any case, turned out to be erroneous: it ignores the fact that quantity alone cannot tell us anything about the actual strain of a job or, therefore, how long a worker needs for recreation. If the struggle for shorter working hours does not take qualitative differences into account, it is very likely that whole groups of employees – such as the working poor, migrant workers and so-called 'entreployees' – will not have a realistic opportunity to participate in democratic will formation in a way that satisfies what is normatively demanded. Given the pressures of today's work life, they will quite simply lack the time to engage with political questions as well-informed participants in democratic practices of deliberating, exchanging opinions and formulating positions.

None of this is to say that our aim is simply the restoration of the 'salarial society' of the 1960s.[13] The measures needed to remove the economic and temporal obstacles created by precarious employment and ever-increasing performance expectations might look like attempts to recover lost ground rather than ways of introducing a new social division of labour. But this impression vanishes when we now go on to ask how we are to remove the obstacles to democratic participation arising in relation to the remaining three dimensions. Here it also becomes clear that interventions in one dimension require improvements in another.

This mutual dependence is particularly striking in the case of the third dimension. I have claimed that people whose work is not sufficiently recognized, or is even looked down upon, will find it difficult to believe in the worth of their own convictions, and thus to be self-confident participants in public will formation. Some might object that recent decades have seen managers in capitalist businesses and public administrations often very eloquently praising their employees to boost their morale and loyalty. The appreciation I have in mind, however, is not merely symbolic – not a matter of verbal nicety. Such rituals of recognition make no 'material' difference at all, and are therefore purely ideological. Unless they come along with significant financial rewards or substantial improvements in the organization of work, the recipients usually realize quite quickly that such praise is a mere strategy to increase performance or create identification with the aims of the business.[14] Of course, a good atmosphere and a supportive and affirmative culture may still have a positive effect on job satisfaction, but these are superficial effects: they do not touch the core of the problem of insufficient recognition of contributions to social labour.

An adequate treatment of this problem must first draw a distinction between the appreciation of individual contributions and the contributions made by a whole professional and occupational sector. The first kind of recognition relates to an individual's work contribution within the social division of labour. This work can be done more or less well, and those who are in a position to judge this are usually customers, colleagues and superiors. Such judgements should make use of general criteria, even if the validity of these criteria is difficult to evaluate for those without the contextual knowledge and familiarity with the nature of the work.

The second kind of recognition relates to work done by individual professional groups. Here, the political community at large is responsible for bestowing such recognition. Implicitly or explicitly, a polity must always decide how it values the various kinds of effort that uphold its form of life. Only the second kind of recognition is relevant to our interest in fostering democratic participation. As a rule, it is workers in sectors that are disdained by society who begin to doubt their ability to participate in democratic practices. However, a particular profession's level of social recognition is not easy to measure. Cultural knowledge, symbolic gestures and institutional commitments all play a role and the overall degree of recognition results from a complicated and mutable relationship to these elements. The salary level may give us a good initial indication, but its significance is limited by the fact that it is determined chiefly by economic demand,[15] which rarely corresponds to the degree of general esteem. Indeed, there are often glaring discrepancies between the two: professional activities that yield huge financial rewards may nevertheless conflict with society's values and thus be penalized with some contempt. We need only think of the sudden and dramatic reputational damage suffered by managers of many influential banks after the financial crisis in 2008, despite the fact that their income was largely unaffected.[16] A better indicator might be the level of general esteem, attention and material privilege that a sector enjoys within the polity. A positive development in these three aspects often signals a shift in what we might call the 'moral economy' of a polity: that an occupational area that hitherto enjoyed little esteem will from now on be more valued, more visible and looked after better. This is what happened to housework: once done almost exclusively by women, it remained largely invisible before the feminist movement put it centre stage, and thus ensured that it received more recognition within society's system of values.

The example of housework also makes clear that there is no necessary correspondence between the social esteem enjoyed by an occupational area and its 'use value', that is, its usefulness within the social division of labour. Services such as cooking, cleaning and childcare have always been indispensable for social reproduction, and yet for 'ideological' reasons they enjoyed little public esteem and were mostly ignored throughout the history of modern capitalism.[17] It is generally difficult to identify the reasons why a particular society has a high regard for certain occupations and a low regard for others.[18] The qualifications a job requires, and thus the intellectual abilities the employees are assumed to have, obviously play a substantial role. Of only minor significance, by comparison, are the effort a job requires and the job's importance for maintaining the material basis of our cultural form of life. For instance, carers for the sick and elderly, firefighters, refuse collectors, bus and subway drivers, and those working at supermarket checkouts are not usually held in particularly high esteem, but their work is crucial for our health and well-being and requires a high level of manual, intellectual and/or communicative skill.[19]

The example of housework also neatly illustrates the psychological consequences for those who do work that does not enjoy a high level of social recognition. Traditionally there was very little social appreciation of the daily activities of 'housewives' and it was therefore commonly assumed that they did not possess any socially useful or valuable skills. They thus lacked the self-confidence to play an active role in political debate. To generalize from this example, we might say that there is a social mechanism whereby a lack of recognition and tacit disregard for a whole class of work activities lead to epistemic self-doubt among the workers themselves. When an occupation is seen as requiring little intellectual ability and the employees as therefore lacking sound political judgement, these individuals will sooner or later begin to doubt that they have a voice in democratic debate. This close connection between low social esteem and epistemic self-doubt can certainly be broken, for instance by way of a 'counterculture of dignity' or through interest groups.[20] But without such countermeasures, the negative effects will probably set in rapidly. In seeking to participate as equals in democratic will formation, employees who work in areas that society holds in low regard will struggle to overcome significant psychological inhibitions. This situation is utterly unjustifiable, and a democratic labour politics must therefore try to change it. It must look for ways of influencing society's value system so that those doing hard, indispensable and self-abnegating work for society receive the esteem they deserve.[21]

Of course, such a 'revaluation' in society's value system cannot simply be decreed by the state. Cultural value systems are historically grown textures of widely shared convictions and cannot be readjusted simply by public reasoning. They do not immediately give in to the pressure of argument: they are internalized patterns of response that have become part of a community's second nature, and they can be altered only through long-term learning processes. The problem is even deeper when it comes to the way a culture views the social status and qualitative requirements of a whole area of work. It would not suffice to remove the existing hierarchical order and ensure that work that serves our basic well-being was on a par with other professional areas. In addition, those who do this work would also need to be convinced that they deserve this new-found esteem. Adam Smith already knew that people are not usually satisfied simply because they receive praise or recognition, and that real self-respect develops only when people actually feel worthy of such praise and consider their achievements to be 'objective' accomplishments.[22] This is important for the issue of the widespread lack of recognition of professions that are important for the functioning of society, because it means that attempts to persuade the public to recognize the worth of such professions, even if successful, will not be enough. If labour relations remain unchanged – if labour relations do not convey to the workers that they genuinely deserve higher esteem – then the workers' feeling of self-worth will not increase. Improved public esteem for a particular profession will have a positive effect only if it is accompanied by enduring improvements to working conditions and the organization of work.

It is this difficulty that points to the very close connection between the third and fifth dimensions – the psychological and intellectual. The former has a negative impact on a worker's capacity for democratic participation when the work is not socially recognized. The latter has a negative impact when the work is repetitive, unstimulating and intellectually unchallenging – when it does not allow workers to realize their creative and intellectual potential, so that they come to doubt their ability to initiate change. The close connection between tedious work and a lack of recognition consists in the fact that these factors can only be improved in tandem. If work remains monotonous, intellectually undemanding and soul-destroying – as much work in the service sector and industrial production often unfortunately is – workers will not be able to develop more self-respect. If working conditions do not change, symbolic expressions of public esteem will be ineffectual. How should someone who day in, day out handles parcels under strict supervision, who is ordered to make one food delivery after another, who has to care for seriously ill patients in a cost-cutting hospital that piles ever-increasing time pressure on its workers and leaves them little room to show empathy – how should people working under such conditions be proud of their work and derive feelings of well-deserved recognition from it? Such recognition is possible only if an increase in social esteem for these jobs – jobs that public opinion often sees as simple and unskilled, but that in fact involve sacrifice, commitment and tact, and whose value for our well-being cannot be overestimated – goes hand in hand with a qualitative reorganization of these professional areas.

This brings us to the factor that will perhaps be of particular importance in the struggle to create labour relations that are more conducive to democracy: the social factor. Here, the task is to reconfigure the social division of labour so that every position within it allows for participation in democratic exchange. Even if we imagine that all other interventions at our disposal had been deployed, addressing the social factor would remain crucial. That is, if social policy measures and legal reforms guaranteed the economic independence of all wage labourers; if a redistribution of tasks reduced working hours for all employees, leaving them enough time to get hold of and digest political information; if experience had finally made clear to the public the worth of essential services and work activities and they therefore received the recognition and support they deserve; and if the introduction of temporally limited, obligatory public service had created more understanding for the hardship suffered by other social groups – even if all this had been achieved, there would still be many types of work whose draining monotony, lack of individual agency, and isolation would make it hard for workers to participate in democratic will formation to the normatively demanded extent. To remove the disadvantages associated with such jobs, we would require interventions in the division of labour far more radical than any of the improvements enumerated so far. The way the social division of labour delineates workplaces from each other, and the way they relate to each other, would need to be reconfigured, so that none of the work is as intellectually one-sided, draining, tiring and unstimulating as is currently the case in many areas of the service and production industries. It is difficult even to conceive of such a radical reorganization of the division of labour. Fortunately for us, however, Émile Durkheim was already dealing with similar problems 130 years ago. Although his work on the division of labour in society was written when labour conditions and business structures were, by our standards, idyllic, transparent and small-scale, it nevertheless contains some useful suggestions for how we might reduce the division of labour and hence its negative effects.

Durkheim examined not only the legal rights of wage labourers but their professional environment, asking whether it was a space of fair social cooperation that was thus conducive to democracy. He did this for the same reason that we have mentioned several times already, namely that the self-respect, intellectual initiative and social skills required for people to see themselves as free and equal citizens, as fully fledged members of a society that is based on the division of labour, require in turn that their occupations be sufficiently stimulating and complex. For Durkheim, even giving workers as many individual and collective rights as possible will not be enough, for these rights say nothing about the quality of individual workplaces and how challenging they are. On the basis of this premise, Durkheim reflected on how the division of labour and its interweaving of occupational areas would have to change if every employee was to develop the abilities required for democratic participation.[23] He made myriad suggestions, but two sets of proposals stand out as particularly relevant, even if they are tailored to the older, industrialist society. First, he recommended that each role be augmented with further responsibilities until the worker can understand how the role fits within the network of other roles. Such a reconfiguration of professions – away from a model that breaks down work into ever smaller and more repetitive operations – would be in the interests of wage labourers, Durkheim believed, because it would allow them to understand the value of their work to society at large.[24] In other words, for Durkheim, only those who can see, in their workplace, what they are contributing to the reproduction of society can have a sense of the value of their work as something worthy of recognition. Crucially, this is possible only if one's role is rich enough to be understood as an independent contributor to the overall process of cooperation, one that is more or less complete in itself. We saw in the second excursus, on the concept of the division of labour, that Durkheim's ideas about a necessary reconfiguration of professions are not unfounded or unrealistic. We saw that professions are the result of an arbitrary and power-based bundling of activities into entities that are alleged to be functionally useful. There is therefore no reason why we should be prevented by technological necessity from rebundling the existing job profiles. It is not clear whether Durkheim appreciated the fluidity of the delineations between occupational fields, but he seems to have assumed that there are no structural obstacles to loosening and expanding them so as to render more transparent the cooperation that the division of labour embodies. However, any expansion of occupational areas must not covertly serve the purpose of increasing efficiency. As Georges Friedmann's pathbreaking study on mechanized production points out, we must carefully examine any apparent attempt to alleviate the effects of the division of labour to see whether its aim is really to reduce monotony and fragmentation, or whether in fact its hidden agenda is to increase individual productivity.[25]

Durkheim's second measure for improving wage labour in line with this normative principle is all of a piece with his first, but it has a different aim, which he considers just as important as increasing the transparency of the division of labour: namely, making individual tasks complex and rich enough so that the individual's mental and intellectual capacities are not stifled. Like Adam Smith and Hegel before him, and many others after him,[26] Durkheim was convinced that the monotony and intellectual one-sidedness of wage labour severely limit the worker's ability to participate, proactively and self-confidently, in the social negotiations that determine the rules by which society is governed. By now we are well acquainted with the argument that he uses to support this claim. In short, those who have to carry out the same intellectually undemanding operations over weeks, months and years are in danger of losing the mental and intellectual skills necessary for participation in the processes of democratic will formation. To avoid this, he again suggests modifying the set of tasks in particularly negatively affected occupational areas by adding tasks from neighbouring areas. To give some contemporary examples, those working at supermarket checkouts could also check stocks and order supplies, cleaners could also carry out simple repairs or do gardening work, and assembly-line workers in the meat industry could also be put in charge of quality control. The purpose of expanding individual professions by adding related tasks is always the same: Durkheim wants to ensure that individual jobs do not become so intellectually impoverished and undemanding that employees lose the ability, courage and self-confidence to act as equals in society's processes of will formation.

The two measures suggested by Durkheim, however, do not touch upon an aspect of work that is at least as important today as the aspects they were meant to address in his time. Chapter 6's survey of recent trends in the social organization of labour showed clearly that work is increasingly characterized by an isolation of individual tasks. Work that previously required and relied on communication, cooperation and intellectual exchange can today more easily be separated out, with each task made the responsibility of a single person in the interests of more efficient control. This threatens to reduce motivations to engage in cooperative behaviour at work, and thus widens the gap between social roles and behavioural expectations in the world of work and those in the democratic public sphere. Competitiveness and looking at one's own interests and well-being are qualities that are essential in the workplace, but in the democratic public sphere, where citizens need to strive towards the common good, they need to be shed. To soften the effects of this contradiction – perhaps even to resolve it – the pronounced isolation of labour would need to be reversed. We would require organizational forms that are based more firmly in cooperation and closely integrated work. In industrial sociology, group and team work has for a long time been seen as a first step in this direction – as a kind of preliminary introduction to the democratic attitude. Durkheim, however, despite all his emphasis on syndicalism and the integrative role of groups, scarcely mentions this approach.

In the history of sociology, Durkheim is seen as the great proponent of 'occupational groups', but group or team work does not really figure in his account of how the division of labour might be made more democratic and roles less qualitatively distinct. He focuses almost exclusively on a group's task of negotiating the interests of a particular profession with other interest groups and establishing an agreement that turns its particularist interest into something that is useful for the common good.[27] The idea that it might also make sense to put work activities into the hands of groups of cooperating individuals instead of individual employees is nowhere to be found in his study. His proposals for reforming the division of labour are so focused on the enrichment of individual activities that he does not even begin to consider whether the coordination of sub-tasks among members of a group might not be just as good a way of fostering cooperative and democratic behaviour. In the twentieth century, conceptions of group working were occasionally put forward as promising counter-models to the repetitive and isolating assembly-line work of the large-scale Taylorist factory.[28] After some branches of the automotive industry introduced so-called production islands in addition to assembly lines, working in teams was briefly seen, especially in the 1970s and 1980s, as the best way to overcome alienating working conditions within the capitalist framework.[29] Since then, however, this idea seems to have disappeared again. Apparently, few now believe that the necessary preconditions for participation in democratic practices could be fostered just as well by making various tasks the responsibility of an autonomous group. Organizing social labour as cooperative group work, however, is probably the best way to give workers the opportunity to learn what it means to take up the perspective of another person and to take that person's judgement into consideration when forming their own. Management might reserve the right to have the last word, and so the scope for individual decisions on processes and temporal patterns might be limited, but even such a limited form of cooperation would still be better for democracy than work done in complete isolation, and under digital surveillance, at an assembly line, at a control panel or with a mop in hand. Organizational measures that allow parts of a task to be distributed among the members of a group – provided the task permits it and employees are happy with a closer integration of their activities – are therefore as much a part of

democratic labour politics as is Durkheim's tool of reducing the qualitative differences between individual jobs within the division of labour.
In today's service sector, there is a clear tendency towards standard-
izing areas of work by reducing jobs to the smallest possible number of
operations, and allocating these to lowly paid individual cleaners, parcel
delivery drivers or checkout operators.[30] This trend towards cost-cutting
rationalization should be opposed in part through the re-establishment
of the group as the original subject of work.

In this case, too, we must bear in mind that measures that aim at the
communitarization of work can easily be seized upon by businesses as
ways of increasing employees' motivation and thus their productivity.
Like many of the suggestions I detail here, group work initiatives are
Janus-faced: in the absence of public control and oversight, they can be
used – or rather abused – to encourage individual members of a group
to increase their productivity by introducing mechanisms of mutual
control and motivation within groups. The likelihood of abuse will
be reduced, however, if the group is authorized by works council rules
to autonomously decide on the pace of work and the distribution of
tasks. If a group of cooperating individuals can draw on its members'
knowledge and experience in determining how best to carry out a work
assignment and meet a deadline, it is down to them to determine the
pace of work and distribution of tasks accordingly.

This brings us to the fourth of the levers for improving the working
sovereign's opportunities to make use of its democratic rights. Many
employees find it difficult to participate in processes of public will
formation with the necessary self-confidence because at work they are
conditioned to follow orders and have no participatory rights at all. I
called this kind of adverse effect 'social', because it undermines workers'
ability to see themselves as members of a democratic polity not just in
the political arena but also at their workplace. If workers have to follow
management's instructions obediently and unquestioningly, they will
not be able to suddenly become mature citizens when they step onto the
public stage of democratic deliberation. Measures that aim to mitigate
the effects of this discrepancy should therefore be a central concern of
democratic labour politics. In thinking about such measures, the basic
rule is that the gap between the different behavioural expectations of
the two spheres will diminish to the extent that employees are given the

right to decide matters at their workplace. Under contemporary social and economic conditions, there are obviously very narrow limits for the application of this rule. At issue are improvements to the organization of labour within, not outside, the labour market, and any such improvements will thus have to be effective under conditions of the continuing private ownership of the means of production. These improvements would therefore aim to achieve participation, but not autonomy. If there is no realistic prospect of a feasible economic system based mainly on producer and service cooperatives, a democratic labour politics can only fight for more participation.

Participation is a broad and vague concept that can refer to various levels of decision-making within a business, public administration or service provider. Employees may be given a say over an organization's high-level aims and the level of financial rewards, or their participatory rights may extend right down to the rules governing everyday work processes. The ways in which employees may participate are as diverse as the levels at which they may be involved: from direct individual participation to the delegation of the employees' voice to a body representing their interests. The various forms of participation that already exist in some European countries mainly concern the higher levels of decision-making and are based on the indirect involvement of employees through trade unions that represent their interests.[31] For the negotiation of wages, working times or business aims, indirect participation through trade union representatives on executive boards may in fact be strategically advantageous, for these decisions require specialist knowledge and must often be taken quickly, and the compromises reached may apply across whole sectors. Nevertheless, from the perspective of democratic labour politics, this model also has significant disadvantages, especially in low-wage sectors where, because of low membership numbers and solid resistance from employers, trade unions have little power.[32] To the extent that negotiations with employers are led by academically trained specialists whose behaviour and habitus increasingly diverge from those of the employees, this form of participation will be less able to fulfil the function with which we are concerned: enabling and encouraging wage labourers to engage in democratic practices. The inexorable bureaucratization of trade unions is the price they pay for their state-backed bargaining power. At the same time, it inevitably leads to an impoverishment of their moral social role. Accreditation by the state carries with it the need to follow the organizational principles and hierarchical decision-making systems of public administrations.[33] As a consequence, the many diverse wage labourers that trade unions seek to represent come to be treated as exchangeable union members who will willingly follow the leadership's course. In the interests of efficiently conducted negotiations, trade unions will have to disregard the specific demands of certain groups of dissatisfied workers or rebellious employees, which would otherwise jeopardize the formulation of overarching goals and strategies for achieving them. This compulsion to generalize trade union agendas has an almost paradoxical effect: trust in possessing the power to bring about social change is generated not among individual wage labourers, but within the trade union apparatus. A trade union politics that focuses on issues of money and time will therefore not significantly reduce the gap between the imposed immaturity of the workplace and the normatively demanded maturity of the political sphere. Imperceptibly, in fact, the gap solidifies and becomes permanent. Even those workers who become trade union members are almost as passively exposed to the decisions of higher union functionaries as they are to the work directives of their managers, superiors or boards of directors – the difference, of course, is that the trade union officials take themselves to be acting in the best interests of the dependent labourers.

I do not wish to deny the sociopolitical importance of trade unions in representing the interests of employees. In fact, the importance of their function can hardly be overestimated. For the time being, they remain indispensable in the battle against the increasing economic and temporal disadvantages that, as we have seen, wage labourers are suffering once again. Lest we forget, trade unions are more or less the only remaining civil society organizations that manage to keep a spirit of solidarity alive among large numbers of wage labourers – even if they increasingly struggle to do so.[34] They are far from obsolete. However, they rarely, if ever, fulfil their social and moral purpose of familiarizing employees with democratic practices through involvement in union decision-making. Changing this would require much more effort to achieve bottom-up rather than top-down decision-making. But this would mean trade unions making the case for working conditions that permit labourers to participate and have a voice in decision-making at the workplace.

The process that teaches employees to see themselves as socially effica-
cious and capable of cooperation must begin at the material base of the
relations of production and services – that is, at the level of decisions
regarding everyday work. It more or less goes without saying that, in a
capitalist economy based on private property, such a practice of direct,
'on the ground' participation would make little headway. It could not
interfere with mandated performance levels, remuneration or working
times. In a capitalist system, these would still need to be set by either
an executive board, preferably with the involvement of trade unions,
or by the management or individual entrepreneur. Beyond these issues,
however, whatever questions remain – the detail of work processes,
the distribution of tasks, and breaks – would be in better hands with
employees, who have the appropriate knowledge and skills to make
informed decisions in these areas. In addition, the experience of having
relative autonomy in planning the execution of a task from beginning
to end would increase their self-respect; they would realize that they
can take the initiative and rely on their cognitive and social abilities.
One might say that the greater the workers' freedom in organizing and
shaping their work, the greater their confidence that their opinions
and interests will count in the process of democratic will formation.
If, however, there is no worker participation at the level of basic labour
relations, they will experience nothing to make them develop any trust
in the democratic practices of opinion formation.

Cooperation within a team is therefore not enough. Rather, a
democratic labour politics must take the self-organizing and relatively
autonomous work group as its empirical model and normative vantage
point.[35] Any effort to improve the conditions of market-based labour
must take this as its point of departure in the battle for more participation in the workplace. This policy option is well supported by strong
empirical evidence showing that employees desire to have more of a say
in the design and organization of their work.[36] We must bear in mind,
though, that a policy of introducing participation at the fundamental
level of the organization of work must at the same time aim to reconcile
labour relations in general with the principles of democratic practice.
Direct participation would require no major institutional changes,
because many of the conditions for it already exist. As Philipp Staab
has pointed out, it would be straightforward to allow a cleaning team,

parcel delivery team or one branch of a business to do its work autonomously and cooperatively within the division of labour.[37] The main obstacle is the radical economic strategies of businesses that are hell-bent on increasing individual performance by fragmenting all work into the smallest possible elements, to be allocated to individual employees whose performance can then be quantified and controlled. The battle against this cost-cutting, profit-maximizing capitalist rationalization must therefore be at the heart of any labour policy that aims to bring the labour market into the democratic fold from within.

Let me recapitulate and conclude. Given contemporary social relations, anyone interested in democratic labour policies has two strategies for pursuing the long-term aim of establishing conditions that are more conducive to democratic participation: they can try to introduce democratic alternatives to the capitalist labour market, or they can try to improve the existing capitalist labour market by introducing legal restrictions, social policies or a reconfigured division of labour. As I have mentioned, pursuing these strategies in combination would increase our chances of success. Perhaps attempts to circumvent the labour market and to reform it could support each other and become a single project. Integrating the strategies in this way would also mitigate the weaknesses of each approach. An exclusive focus on circumventing the labour market risks losing sight of historical limitations and thus ultimately not achieving very much. An exclusive concentration on labour market reform, by contrast, might place too much emphasis on contemporary circumstances and thus rule out the possibility of more radical change. The one lacks a sense of proportion and realism, the other a sense of direction and imagination. Each side must therefore be slightly modified, so that its measures can complement and reinforce, rather than impede, those of the other. In other words, proposals for democratic alternatives to the labour market should adopt a modicum of the sober realism that they too often lack, and strategies for labour market reform could do with more of the utopian enthusiasm that they, in turn, too often lack.

Suppose that proponents of the two strategies were to meet in the middle, so that labour market reforms not only took the status quo as their point of departure but included an experimental element that looked to future possibilities. Were this to happen, the self-perceptions of the two sides, and the way that each perceives the other, might change.

Producer cooperatives and self-administered businesses do not have to be conceived of as entirely opposed to labour market reforms; they could be understood as complementing and spurring on such reforms. Mutual suspicion could give way to mutual support: those who envision the complete democratization of work could reveal to the other side new possibilities amid all the obstacles; those advocating reforms of the labour market could show the other side how small the space for far-reaching changes can sometimes be.

Of course, we cannot categorically exclude the possibility that one day we will be able to create labour relations that constitute a genuinely 'democratic economy'. We may always hope that all the contradictions we have found between the promise of democratic participation and the reality of the social division of labour will eventually be resolved by the appropriate labour relations. But this does not relieve us of our duty here and now, and for the foreseeable future, to concentrate on reducing the gap between political democracy and the social division of labour as far as we are able to do so. From my perspective, the middle way that I have just described is not just the only possible one; it is the moral order of the day.

Given our social circumstances as we find them, however, even taking the initial steps along this path will be no mean feat. As I have mentioned, political attention has long since shifted away from the challenges of the world of work, and it would be misguided to count on the public taking a keen interest in labour policy. So, too, would it be wrong to expect a collective uprising by wage labourers against their precarious employment conditions. An atmosphere of anxious endurance and tacit acceptance seems to have descended on the world of work like a dust cloud – as though most people assume that any public outcry would only make things worse. In Chapter 7, I argued that we should not be deceived by this superficial impression, and I pointed to the many small acts of silent resistance that take place every day, and that are rooted in and orchestrated by countercultures within the world of work. They reveal people's collective interest in defending their dignity, in not being cowed.[38] For all that, a democratic labour politics cannot justify itself with reference to a wave of moral outrage haunting Europe today. In retrospect, this situation is rather unusual. In the post-war period, working conditions were never simply accepted without protest in this way. And working conditions are significantly worse now than they were fifty or sixty years ago, when collective resistance was routine.

In our era of inertia, when there are few hopeful visions for the future, and when most simply bide their time, the political agenda I have outlined here has no reason to display excessive self-confidence or show overweening revolutionary ambition. It must go back to the beginnings, must cautiously set out from the places where the quiet resistance of the working sovereign is to be found, and it must support this resistance with moral argument until, perhaps, one day, it will grow into a visible counter-movement. I do not mean that a politics not borne aloft by the revolutionary masses can only ever be 'a slow, powerful drilling through hard boards', as Max Weber thought.[39] But a politics that is convinced that this great achievement – the democratic sovereignty of the people – demands the urgent improvement of labour relations could do with a dose of Weber's realism.

Notes

Preliminary Remarks

1 This deficiency is pointed out by Karl Marx in *On the Jewish Question*, which repeatedly speaks about the '*secular contradiction between the political state and civil society*', meaning by 'civil society' – following Hegel – the capitalist relations of work and production. Karl Marx, *On the Jewish Question*, in *Early Writings*, London: Penguin, 1992, pp. 211–41; here: p. 226. More recently, Elizabeth Anderson postulates the same 'contradiction', albeit from within a very different theoretical framework, in her *Private Government: How Employers Rule Our Lives (and Why We Don't Talk about It)*, Princeton NJ: Princeton University Press, 2017, pp. 41f.

2 This also contradicts Ernst-Wolfgang Böckenförde's famous dictum according to which the modern 'liberal, secularized state is sustained by conditions it cannot itself guarantee'. Ernst-Wolfgang Böckenförde, 'The Rise of the State as a Process of Secularization', in *Religion, Law, and Democracy: Selected Writings*, Oxford: Oxford University Press, 2020, pp. 152–67; here: p. 167. I would argue that the democratic state under the rule of law has two tools at its disposal – education and labour policy – which it can use, if not to guarantee the cultural and intellectual conditions that sustain democracy, then at least to improve the likelihood of their emergence.

3 See Axel Honneth, 'Work and Instrumental Action', *New German Critique* 26, Critical Theory and Modernity (1982), pp. 31–54; Axel Honneth, 'Labour and Recognition: A Redefinition', in *The I in We: Studies in the Theory of Recognition*, Cambridge: Polity, 2012, pp. 56–74.

Part I

1 James Tully, *An Approach to Political Philosophy: Locke in Contexts*, Cambridge: Cambridge University Press, 1993, p. 260.

2 John Rawls is without a doubt the political philosopher who puts the strongest emphasis on this connection. See e.g. his *Justice as Fairness: A Restatement*, Cambridge MA: Harvard University Press, 2001, esp. §2. Also: Amy Gutmann and Dennis Thompson, *Democracy and Disagreement*, Cambridge MA: Harvard University Press, 1996; especially chapter 8. Russell Muirhead, *Just Work*, Cambridge MA: Harvard University Press, 2004; esp. chapter 1. However, Rawls never discusses what follows from this, his central thesis, for social labour relations themselves. I shall return to this question in Chapter 3.

3 Georg Wilhelm Friedrich Hegel, *Elements of the Philosophy of Right*, Cambridge: Cambridge University Press, 1991, §253, p. 271. On the idea that work gives the worker the social status of being 'free', see among others Robert J. Steinfeld, *The Invention of Free Labour: The Employment Relation in English and American Law and Culture 1350–1870*, Chapel Hill: University of North Carolina Press, 1991.

4 Jürgen Osterhammel, *The Transformation of the World: A Global History of the Nineteenth*

Century, Princeton NJ: Princeton University Press, 2014, esp. chapter XIII. To get a vivid impression of the conditions that characterized early industrial work, it suffices to take a look at Friedrich Engels, *The Condition of the Working Class in England*, Oxford: Oxford University Press, 1993 [1845].

5 Karl Marx, *Wage Labour and Capital*, New York: International Publishers, 1933, p. 16.

1 Three Resources for a Critique of Contemporary Labour Relations

1 Moses I. Finley, *The Ancient Economy*, Berkeley: University of California Press, 1973, p. 81. See also Hannah Arendt, *The Human Condition*, Chicago: University of Chicago Press, 1998, pp. 81–5, and Herbert Applebaum, *The Concept of Work: Ancient, Medieval, and Modern*, Albany: SUNY, 1992, pp. 167–75.

2 See especially Werner Conze, 'Arbeit', in Otto Brunner, Werner Conze and Reinhart Koselleck (eds), *Geschichtliche Grundbegriffe: Historisches Lexikon zur politisch-sozialen Sprache in Deutschland*, vol. 1, Stuttgart: Klett-Cotta, 1972, pp. 154–215. Another treasure trove of material on the changing meaning of 'work' throughout the so-called 'Sattelzeit', the bridging period between roughly 1750 and 1850, is Jörn Leonhard and Willibald Steinmetz (eds), *Semantiken von Arbeit: Diachrone und vergleichende Perspektiven*, Cologne, Weimar, Vienna: Böhlau, 2016.

3 From then on, the 'opposite of work' was, as Richard van Dülmen succinctly puts it, 'not poverty but unemployment, a condition that does not permit the human individual to be fully human and partake of the common good'. Richard van Dülmen, '"Arbeit" in der frühneuzeitlichen Gesellschaft', in Jürgen Kocka and Claus Offe (eds), *Geschichte und Zukunft der Arbeit*, Frankfurt am Main: Campus, 1999, p. 82. A very good short survey of the changing value of work can be found in Michael S. Aßländer and Bernd Wagner, 'Einführung: Philosophie und Arbeit', in Michael S. Aßländer and Bernd Wagner (eds), *Philosophie der Arbeit: Texte von der Antike bis zur Gegenwart*, Berlin: Suhrkamp, 2017, pp. 11–26.

4 Georg Simmel offers an impressive account of this gradual process of the emancipation of work from paternalism and personal dependence in *The Philosophy of Money*, London: Routledge, 2011 [1900/1907], pp. 305–83. An altogether different account, one that describes this process in unambiguously negative terms, is given by Marx under the heading of 'primitive accumulation'. Karl Marx, *Capital: Volume I*, London: Penguin, 1990, pp. 873–930. An excellent examination of the emergence of 'free labour' in the Anglo-Saxon world from the perspective of legal history is Steinfeld, *The Invention of Free Labour*.

5 Transl. note: Marx distinguishes two *aspects* of labour under capitalist conditions: 'Entfremdung' (estrangement) and 'Entäußerung' (alienation). However, 'Entfremdung' is sometimes also translated as 'alienation'. Marx's terminology is not perfectly clear. He says about the two terms: 'if the product of labour is alienation, production itself must be active alienation, the alienation of activity, the activity of alienation. In the estrangement [Entfremdung] of the object of labour is merely summarized the estrangement, the alienation, in the activity of labour itself.' *Economic and Philosophical Manuscripts*, in *Early Writings*, p. 326. Thus, we may say estrangement names the fact that the labourer is separated from his own activity, alienation the fact that the product of his activity is separated from him. But then by listing both terms here and in other places, he also blends the two aspects into one.

6 See the excerpts from Auguste Blanqui, Charles Fourier and Louis Blanc in Michael

Vesters collected volume *Die Frühsozialisten 1789–1848*, 2 vols, Reinbek: Rowohlt, 1970; here: vol. 1.

7 Marx, *Economic and Philosophical Manuscripts*, pp. 279–400. On 'estranged labour', see pp. 322–34.

8 The discussion of Marx's conception of estranged labour covers so many different aspects (essentialism, labour as reification, the influence of Locke's theory of property, etc.) that I only want to mention one important contribution in each case. On the question of whether Marx employed a questionable understanding of labour as 'reification', see Ernst Michael Lange, *Das Prinzip Arbeit: Drei metakritische Kapitel über Grundbegriffe, Struktur und Darstellung der Kritik der politischen Ökonomie von Karl Marx*, Berlin: Ullstein, 1980. On the question of whether Marx's idea that the worker is estranged from what he produces illegitimately draws on premises from Locke's theory of property, see Gerald A. Cohen, 'Marxism and Contemporary Political Philosophy, or: Why Nozick Exercises Some Marxists More than He Does Any Egalitarian Liberals', in *Canadian Journal of Philosophy* 16 (1990), pp. 363–87. For a succinct discussion of whether Marx employs essentialist ideas about the human species, see Will Kymlicka, *Contemporary Political Philosophy*, Oxford: Clarendon Press, 1990, pp. 187–92. The interesting suggestion that Marx's notion of estranged labour amounts to the claim that human labour was originally a being-active-for-each-other has been made by Daniel Brudney: 'Two Marxian Themes: The Alienation of Labour and the Linkage Thesis', in Jan Kandiyali (ed.), *Reassessing Marx's Social and Political Philosophy: Freedom, Recognition, and Human Flourishing*, Routledge: London, 2018, pp. 211–38. See also the strong criticism of Marx's idea of non-estranged labour in Raymond Geuss, *A Philosopher Looks at Work*, Cambridge: Cambridge University Press, 2021, pp. 121–8.

9 See William Morris, *News from Nowhere and Other Writings*, London: Penguin, 1993 [1890]; John Ruskin, *The Stones of Venice*, vol. 2, London: Smith, Elder and Co., 1906 [1853], pp. 150f. On this tradition, which criticizes the modern estrangement of labour in a romantic and artisanal spirit, see David A. Spencer, *The Political Economy of Work*, London: Routledge, 2009, pp. 39–46.

10 Numerous publications have helped to popularize Marx's idea of estranged labour, among them Erich Fromm, *Marx's Concept of Man*, New York: Frederick Ungar Publishing, 1961.

11 Marx, *Economic and Philosophical Manuscripts*, p. 326: 'He is at home when he is not working, and not at home when he is working.'

12 Ibid., p. 325.

13 I owe this point to discussions with Joseph Hamilton after my seminar on the philosophical concept of labour at Columbia University.

14 On this obvious point, see Richard J. Arneson, 'Meaningful Work and Market Socialism', *Ethics* 97:3 (1987), pp. 517–45. Raymond Geuss also puts the point succinctly: 'For Marx, however, alienation is not in the first instance a concept of individual psychology. It refers to a real state of affairs, an ontological condition – that is, the worker is alienated not because she *experiences* a loss of meaning or *feels* as if her work life is out of her control or *views* herself as separated from her product. Rather, she is alienated because she actually *is* separated from her product.' Geuss, *Work*, p. 123. For a similar argument, see Allen Wood, *Karl Marx*, London: Routledge, 1981, p. 23.

15 See Andrea Veltman, *Meaningful Work*, Oxford: Oxford University Press, 2016, chapter 4.

16 For a good survey of the various ways in which work is considered intrinsically valuable from an ethical perspective, see Anca Gheaus and Lisa Herzog, 'The Goods of Work (Other than Money)', *Journal of Social Philosophy* 47:1 (2016), pp. 70–89.

17 Specifically on this idea, see Lange, *Das Prinzip Arbeit*, chapter 1. A critical and noteworthy discussion of Lange's thesis that Marx was following Hegel with his concept of work and 'model of estrangement', and thus was committed to untenable metaphysical assumptions, can be found in Hans-Christoph Schmidt am Busch, *Hegels Begriff der Arbeit*, Berlin: Akademie Verlag, 2002, pp. 40–6. Beate Rössler is also of the opinion that there is a version of Marx's theorem of estrangement that can do without reference to the 'objectification' of skills and abilities in 'actual objects being produced': 'Although many commentators still cling to the idea of skilled craftsmanship as the ultimate in gratifying and meaningful work, it seems much more plausible not to reduce the idea of objectification to actual objects being produced ... but rather to interpret it in the sense that the abilities, ideas, aims, and talents of the worker – his "individuality" – can be objectified in interaction with the external world in different, even abstract, forms.' Beate Rössler, 'Meaningful Work: Arguments from Autonomy', *Journal of Political Philosophy* 20:1 (2012), pp. 71–93; here: p. 88.

18 See e.g. Ruth Yeoman, *Meaningful Work and Workplace Democracy*, Basingstoke: Palgrave, 2014, chapter 1.

19 See e.g. Werner Sombart, *Why Is There No Socialism in the United States?*, London: Routledge, 1976 [1906]. Max Weber repeatedly expressed a similar view.

20 See Alex Gourevitch, *From Slavery to the Cooperative Commonwealth: Labor and Republican Liberty in the Nineteenth Century*, Cambridge: Cambridge University Press, 2015, chapter 3.

21 See Steinfeld, *The Invention of Free Labour*, and Osterhammel, *The Transformation of the World*, chapter XIII.

22 Gourevitch, *From Slavery to the Cooperative Commonwealth*, pp. 68f.

23 Ibid., pp. 77–81.

24 Ibid., pp. 86–8.

25 On these discussions, see ibid., pp. 88–96.

26 See ibid., pp. 118–26.

27 Dewey's concept of freedom is less individualist than that of the republican tradition. It focuses more on the communicative idea that individual freedom depends on uncoerced cooperation with all other members of a community. See John Dewey, *The Public and Its Problems*, in *The Later Works, 1925–1953*, vol. 2, Carbondale: Southern Illinois University Press, 1988, pp. 235–372. On his definition of freedom, see ibid., p. 155.

28 Anderson, *Private Government*.

29 On the first of these options, see e.g. Alex Gourevitch, 'Labor Republicanism and the Transformation of Work', *Political Theory* 41:4 (2013), pp. 591–617. On the second option, see Elizabeth Anderson, 'Reply to Commentators', in *Private Government*, pp. 119–44.

30 Anderson, *Private Government*, pp. 45f.

31 Ibid., p. 128.

32 See Axel Honneth, *Freedom's Right: The Social Foundations of Democracy*, Cambridge: Polity, 2014, pp. 255–304.

33 I owe this clarification to discussions with Robin Celikates after my Benjamin Lectures.

34 See Adam Smith, *An Inquiry into the Nature and Causes of the Wealth of Nations*, Ware: Wordsworth, 2012 [1776], pp. 777–9.

35 Hegel, *Elements of the Philosophy of Right*, §§196–8 and §§250–6, pp. 231–3 and pp. 270–4.

36 See Émile Durkheim, *The Division of Labor in Society*, Glencoe IL: The Free Press, 1960

[1893]. On Durkheim and the tradition of solidarism in France, see Christian Gülich, *Die Durckheim-Schule und der französische Solidarismus*, Wiesbaden: Springer, 1991. See also G. D. H. Cole, *Labour in the Commonwealth: A Book for the Younger Generation*, London: Headley Brothers, 1918.

37 On the metaphysical connotations, see Lange, *Das Prinzip Arbeit*, chapter 1.

38 Beate Rössler, it seems to me, does not avoid the tendency to take the criterion of 'absence of estrangement' in merely subjective terms when trying to link the critique of estrangement (Marx) with the value of autonomy (in her case: Kant): 'Thus, alienated work is alienated because it is work which cannot be seen by the subject as a possible self-realization of his abilities and talents, or as an actualization and externalization of those talents and interests. Meaningless, monotonous work forecloses the possibility for the subject to endorse the work and its value.' Rössler, 'Meaningful Work', p. 88. Thus, whether work is meaningful or non-estranged is down to the judgement of the working subject.

39 Ruth Yeoman happily concedes this point at an inconspicuous place in her book *Meaningful Work and Workplace Democracy*, p. 206.

40 This problem can only be avoided by taking being-active-for-each-other as the 'proper' form of labour. See Brudney, 'Two Marxian Themes', pp. 216f. This, however, only swaps one problem for another, for now labour's essential characteristic is taken to be a single purpose, which neglects all the other motivations that there might be.

41 See e.g. the commentary by Tyler Cowen, 'Work Isn't So Bad After All', in Anderson, *Private Government*, pp. 108–16.

42 On the thesis that the design of the material substance of work and modes of production are relatively independent from the capitalist organization of labour, and therefore are the outcome of political battles and negotiations, see Michael J. Piore and Charles F. Sabel, *The Second Industrial Divide: Possibilities for Prosperity*, New York: Basic Books, 1984. I shall return to this study in more detail in the second excursus, 'On the Concept of the Social Division of Labour'.

43 On this objection, see Richard Arneson's thought experiment: 'To illustrate the point, imagine a market economy whose firms are labor-managed in the sense that ultimate decision-making power is vested in a majority vote of the enterprise work-force. Within each firm, workers decide by majority vote to eschew participation in managerial tasks. Jobs for the most part are dirty, exhausting, subject to close supervision, devoid of challenge or interest. High wages are the compensation that firm members accept as a trade-off for these disamenities.' Arneson, 'Meaningful Work and Market Socialism', p. 518.

44 Beate Rössler's approach (and also that of Adina Schwartz, 'Meaningful Work', *Ethics* 92:4 [1982], pp. 634–46) attempts to combine these two perspectives. But it seems to me that this is possible only at the price of understanding the criterion for 'meaningful' work in purely subjective terms: that is, the judgement as to whether a particular kind of work is meaningful or meaningless is entirely down to the subjects carrying out the work (as already mentioned in note 38 above).

45 The normative paradigm that thus emerges is narrower than an approach that seeks employees' sufficient inclusion in all social practices that are part of the political community's shared culture. The approach developed here proposes that the world of work must facilitate inclusion in just one social practice, namely participation in the processes of democratic will formation. Hauke Behrendt has put forward a very interesting proposal

for a wider concept of social inclusion in connection with the world of work: *Das Ideal einer inklusiven Arbeitswelt: Teilhabegerechtigkeit im Zeitalter der Digitalisierung*, Frankfurt am Main: Campus, 2018; see esp. chapter 5.

46 See John Dewey, *Human Nature and Conduct: An Introduction to Social Psychology* (*The Middle Works: 1899–1924*, vol. 14), Carbondale: Southern Illinois University Press, 2008, pp. 154–63.

2 A Forgotten Tradition

1 Cole, *Labour in the Commonwealth*, p. 35.

2 Smith, *Wealth of Nations*, pp. 777f.

3 Ibid., p. 778.

4 Ibid.

5 See Anderson, *Private Government*, pp. 17–22. On this point in Smith, see Donald Winch, *Adam Smith's Politics: An Essay in Historiographic Revision*, Cambridge: Cambridge University Press, 1978, pp. 113–20.

6 Smith, *Wealth of Nations*, pp. 758–84.

7 See the instructive comparison of Hegel and Smith in Lisa Herzog, *Inventing the Market: Smith, Hegel and Political Theory*, Oxford: Oxford University, 2013. I also learned a lot from Thimo Heisenberg's essay 'Hegel on the Value of the Market Economy', *European Journal of Philosophy* 26 (2018), pp. 1283–96. More recently, I have tried to show that Hegel was probably unable to make up his mind between an optimistic view of the market – a view that out-Smiths Smith, so to speak – and a deeply pessimistic view that anticipates Marx, and that thus, at a loss, he oscillated between the two alternatives: Axel Honneth, 'Reality or Appearance of Ethical Life? Hegel's Analysis of the Market Economy', *Ethics in Progress* 13:1 (2022), pp. 10–23.

8 Hegel, *Elements of the Philosophy of Right*, §253, p. 271.

9 On corporations, see ibid., §§250–6, pp. 270–4.

10 On Hegel's notion of 'corporation', see the contributions in Sven Ellmers and Steffen Herrmann (eds), *Korporation und Sittlichkeit: Zur Aktualität von Hegels Theorie der bürgerlichen Gesellschaft*, Paderborn: Fink, 2017. See also Carsten Herrmann-Pillath and Ivan Boldyrev, *Hegel, Institutions and Economics: Performing the Social*, London: Routledge, 2014.

11 Hegel, *Elements of the Philosophy of Right*, §243, p. 266.

12 On the concept of 'fair value', see Rawls, *Justice as Fairness*, §45, pp. 148–50.

13 These three normative conditions can be derived indirectly from Durkheim's analysis of abnormal forms of the division of labour. See Durkheim, *The Division of Labor in Society*, Book III, chapters 1 and 2.

14 Émile Durkheim, *Physik der Sitten und des Rechts: Vorlesungen zur Soziologie der Moral*, Frankfurt am Main: Suhrkamp, 1999. See in particular the first three lectures.

15 See Jens Beckert, *Beyond the Market: The Social Foundations of Economic Efficiency*, Princeton NJ: Princeton University Press, 2002, especially the sections on 'Professional Groups' and 'Cooperation and Morality', pp. 119–25. See also p. 167.

16 See Gülich, *Die Durkheim-Schule und der französische Solidarismus*.

17 Cole, *Labour in the Commonwealth*. On Cole, see the short account in Carole Pateman, *Participation and Democratic Theory*, Cambridge: Cambridge University Press, 2014, pp. 33–42. An extensive treatment of Cole's life and work is Luther Pieri Carpenter, *G. D. H. Cole: An Intellectual Biography*, Cambridge: Cambridge University Press, 1973.

18 G. D. H. Cole, *Self-Government in Industry*, London: Routledge, 2010 [1918].

19 G. D. H. Cole, *Guild Socialism Restated*, London: Routledge, 2017 [1920].

20 Hegel, *Elements of the Philosophy of Right*, §255 (Addition), p. 273.

21 See e.g. Constance Reavely and John Winnington, *Democracy and Industry*, London: Chatto and Windus, 1947; Pateman, *Participation and Democratic Theory*; Georges Friedmann, *Où va le travail humain?* Paris: Gallimard, 1950, esp. part III, chapter III. Interesting suggestions that point in a similar direction can also be found in Marion Young, *Justice and the Politics of Difference*, Princeton NJ: Princeton University Press, 2011, chapter 7.

22 John Stuart Mill, *Principles of Political Economy: With Some of Their Applications to Social Philosophy*, vol. II, London: Longmans, Green, Reader and Dyer, 1871, Book IV, chapter 7, §6, pp. 352–75. As far as I can see, John Dewey does not come to a definite conclusion regarding the direction of the required reforms or the direction in which capitalist labour relations should be transcended. He was convinced that the capitalist economy would undermine democratic action because of its institutional orientation towards the pursuit of self-interest, but in the course of his life, he considered several ways in which this ill could be removed through economic reform. See on the one hand John Dewey, *Individualism, Old and New*, in *The Later Works, 1925–1953*, vol. 5, Carbondale: University of Southern Illinois Press, 1984, pp. 41–124, and on the other John Dewey and James H. Tufts, *Ethics* [1932], in John Dewey, *The Later Works, 1925–1953*, vol. 7, Carbondale: University of Southern Illinois Press, 1985, chapter 22. A very good survey of Dewey's vacillation is given by Robert B. Westbrook, *John Dewey and American Democracy*, Ithaca: Cornell University Press, 1991, chapter 12. A forceful attempt at making Dewey's ideas on the necessity of labour reform fruitful for contemporary political thought is made by Emmanuel Renault in an unpublished book manuscript he kindly put at my disposal: *Penser les enjeux du travail avec John Dewey*, 2021. Another US author who, between the two world wars, helped to keep alive the idea that political democracy requires participatory labour relations was William Edward Burghardt Du Bois. In his historical study on the stages of social reconstruction after the American Civil War, he tried to show that reconstruction was doomed to fail because the 'white' workers' movement's racism meant that it was unable to unite its fight against wage labour with the 'black' movement's rebellion against slavery. See W. E. B. Du Bois, *Black Reconstruction in America 1860–1880*, New York: Simon & Schuster, 1992 [1935], especially chapter XIII.

23 On the prehistory of programmes for the humanization of the world of work, mainly in Germany, see the fascinating study by Joan Campbell, *Joy in Work, German Work: The National Debate, 1800–1945*, Princeton NJ: Princeton University Press, 1989. On the period after the end of the Second World War, see Nina Kleinöder, Stefan Müller and Karsten Uhl, 'Humanisierung der Arbeit': Aufbrüche und Konflikte in der rationalisierten Arbeitswelt des 20. Jahrhunderts*, Bielefeld: transcript, 2019. On the 1960s and 1970s, see Yves Delamotte and Kenneth F. Walker, 'Humanization of Work and the Quality of Working Life – Trends and Issues', *International Journal of Sociology* 6:1 (1976), pp. 8–40.

24 Milojko Drulović, *Arbeiterselbstverwaltung auf dem Prüfstand: Erfahrungen in Jugoslawien*, Berlin: Dietz, 1976.

3 Democracy and the Question of a Fair Division of Labour

1 John Rawls, *A Theory of Justice*, Revised Edition, Cambridge MA: Harvard University Press, 1999, p. 229.

2 See Dewey and Tufts, *Ethics*, chapter 22.

3 See Friedrich Kambartel, 'Bemerkungen zur politischen Ökonomie', in *Philosophie und politische Ökonomie*, Göttingen: Wallstein, 1998, pp. 11–40; here: pp. 25f.

4 See Rawls, *Justice as Fairness*; Jürgen Habermas, *Between Facts and Norms: Contributions to a Discourse Theory of Law*, Cambridge MA: MIT, 1996.

5 Rawls, *Justice as Fairness*, §45, pp. 148–50.

6 Habermas, *Between Facts and Norms*, chapter 9.2, pp. 409–18.

7 Habermas at least makes brief reference, following a quotation from Spiros Simitis, to the importance of the legal regulation of labour relations for equal opportunities, but he does not pursue the matter further. See ibid., pp. 413f. Rawls has frequently been criticized for ignoring labour relations that disadvantage workers. The most recent examples are: Jahel Queralt and Iñigo González-Ricoy, 'The Ballot and the Wallet: Self-Respect and the Fair Value of Political Liberties', *European Journal of Philosophy* 29:2 (2021), pp. 410–24. Rafeeq Hasan, 'Rawls on Meaningful Work and Freedom', *Social Theory and Practice* 41:3 (2015), pp. 477–504. An older critique, which was pathbreaking at the time, is Gerald Doppelt, 'Rawls' System of Justice: A Critique from the Left', *Noûs* 15 (1981), pp. 259–307.

8 There is, however, a very interesting passage in Rawls's *Justice as Fairness* (pp. 178f.) in which, with reference to J. S. Mill's suggestion of putting more of the administration and leadership of businesses into the hands of the workers, Rawls says: 'Would worker-managed firms be more likely to encourage the democratic virtues needed for a constitutional regime to endure? If so, could greater democracy within capitalist firms achieve much the same result? I shall not pursue these questions. I have no idea of the answers, but certainly these questions call for careful examination. The long-run prospects of a just constitutional regime may depend on them.'

9 There may be other reasons for Rawls's and Habermas's relative neglect of the quality of labour relations. One is that the currently dominant economic theory, which is a point of reference for both authors, albeit to different degrees, is utterly uninterested in the quality of labour relations – unlike, incidentally, the classic authors of the discipline, for whom it was a central concern.

10 Regarding the literature on such alternatives, I mention as an initial reference Johannes Berger and Claus Offe, 'Die Zukunft des Arbeitsmarktes: Zur Ergänzungsbedürftigkeit eines versagenden Allokationsprinzips', in Claus Offe (ed.), 'Arbeitsgesellschaft': *Strukturprobleme und Zukunftsperspektiven*, Frankfurt am Main: Campus, 1984, pp. 87–117. I shall return to this important text.

11 Jürgen Habermas, *The Theory of Communicative Action*, vol. 2, Boston: Beacon Press, 1987, pp. 303–31. I leave aside the question of whether Habermas's neglect of the sphere of work and its political and moral importance is rooted in his early decision to conceive of work purely in terms of 'instrumental action' and thus to look at it exclusively from the perspective of purposive rationality. A detailed analysis of the conception of the market in Habermas's *Theory of Communication Action* can be found in Timo Jütten, 'Habermas and Markets', *Constellations* 20:4 (2013), pp. 587–603. The thesis that Habermas retained this idea of the market as a 'norm-free' sphere in his later democratic theory, as presented in *Between Facts and Norms*, is put forward by William A. Forbath, 'Short Circuit: Habermas' Understanding of Law, Politics, and Economic Life', in Michel Rosenfeld and Andrew Arato (eds), *Habermas on Law and Democracy: Critical Exchanges*, Berkeley: University of California Press, 1998, pp. 272–86.

12 Rawls, *Justice as Fairness*, pp. 64ff. Habermas, *Between Facts and Norms*, chapter 9.2. pp. 409–18.

13 'Surely what is of genuine moral concern is not formal but substantive. It is whether people have good lives, and not how their lives compare with the lives of others.' Harry Frankfurt, 'Equality and Respect', *Social Research* 64:1, The Decent Society (1997), pp. 3–15.

14 For a good survey of the manifold forms of discrimination, including with regard to the labour market, see Ulrike Hormel and Albert Scherr (eds), *Diskriminierung: Grundlagen und Forschungsergebnisse*, Wiesbaden: Springer, 2010.

15 This deficiency is more significant in the case of Rawls's theory of justice than in Habermas's democratic theory, because Rawls claims explicitly, and much more force-fully than Habermas, that his conception of justice, which is compulsory for democratic societies, is tied to the premise that everyone in this society can see themselves as a member of a 'fair' system of social cooperation that exists over many generations (see e.g. Rawls, *Justice as Fairness*, §2, pp. 5–8). This reference to a presupposed system of cooperation means that the social division of labour is subject to the normative demand of fairness, but there is never any explanation of what this means in practice. It is not enough merely to refer, as Rawls does, to the legal guarantee of a free choice of profession. Even if there is such free choice (on this question see 'Excursus II' below), it takes place under the conditions of a given division of labour whose origin and shape is taken for granted and not subjected to any further normative scrutiny. Rawls is certainly right to tie the credibility and meaning of his two principles of justice to the condition of a fair division of labour, but doing so subjects his theory to a normative demand that he seems unwilling to confront, for to confront it would require him to reflect on criteria that lie outside of his 'political' conception of justice. These would be criteria that would make it possible to judge whether the social division of labour is 'fair' or 'just', or at what point we could say it had become so. To respond to this objection by saying that such criteria are provided by the political idea of justice as fairness would be viciously circular, because this idea can claim to be justified only to the extent that a fair division of labour already exists, and so it cannot be used to assess the fairness of the division of labour. For such an assessment, we require independent standards that are much more closely aligned with the world of social labour, and that therefore make it possible to judge whether the system of social cooperation is just or fair enough for the application of the political conception of justice. On the role of the presupposition of a 'fair system of cooperation' in Rawls's theory of justice, see Jochen Ostheimer, *Liberalismus und soziale Gerechtigkeit: Zur politischen Philosophie von Rawls, Nozick und Hayek*, Paderborn: Ferdinand Schöningh, 2019, chapter 2.4.

16 A comparison can again be made with Hauke Behrendt's interesting approach (see chapter 1, note 45). Within the broader framework of his concept of inclusion, he identifies three categories of necessary conditions: institutional, intersubjective and material. These must be fulfilled in order to enable employees' 'effective' participation in social practices. See Behrendt, *Das Ideal einer inklusiven Arbeitswelt*, pp. 183–8.

17 I shall separately address the question of whether such freedom from anxiety would be better guaranteed by decoupling livelihood from gainful employment through the intro-duction of an unconditional basic income. See Chapter 7.

18 Transl. note: *Little Man – What Now?* is a novel by the German writer Hans Fallada. It was published in 1932 and describes the economic hardship of the years following the

1929 stock market crash through the story of a young couple trying to make a living. The novel was highly popular in Germany and the title has become proverbial.

19 Carole Pateman calls this trust in the relevance of one's own political convictions, which can be gained only in the workplace, 'a sense of political efficacy'. See Pateman, *Participation and Democratic Theory*, pp. 45–66. Albert Bandura's psychological concept of 'self-efficacy' expresses a similar thought. See his *Self-Efficacy: The Exercise of Control*, New York: Worth, 1997.

20 On the connection between policies on working hours and political participation, see Karl Hinrichs, Claus Offe and Helmut Wiesenthal, 'Der Streit um die Zeit – Die Arbeitszeit im gesellschaftspolitischen und industriellen Konflikt', in Offe (ed.), *Arbeitsgesellschaft*, pp. 141–66; esp. pp. 165f.

21 Even these three activities are not enough by themselves, as has been demonstrated with refreshing clarity by Michael Walzer, 'Deliberation – and What Else?', in *Politics and Passion: Towards a More Egalitarian Liberalism*, New Haven: Yale University Press, 2004, pp. 90–109.

22 In his still highly rewarding book on human problems of automation, Georges Friedmann introduced the term 'industrial fatigue' into sociological discussions of the phenomenon. From the 1950s onwards, the conclusions of his book served as the normative guidelines in West German industrial sociology. Georges Friedmann, *Industrial Society: The Emergence of Human Problems of Automation*, Glencoe IL: Free Press, 1955; see esp. pp. 77–92.

23 On the complex theme of the influence of social hierarchies and power disparities on a person's epistemic self-confidence, see the fascinating study by Miranda Fricker, *Epistemic Justice: Power and the Ethics of Knowing*, Oxford: Oxford University Press, 2007. On the role of humiliation in the symbolic reproduction of social inequality and the feelings of inferiority thus caused, see Sighard Neckel, *Status und Scham: Zur symbolischen Reproduktion sozialer Ungleichheit*, Frankfurt am Main: Campus, 1991; esp. chapters VI and VIII. Important material on the 'psychological' aspect of the impairments resulting from one's position in the social division of labour can also be found in Ursula Holtgrewe, Stephan Voswinkel and Gabriele Wagner (eds), *Anerkennung und Arbeit*, Konstanz: UVK, 2000. See also Young, *Justice and the Politics of Difference*, chapter 7. On the whole thematic complex, see Chapter 9.

24 See Rawls, *A Theory of Justice*, pp. 386–91.

25 On the importance of Rousseau in this context, see Frederick Neuhouser, *Rousseau's Critique of Inequality*, Cambridge: Cambridge University Press, pp. 214f.

26 Rawls, *A Theory of Justice*, p. 386.

27 Ibid., p. 387. Jeffrey Moriarty has put forward the interesting thesis that, in the course of developing his theory, Rawls relinquished his original, optimistic idea that the necessary degree of self-respect can be gained through private activities that involve recognition from clubs or small social groups. See Jeffrey Moriarty, 'Rawls, Self-Respect, and the Opportunity for Meaningful Work', *Social Theory and Practice* 35:3 (2009), pp. 441–59. On this thematic complex, see also Arto Laitinen, 'Social Bases of Self-Esteem: Rawls, Honneth and Beyond', *Nordicum – Mediterraneum* 7:2 (2012), and Doppelt, 'Rawls' System of Justice'. Arneson ('Meaningful Work and Market Socialism', p. 30) rightly rejects as implausible Doppelt's assumption that such 'self-esteem' can be gained only through 'meaningful work'. But Arneson still holds on to Rawls's premise that a sense of self-esteem is indispensable if one is to pursue one's personal plans with confidence. However, if we claim instead that self-esteem is necessary for confident participation in

democratic discussion, it becomes clear why the opportunity to develop a sense of self-esteem depends on work activities that are generally valued. Thus, the question of why the development of self-esteem is necessary determines where and how self-esteem can actually be developed.

28 On the nineteenth-century history of the association of specific activities with the female gender and the devaluation of these activities, see Joan W. Scott, 'The Woman Worker', in Georges Duby and and Michelle Perrot (eds), *A History of Women in the West* (5 vols), vol. 4: *Emerging Feminism from Revolution to World War* (ed. Geneviève Fraisse and Michelle Perrot), Cambridge MA: Harvard University Press, 1994, pp. 399–426.

29 For a wonderful attempt at undermining the usual hierarchies between, for example, intellectual and manual labour, and skilled and unskilled work, by closely examining, with specific reference to US conditions, the intellectual effort involved in so-called simple professions (plumbing, carpentry, waitressing), see Mike Rose, *The Mind at Work: Valuing the Intelligence of the American Worker*, New York: Viking, 2004; esp. pp. 141–66.

30 On the school as a place that fosters democracy, see Axel Honneth, 'Education and the Democratic Public Sphere: A Neglected Chapter of Political Philosophy', in *The Poverty of Our Freedom*, Cambridge: Polity, 2023, pp. 126–40.

31 Hegel, *Elements of the Philosophy of Right*, §243, p. 266.

32 See the classic study by Melvin Kohn and Carmi Schooler, *Work and Personality: An Inquiry into the Impact of Social Stratification*, Norwood: Ablex Publishing, 1983. See also Melvin Kohn, 'Job Complexity and Adult Personality', in Neil J. Smelser and Erik H. Erikson (eds), *Themes of Work and Love in Adulthood*, Cambridge MA: Harvard University Press, 1980, pp. 193–210; Arthur Kornhauser, *Mental Health of the Industrial Worker: A Detroit Study*, New York: John Wiley & Sons, 1965. Important observations on the mental impact of highly repetitive and monotonous work can also be found in Friedmann, *Industrial Society*, part 2; esp. chapters 1–4.

33 See Excursus II: On the Concept of the Social Division of Labour.

34 On the problem of finding an appropriate definition of 'work' that is neither too narrow nor too broad, see John W. Budd, *The Thought of Work*, Ithaca: Cornell University Press, 2011, p. 2: 'A meaningful definition of work, therefore, needs to lie somewhere between the overly narrow focus on paid employment and the excessively broad inclusion of all human activity.'

Excursus I: On the Concept of Social Labour

1 Martin Luther King, Jr., 'All Labor Has Dignity', in *All Labor Has Dignity*, ed. Michael K. Honey, Boston: Beacon Press, 2011, pp. 171f. I would like to thank Joseph Hamilton for pointing me to this speech.

2 This excursus is intended as only a brief reconstruction of the intellectual history of the concept of labour in modernity, and of the gradual transformation and broadening of the understanding of what constitutes the substance of labour in the social imaginary. The social understanding of what count as the core operations of work does not say anything, however, about how these activities are actually publicly valued and financially rewarded. What follows is largely identical with a previously published article: Axel Honneth, '"Labour": A Brief History of a Modern Concept', *Philosophy* 97:2 (2022), pp. 149–67. Transl. note: The existing translation has been consulted for this new translation.

3 See John Locke, *Two Treatises of Government*, London: Whitmore and Fenn, 1821 [1689], pp. 208–30; especially pp. 209f. and pp. 221–5.

4 Whether Locke thought the hunting and gathering practised by the indigenous peoples of North America added value to natural objects, and therefore created a right to property, is an interesting question. His remarks on the matter are ambivalent (see ibid., pp. 216–24), and thus can be construed as justifying the appropriation of land by white settlers. On this still highly relevant question, see Gurminder K. Bhambra and John Holmwood, *Colonialism and Modern Social Theory*, Cambridge: Polity, pp. 32–8 and pp. 65–71.

5 On this contradiction in Smith, see the introduction by Erich W. Streissler in Adam Smith, *Untersuchungen über Wesen und Ursache des Reichtums der Völker*, Tübingen: Mohr Siebeck, 2005, pp. 1–31.

6 Smith, *Wealth of Nations*, p. 326.

7 See Osterhammel, *The Transformation of the World*, p. 696.

8 'Thus, by those means [formative *doing*], the working consciousness comes to an intuition of self-sufficient being *as its own self.*' Georg Wilhelm Friedrich Hegel, *The Phenomenology of Spirit*, Cambridge: Cambridge University Press, 2018, p. 115.

9 Hegel, *Elements of the Philosophy of Right*, §203, p. 236.

10 An exception is the 'estate of commerce', which certainly includes services but which Hegel subsumes under the producing estate of trade and industry. See ibid., §204, pp. 236f.

11 I do not wish to claim that Marx did not take note of other forms of social labour, only that his normative conception of the essence of human labour is tied to the manufacturing of products. Daniel Brudney sees this limitation of Marx's concept of work as expressing a 'productivism' that was typical of Victorian England. Brudney, 'Two Marxian Themes', p. 218.

12 Marx, *Economic and Philosophical Manuscripts*, p. 329.

13 See Sven Beckert, *Empire of Cotton: A Global History*, London: Vintage, 2015.

14 Following Miranda Fricker, I use the term 'social imagination' for social meanings that circulate below the threshold of explicit linguistic articulation. See Fricker, *Epistemic Injustice*, pp. 37f.

15 On the emergence in the literary imagination of an industrial proletariat as a revolutionary class, see Patrick Eiden-Offe, *Die Poesie der Klasse: Romantischer Antikapitalismus und die Erfindung des Proletariats*, Berlin: Matthes & Seitz, 2017; on the cult surrounding industrial workers, see especially pp. 220–4. An English edition is forthcoming: *The Poetry of Class: Romantic Anti-Capitalism and the Invention of the Proletariat*, Leiden: Brill, 2024.

16 The great exception is John Stuart Mill. In volume I of his *Principles of Political Economy* (London: Longmans, Green and Co., 1909 [1848]), he takes great care to distinguish between the various forms of labour that are needed – 'directly' (p. 29) or 'indirectly' (p. 31) – 'in the production of an article fitted for some human use' (p. 29). Mill considers not only the labour of 'officers of government, of the army and navy, of physicians, lawyers, teachers, musicians, dancers, actors', but also the labour of 'domestic servants', because they all possess social 'utility' (pp. 44f.); they consist in 'a pleasure given, an inconvenience or a pain averted' (p. 46). He therefore does not want to use the term 'unproductive' as a pejorative term ('as a term of disparagement', p. 44), and suggests that we 'should regard all labour as productive which is employed in creating permanent utilities, whether embodied in human beings, or in any other animate or inanimate objects' (p. 48), irrespective of whether an object is produced or a service rendered. Given

that Mill takes such pains to differentiate between the different kinds of labour that are useful for society, it is striking that he has nothing to say about the unpaid labour of cooking, looking after children and cleaning done by women in the household – in fact, nowhere does his captivatingly precise argumentation mention women at all. (Mill's special position within the history of the modern concept of labour was pointed out to me by Michael S. Aßländer.)

17 See Émile Zola, *The Ladies' Paradise*, Oxford: Oxford University Press, 1995 [1882/83] and *The Belly of Paris*, Oxford: Oxford University Press, 2007 [1873]. See also Chapter 4, p. 73.

18 There are some excellent recent studies on the specific demands of certain occupations, especially concerning the coordination of intellectual and manual activities in the case of, for instance, hairdressers and waiters. See the pathbreaking book by Mike Rose, *The Mind at Work*, chapters 1 and 2.

19 On the cultural and social heterogeneity of service and administrative occupations in Germany, see Jürgen Kocka, *Die Angestellten in der deutschen Geschichte 1850–1980: Vom Privatbeamten zum angestellten Arbeitnehmer*, Göttingen: Vandenhoeck & Ruprecht, 1981. See also Hans Speier, *Die Angestellten vor dem Nationalsozialismus*, Göttingen: Vandenhoeck & Ruprecht, 1977.

20 See Max Weber, *Economy and Society: An Outline of Interpretive Sociology*, Berkeley: University of California Press, 1978, pp. 956–1005. On the history of industrial and state bureaucracy in Germany, see Kocka, *Die Angestellten in der deutschen Geschichte*, chapter 2.

21 On the complicated history of the concept of 'employee' as opposed to 'worker', see Kocka, *Die Angestellten in der deutschen Geschichte*, chapter 4. The distinction between 'blue collar' and 'white collar' workers in the English-speaking world does not fully correspond to that between 'workers' and 'employees' because it is much more closely associated with the relation between the 'proletarian' working class and the 'professional' middle classes. See C. Wright Mills, *White Collar: The American Middle Classes*, Oxford: Oxford University Press, 1951.

22 A good survey of the living and working conditions of domestic servants in big cities between the late eighteenth century and the early twentieth century is provided by Heidi Müller in a study that was published in connection with an exhibition at the Berliner Museum für Deutsche Volkskunde: *Dienstbare Geister: Leben und Arbeitswelt städtischer Dienstboten*, Berlin, 1985. It mentions an investigation of the situation of female domestic servants in Berlin that Oskar Stillich carried out in 1900. The investigation was sabotaged by employers, so only 10 per cent of the questionnaires were returned (ibid., p. 7). Despite this meagre empirical base, Stillich was able to show how miserable the situation of female servants was. See Oskar Stillich, *Die Lage der weiblichen Dienstboten in Berlin*, Berlin: Akademischer Verlag für soziale Wissenschaften, 1902; on the boycott of the study, see pp. 76f.

23 Scott, 'The Woman Worker', p. 411. As Scott spells out, a conclusion was drawn from the inferiority of wages to the inferiority of work: women working in the domestic services sectors were lowly paid, and their work seen as less productive, and this was then projected onto women working in industry; see ibid., pp. 411f.

24 See Arendt, *The Human Condition*. There are no references to care workers or servants at all. According to Arendt's criteria, their work is neither 'labour' nor 'production'.

25 An observation in the travelogue of Marianne Weber throws a spotlight on the new

situation in which bourgeois housewives found themselves: 'To understand what a life without servants means for cultured people under the conditions of today's private homes, one has to see it with one's own eyes. What an extraordinary luxury for instance cleanliness is, you will only recognize once you have lived for some time in such a household with several children.' Quoted after Dirk Kaesler, 'Man sieht nur, was man zu wissen glaubt: Max und Marianne Weber im Amerika der Jahrhundertwende', in Frank Keller and Wolfgang Knöbl (eds), *Amerika und Deutschland: Ambivalente Begegnungen*, Göttingen: Wallstein, 2006, pp. 10–29; here: p. 10.

26 See Osterhammel, *The Transformation of the World*. p. 696.

27 '*Stand* der Frau – ist *Hausfrau*'. Georg Wilhelm Friedrich Hegel, *Grundlinien der Philosophie des Rechts*, Werke, vol. 7, Frankfurt am Main: Suhrkamp, p. 320. Transl. note: This is a handwritten marginal note by Hegel to §167. Hegel's handwritten notes are not included in the English edition.

28 See Barbara Greven-Aschoff, *Die bürgerliche Frauenbewegung in Deutschland 1894–1933*, Göttingen: Vandenhoeck & Ruprecht, 1981, part A, chapter V.

29 See Andrea Komlosy, *Arbeit: Eine globalhistorische Perspektive. 13. bis 21. Jahrhundert*, Vienna: Promedia, 2014. This study also contains useful references to further literature. See also Adelheid Biesecker and Uta von Winterfeld, 'Vergessene Arbeitswirklichkeiten', in Ulrich Beck (ed.), *Die Zukunft von Arbeit und Demokratie*, Frankfurt am Main: Suhrkamp, 2000, pp. 269–86.

30 As mentioned above, John Stuart Mill had already begun to tear down the distinction between 'productive' and 'unproductive' labour (see note 16). His conception of 'productive' labour, which aims to be as objective as possible, defines it as the creation of 'permanent utilities' (*Principles of Political Economy*, vol. I, p. 48). Thus, weaving a tablecloth for use in one's own household must also be seen as 'productive' because it creates a 'permanent utility' for the family. At the same time this point shows that Mill's distinction is not appropriate for drawing a line between gainful employment and housework.

31 See Sabine Gürtler, 'The Ethical Dimension of Work: A Feminist Perspective', *Hypatia* 20 (2005), pp. 119–34. See also Ilona Ostner and Elisabeth Beck-Gernsheim, *Mitmenschlichkeit als Beruf: Eine Analyse des Alltags in der Krankenpflege*, Frankfurt am Main: Campus, 1996. A fundamental and far-reaching attempt at expanding the dominant concept of labour by including caring and nursing professions can be found in Marlène Jouan, 'Ce qui compte comme "travail": La distinction entre travail productif et travail reproductif au prisme de la circulation transnationale de la gestation pour autrui', in Alexis Cukier, Katia Genel and Duarte Rolo (eds), *Le sujet du travail: Théorie critique, psychanalyse et politique*, Rennes: Presses universitaires de Rennes, 2022, pp. 103–23.

32 This useful categorization has been suggested by Martin Baethge, 'Die Arbeit in der Dienstleistungsgesellschaft', in Adalbert Evers, Rolf G. Heinze and Thomas Olk (eds), *Handbuch Soziale Dienste*, Wiesbaden: Springer, 2011, pp. 35–61, here: p. 45.

33 On the category of 'voluntary work', see the survey in Rolf G. Heinze and Christoph Strünck, 'Die Verzinsung des sozialen Kapitals: Freiwilliges Engagement im Strukturwandel', in Beck (ed.), *Die Zukunft von Arbeit und Demokratie*, pp. 171–216.

34 On the problem of finding an appropriate concept of labour, see Budd, *The Thought of Work*, p. 2.

35 See Johánn P. Árnason, *Praxis und Interpretation: Sozialphilosophische Studien*, Frankfurt am Main: Suhrkamp, 1988, especially pp. 45–53. See also the contributions in Leonhard

and Steinmetz (eds), *Semantiken von Arbeit*. Of course, it might be objected that there is a core area of activities that are required for the reproduction of *any* society and that only these should therefore count as necessary: preparing food and acquiring the raw materials for this, erecting some form of housing, caring for the sick, passing on cultural practices to the next generation and so on. But in different societies these requirements are covered by very different practices and in very different social constellations. In the case of caring for the sick, think of magic, collective rituals or various forms of therapy. This shows that it is impossible to speak, objectively and independently of any interpretation, of a fundamental set of activities that is required for social reproduction. The weakness of today's theories of social reproduction, in my view, is that they abstract from the need for cultural interpretation in establishing what counts as 'necessary' or 'essential' labour. See e.g. Tithi Bhattacharya (ed.), *Social Reproduction Theory: Remapping Class, Recentering Oppression*, London: Pluto Press, 2017; Verónica Gago and Liz Mason-Deese, 'Notes on Essential Labor', *International Labor and Working-Class History* 99 (2021), pp. 24–9.

36 On the difficulty of defining and identifying 'social communities', see Axel Honneth, 'Recht und Sittlichkeit: Aspekte eines komplexen Wechselverhältnisses', in Rainer Forst and Klaus Günther (eds), *Normative Ordnungen*, Berlin: 2021, pp. 42–71.

37 Hegel, *Elements of the Philosophy of Right*, §187, p. 224.

38 I leave aside a perfectly justified question that has been raised in recent years and would complicate matters even further, namely the question of whether and how we should consider the labour done by pets and farm animals that is involved in preserving our social form of life as 'social labour' and thus include it in our conception of a fair system of cooperation. On this topic see Peter Niesen, 'Kooperation und Unterwerfung: Vorüberlegungen zur politischen Theorie des Mensch/Nutztier-Verhältnisses', *Mittelweg 36* 23:5 (2014), pp. 45–58; Bernd Ladwig, *Politische Philosophie der Tierrechte*, Berlin: Suhrkamp, 2020, pp. 225–40. (I would like to thank Peter Niesen for drawing my attention to this problem.)

39 Another example would be the problem mentioned in the previous note: that today the services rendered by animals for the reproduction of our form of life are seen as candidates for inclusion in the concept of 'social labour', and thus should be subject to normative regulation.

40 Coal mining would be an example of a profession that became economically unviable. See e.g. Lutz Raphael, *Beyond Coal and Steel: A Social History of Western Europe after the Boom*, Cambridge: Polity, 2023, pp. 25–7. Professions that might lose their status as serving an indispensable purpose for society are journalists reporting on the stock exchange, think-tank employees, or – should the tax system be simplified – tax advisors. In this context, David Graeber's list of so-called 'bullshit jobs' – paid labour without any visible social value – is useful. See David Graeber, *Bullshit Jobs*, New York: Simon & Schuster, 2018. See also Geuss, *Work*, pp. 147–58. Geuss shows very clearly that drawing the distinction between socially useless and socially useful occupations is an eminently political process of persuading others in public debate by offering generally accepted reasons for a profession's or occupational field's 'objective' usefulness; see ibid., pp. 153f.

41 Continuing the work of the classic Western European and US sociologists, Jürgen Habermas has undertaken an attempt at such an examination in his *Theory of Communicative Action*. My own *Freedom's Right* is also essentially based on an attempt to work out the original functions of social spheres of action.

Part II

1 See e.g. Andrea Komlosy, *Work: The Last 1,000 Years*, London: Verso, 2018; Marcel van der Linden, *Workers of the World: Essays toward a Global Labor History*, Leiden: Brill, 2008; Jan Lucassen, *The Story of Work: A New History of Humankind*, New Haven: Yale University Press, 2021. On the nineteenth century, with a global perspective, see Osterhammel, *The Transformation of the World*, part III, chapter VIII: 'Labor: The Physical Basis of Culture'. On the nineteenth century from a European perspective, see Jürgen Kocka, *Arbeitsverhältnisse und Arbeiterexistenzen: Grundlagen der Klassenbildung im 19. Jahrhundert*, Bonn: Dietz, 1990.

4 A Spotlight on the Nineteenth Century

1 See e.g. this passage from Kant's *The Metaphysics of Morals*: 'an apprentice in the service of a merchant or artisan; a domestic servant (as distinguished from a civil servant); a minor ... all women and, in general, anyone whose preservation in existence (his being fed and protected) depends not on his management of his own business but on arrangements made by another (except the state). All these people lack civil personality' and are thus passive citizens, unlike the active citizens, who have the right to participate in legislation. Immanuel Kant, *The Metaphysics of Morals*, Cambridge: Cambridge University Press, 2017, p. 100. John Stuart Mill still held a similar position, but on the grounds that large parts of the working population continued to lack the general education needed for informed participation in elections. See his *Considerations on Representative Government*, London: Parker, Son and Bourn, 1861, chapter 8: 'On the Extension of the Suffrage'.

2 On the tradition based on this argument, see C. B. Macpherson, *The Political Theory of Possessive Individualism: Hobbes to Locke*, Oxford: Oxford University Press, 1962.

3 On the difficulty of measuring the unpaid work done by women in the nineteenth century, which is practically absent from the available statistical information, see Delphine Gardey, 'Perspectives Historiques', in Margaret Muarani (ed.), *Les Nouvelles frontières de l'inégalité: Hommes et femmes sur la marche du travail*, Paris: Éditions La Découverte et Syros, 1998, pp. 23–38.

4 See Engels, *The Condition of the Working Class in England*.

5 On these developments in Germany, see Hans-Ulrich Wehler, *Deutsche Gesellschaftsgeschichte, vol. 2: 1815–1845/49*, Munich: C. H. Beck, 2008, pp. 162–6.

6 Hegel, *Elements of the Philosophy of Right*, §203, pp. 235f. Thomas Hardy's *Far from the Madding Crowd* contains a wonderful passage that captures the continuing absence, from mediaeval times into the nineteenth century, of any historical dimension from agricultural activity. It talks of the 'functional continuity' of a barn used for sheep shearing: 'One could say about this barn, what could hardly be said of either the church or the castle, akin to it in age and style, that the purpose which had dictated its original erection was the same with that to which it was still applied.' Thomas Hardy, *Far from the Madding Crowd*, London: Smith, Elder & Co., 1874, 2 vols., vol. 1, pp. 240f.

7 On the various forms of employment that were open to propertyless agricultural labourers in Germany, see Wehler, *Deutsche Gesellschaftsgeschichte*, vol. 2, pp. 166–9. See also Ingeborg Weber-Kellermann, *Landleben im 19. Jahrhundert*, Munich: C. H. Beck, 1987, chapter VI.

8 Wehler, *Deutsche Gesellschaftsgeschichte*, vol. 2, p. 166.

9 Wilhelm Heinrich Riehl, *Die Familie*, Stuttgart: Cotta, 1855, p. 29.

10 For an overview, see Roland Bettger, 'Verlagswesen, Handwerk und Heimarbeit', in Rainer A. Müller a. o. (eds), *Aufbruch ins Industriezeitalter*, vol. 2, Munich: Oldenbourg, 1985, pp. 175–83. A broad range of information can be found in Karl Ditt and Sydney Pollard (eds), *Von der Heimarbeit in die Fabrik: Industrialisierung und Arbeiterschaft in Leinen- und Baumwollregionen Westeuropas während des 18. und 19. Jahrhunderts*, Paderborn: Ferdinand Schöningh, 1992.

11 In reality, there was little freedom, as impressively described by Scott, 'The Woman Worker', p. 406. Cf. Goethe's surprisingly detailed but rather romanticizing depiction of cottage industry in a weaver's cottage in *Wilhelm Meister's Journeyman Years, Or, The Renunciants*, in Johann Wolfgang Goethe, *The Collected Works*, vol. 10, Princeton NJ: Princeton University Press, 1995, pp. 96–342; here: pp. 332–42 (Book III, chapter V: 'Lenardo's Diary').

12 The Silesian uprisings entered the collective consciousness in Germany in part because of Heinrich Heine's great poem 'The Silesian Weavers', in *The Poems of Heine: Complete*, London: George Bell and Sons, 1887, p. 395. See also the striking description in Michael Kittner, *Arbeitskampf: Geschichte – Recht – Gegenwart*, Munich: C. H. Beck, 2005, pp. 184–9.

13 On proto-industrialization, see Peter Kreidtke, Hans Medick and Jürgen Schlumbohm, *Industrialisierung vor der Industrialisierung: Gewerbliche Warenproduktion auf dem Land in der Formationsperiode des Kapitalismus*, Göttingen: Vandenhoeck & Ruprecht, 1977.

14 Frederick Engels, 'Preface to the Second Edition', in *The Housing Question*, Paris: Foreign Languages Press, 2021, pp. 1–13; here: p. 8; transl. amended. Transl. note: Engels's *The Housing Question* can also be found in volume 23 of Marx/Engels, *Collected Works*, London: Lawrence & Wishart, 2010, pp. 317–91. However, the volume does not contain the preface to the second edition.

15 Kocka, *Arbeitsverhältnisse und Arbeiterexistenzen*, p. 109. See also Osterhammel, *The Transformation of the World*, pp. 696f. On the working conditions of domestic servants in the nineteenth century, see Rolf Engelsing, *Zur Sozialgeschichte deutscher Mittel- und Unterschichten*, Göttingen: Vandenhoeck & Ruprecht, 1973, and Heidi Müller, *Dienstbare Geister: Leben und Arbeitswelt städtischer Dienstboten*, Berlin: Museum für deutsche Volkskunde, 1985, pp. 24–6.

16 'Unser Blatt' 2 (1899), quoted after Müller, *Dienstbare Geister*, p. 150.

17 On these figures, see ibid., pp. 168f. See also Dorothee Wierling, *Mädchen für alles: Arbeitsalltag und Lebensgeschichte städtischer Dienstmädchen um die Jahrhundertwende*, Bonn: Dietz, 2002.

18 The miserable conditions of domestic servants' accommodation is described poignantly by the maid Hedwig in the famous fourteenth chapter of Theodor Fontane's *The Stechlin*, which is dedicated to the 'perspective from below'. Theodor Fontane, *The Stechlin*, Columbia SC: Camden House, 1995, pp. 111–23; esp. pp. 120–3.

19 See Scott, 'The Woman Worker', pp. 458f.; Müller, *Dienstbare Geister*, pp. 104–10.

20 Zola, *The Ladies' Paradise*. The novels making up Zola's twenty-volume cycle *Les Rougon-Macquart* provide rich material for the study of the lower classes' working life in nineteenth-century France, from agricultural day labourers and washerwomen to the miners. Listed according to date of their first publication, of particular relevance are *The Belly of Paris* [1873]; *The Dram Shop*, Hastings: Delphi Press, 2017 [1877]; *Germinal*, Oxford: Oxford University Press, 1993 [1877]; *The Earth*, Oxford: Oxford University Press, 2016 [1887].

21 See Pierre Devon, 'Proto-Industrialization in France', in Sheilagh C. Ogilvie et al. (eds), *European Proto-Industrialization: An Introductory Handbook*, Cambridge: Cambridge University Press, 1996, pp. 38–48.

22 Michael J. Piore and Charles F. Sabel put forward the interesting thesis that it would have been possible to go down the route of small-scale production in specialized crafts instead of mass production. See their *The Second Industrial Divide*. I shall return to this study in the second excursus, where I discuss the concept of the division of labour.

23 See the survey by Karl Ditt, 'Fabrikarbeiter und Handwerker im 19. Jahrhundert in der neueren deutschen Sozialgeschichtsschreibung', *Geschichte und Gesellschaft* 2 (1994), pp. 299–320; Toni Offermann, *Arbeiterbewegung und liberales Bürgertum 1850–1863*, Bonn: Verlag Neue Gesellschaft, 1979; Craig Calhoun, *The Roots of Radicalism: Tradition, the Public Sphere, and Early Nineteenth-Century Social Movements*, Chicago: University of Chicago Press, 2012.

24 See Wolf Schäfer, 'Wilhelm Weitling im Spiegel der wissenschaftlichen Auseinandersetzungen', in Wilhelm Weitling, *Das Evangelium des armen Sünders/Die Menschheit, wie sie ist und sein sollte*, Reinbek: Rowohlt, 1971 [1846/1838].

25 On Germany, see the summary in Wehler, *Deutsche Gesellschaftsgeschichte*, vol. 2, p. 63.

26 Regarding the changed attitudes to time brought about by the forms of work introduced by the emerging industrial capitalism, see the influential and seminal essay by E. P. Thompson, 'Time, Work-Discipline and Industrial Capitalism', in *Customs in Common*, London: Penguin, 1993 [1991], pp. 352–403.

27 Charles Dickens, *Hard Times*, London: J. M. Dent, 1908, p. 57.

28 Elizabeth Gaskell, *North and South*, Oxford: Oxford University Press, 1934, p. 505.

29 See Eiden-Offe, *Die Poesie der Klasse: Romantischer Antikapitalismus und die Erfindung des Proletariats*.

30 This list is based on Ahlrich Meyer, 'Eine Theorie der Niederlage: Marx und die Evidenz des 19. Jahrhunderts', in Marcel van der Linden and Karl Heinz Roth (eds), *Über Marx hinaus: Arbeitsgeschichte und Arbeitsverhältnisse in der Konfrontation mit den globalen Arbeitsverhältnissen des 21. Jahrhunderts*, Hamburg and Berlin: Verlag Assoziation A, 2009, pp. 311–33. On the inclusion of women in the labour relations of early industrialization in the case of England, see Maxine Berg, 'Women's Work, Mechanization and the Early Phases of Industrialization in England', in Raymond Edward Pahl (ed.), *On Work: Historical, Comparative and Theoretical Approaches*, Oxford: Blackwell, 1988, pp. 61–94.

31 On the importance of slave labour to overseas trade during the early phases of capitalist industrialization, see the excellent exposition by Albert Wirz, *Sklaverei und kapitalistisches Weltsystem*, Frankfurt am Main: Suhrkamp, 1985, chapter 5.

32 See Osterhammel, *The Transformation of the World*, pp. 686–8.

33 Engels, in his highly informative 'The Peasant Question in France and Germany', speaks several times of the 'apathy' of the peasants, which he attributes to social isolation, destitution and personal dependence. Frederick Engels, 'The Peasant Question in France and Germany', in Karl Marx and Frederick Engels, *Collected Works*, vol. 27, London: Lawrence & Wishart, 2010, pp. 481–502; here: p. 483.

34 Hans-Ulrich Wehler, *Deutsche Gesellschaftsgeschichte, vol. 3: 1849–1914*, Munich: Beck, 2006, p. 62.

35 For a survey, see Wolfgang Abendroth, *Sozialgeschichte der europäischen Arbeiterbewegung*, Frankfurt am Main: Suhrkamp, 1965, pp. 11–50. On increasing labour conflict, see Kittner, *Arbeitskampf*, part 2, sections 1–4.

36 Louis Chevalier, *Classes laborieuses et classes dangereuses à Paris pendant la première moitié du XIXe siècle*, Paris 1984 [1958], p. 176. English edition: *Laboring Classes and Dangerous Classes in Paris During the First Half of the 19th Century*, Princeton NJ: Princeton University Press, 1981. Quoted after Robert Castel, *From Manual Workers to Wage Laborers: Transformation of the Social Question*, London: Routledge, 2017, p. 201. See my review of this important book: Axel Honneth, 'Tigersprung in die Vorgeschichte der Arbeit: Zu Robert Castels grundlegendemWerk "Metamorphosen der sozialen Frage"', *Literaturen* 2:1 (2001), pp. 58–9.

37 On the reality behind the term 'pauperism' and on the phantasm of the 'dangerous classes', see the amazing chapter 'The Miserable', in Castel, *From Manual Workers to Wage Laborers*, pp. 196–206.

38 On the debates about pauperism in Germany during the pre-1848 period, see Wehler, *Deutsche Gesellschaftgeschichte*, vol. 2, pp. 281–96. A solid survey of the political debates about the 'social question' in Europe during the second half of the nineteenth century can be found in Ferdinand Tönnies, *Die Entwicklung der sozialen Frage bis zum Weltkriege*, Leipzig: Göschen, 1907. Reprint: Berlin: De Gruyter, 1989 and 2019.

39 On these various motivations and strategies, see Wolfgang J. Mommsen and Wolfgang Mock (eds), *The Emergence of the Welfare State in Britain and Germany 1850–1950*, London: Routledge, 1981.

40 Thomas H. Marshall, 'Citizenship and Social Class', in *Citizenship and Social Class and Other Essays*, Cambridge: Cambridge University Press, 1950, pp. 1–85; see esp. pp. 10–45.

41 See Osterhammel, *The Transformation of the World*, pp. 675f. For a general overview, see Daniel Bell, *The Coming of Post-Industrial Society: A Venture in Social Forecasting*, New York: Basic Books, 1973. Jean Fourastié, *Le Grand Espoir du XXe siècle: Progrès technique, progrès économique, progrès social*, Paris: Presses universitaires de France, 1949. Very informative is Baethge, 'Die Arbeit in der Dienstleistungsgesellschaft'.

42 Osterhammel, *The Transformation of the World*, p. 670.

43 Castel, *From Manual Workers to Wage Laborers*, p. 265.

44 See the sections on 'The Wage-Earning Condition' and 'The Growth-State', ibid., pp. 335–66. In this context, Castel also speaks of the 'gradual growth of the "bourgeois" wage- earner', p. 335.

5 From 1900 to the Threshold of the Present

1 See Louis Althusser, 'Ideology and Ideological State Apparatuses (Note towards an Investigation)', in *Lenin and Philosophy and Other Essays*, New York: Monthly Review Press, 1971, pp. 127–86.

2 See Karin Hausen, 'Die Polarisierung der "Geschlechtscharaktere": eine Spiegelung der Dissoziation von Erwerbs- und Familienleben', in Werner Conze (ed.), *Sozialgeschichte der Familie in der Neuzeit Europas*, Stuttgart: Klett, 1976, pp. 363–96. Scott, 'The Woman Worker'. On the gradual conditioning of 'bourgeois' women for the roles of mother and housewife in the course of the nineteenth century, see the excellent paper by Yvonne Knibiehler, 'Bodies and Hearts', in Fraisse and Perrot (eds), *A History of Women in the West*, vol. 4, pp. 325–68.

3 Bärbel Kuhn, *Haus, Frauen, Arbeit 1915–1965: Erinnerungen aus fünfzig Jahren Haushaltsgeschichte*, St Ingbert: Röhrig, 1994, pp. 88–101. This chapter also clearly demonstrates that it was often only as new commodities or new forms of living were

introduced that new technical appliances were needed. Fitted carpets required vacuum cleaners. Condominiums without cool cellars required fridges, and frozen food a freezer. From the 1980s onwards, ready meals required microwaves.

4 'Just as in the case of the well and washhouse, the loss of the general store meant the loss of a place that previously had offered opportunities for communication.' Ibid., p. 96.

5 See Elisabeth Beck-Gernsheim, 'Vom "Dasein für andere" zum Anspruch auf ein Stück "eigenes Leben": Individualisierungsprozesse im weiblichen Lebenszusammenhang', *Soziale Welt* 34:3 (1983), pp. 307–40.

6 On the following, see Ulrich Kluge, *Agrarwirtschaft und ländliche Gesellschaft im 20. Jahrhundert*, Munich: Oldenbourg, 2005.

7 Elisabeth, the protagonist in Ralf Rothmann's novel *Die Nacht unterm Schnee*, Berlin: Suhrkamp, 2022, p. 96. Transl. note: Ralf Rothmann, born in 1953, is an award-winning German author whose works paint a social panorama of Germany from the Second World War up to the present. *Die Nacht unterm Schnee* (Night under snow) is the last book of a trilogy covering the war and post-war years.

8 On the increasing mechanization of agriculture, see Weber-Kellermann, *Landleben im 19. Jahrhundert*, pp. 360–75.

9 Max Weber, *Die Lage der Landarbeiter im ostelbischen Deutschland*, in *Max Weber Gesamtausgabe*, Abt. 1, vol. 3.2, ed. Martin Riesebrodt, Tübingen: Mohr Siebeck, 1984 [1892], pp. 914f.

10 By 2017, the figure was just 1.4 per cent. See https://www.bauernverband.de /situationsbericht/1-landwirtschaft-und-gesamtwirtschaft/12-jahrhundertvergleich.

11 For a survey of this development in Germany, see Helma Lutz, *Vom Weltmarkt in den Privathaushalt: Die neuen Dienstmädchen im Zeitalter der Globalisierung*, Opladen: Verlag Barbara Budrich, 2007.

12 W. E. B. Du Bois, *The Souls of Black Folk: Essays and Sketches*, Chicago: A. C. McClurg & Co., 1903, p. 94.

13 Siegfried Kracauer, *The Salaried Masses: Duty and Distraction in Weimar Germany*, London: Verso, 1998. Around the same time, Hans Speier, in his 1933 study *Die Angestellten vor dem Nationalsozialismus*, carried out an analysis of the numerous professions that were subsumed under the term 'employee'. An expanded version was published in 1977 (Göttingen: Vandenhoeck & Ruprecht), and an English translation by the author was published in 1986 under the title *German White-Collar Workers and the Rise of Hitler* (New Haven: Yale University Press, 1986). In his excellent survey, Speier distinguishes between 'clerical personnel in small enterprises', 'foremen', 'technical personnel', 'commercial employees in larger establishments', 'saleswomen in one-price stores', 'the lowest personnel in giant enterprises', 'typists', 'machine operators' and 'government employees'. See *German White-Collar Workers*, chapter 1.

14 Kracauer, *The Salaried Masses*, p. 43.

15 See Jan-Otmar Hesse, Roman Köster and Werner Plumpe, *Die Große Depression: Die Weltwirtschaftskrise 1929–1939*, Frankfurt am Main: Campus, 2014.

16 See Carsten Uhl, 'Räume der Arbeit: Von der frühneuzeitlichen Werkstatt zur modernen Fabrik', in *Europäische Geschichte Online* (EGO), edited by Leibniz-Institut für Europäische Geschichte (IEG), Mainz, 2015, http://ieg-ego.eu/de/threads/crossroads /technisierte-lebenswelten/karsten-uhl-raeume-der-arbeit-von-der-fruehneuzeitlichen -werkstatt-zur-modernen-fabrik.

17 See Harry Braverman, *Labor and Monopoly Capital: The Degradation of Work in the*

Twentieth Century, New York: Monthly Review Press, 1998 [1974]; especially chapter 4 on 'Scientific Management', pp. 59–85; Friedmann, *Industrial Society*, part one, chapter 1, pp. 37–66. A sarcastic characterization of Frederick Winslow Taylor's efforts at increasing the productivity of factory work with his methods of 'scientific management' can be found in John Dos Passos's novel *The Big Money*, Boston: Houghton Mifflin, 2000 [1936]; here: pp. 15–37 ('The American Plan'). Simone Weil, in a short speech delivered to workers – of which, unfortunately, we only have the notes taken by a member of the audience – presents her understanding of the purpose and methods of Taylor's system of 'scientific management' with a clarity and intensity that rivals that of Dos Passos's account: Simone Weil, 'La Rationalisation (23 fevrière 1937)', in *La Condition Ouvrière*, Paris: Gallimard: 1951, pp. 178–96.

18 Dos Passos, *The Big Money*, p. 44. In 1934, shortly before the publication of Dos Passos's novel in 1936, Simone Weil began to write her *Factory Journal*, a detailed account of the manual operations she had to perform at or near assembly lines and what piece rates she was paid by various Paris metalworks. Simone Weil, *Factory Journal*, in *Formative Writings 1929–1941*, London: Routledge: 2010, pp. 149–226.

19 Georges Friedmann offers a short sketch of the workers' reaction in his *Industrial Society*: 'Research and the first reactions of workers', pp. 41–3. It is one of the weaknesses of Braverman's study *Labor and Monopoly Capital* that it hardly mentions the industrial workers' resistance to the new methods of production and the new work regime. A good summary of the debates triggered by the introduction of Taylorist methods in the US and Europe is given by Richard Vahrenkamp, 'Frederick Winslow Taylor – Ein Denker zwischen Manufaktur und Großindustrie', in Frederick Winslow Taylor, *Die Grundsätze der wissenschaftlichen Betriebsführung*, ed. Walter Volpert and Richard Vahrenkamp, Weinheim: Belz, 1977, pp. LII–IXC. Transl. note: First publication of Taylor's book: Frederick Winslow Taylor, *The Principles of Scientific Management*, New York: Harper & Row, 1911. For an English translation of Vahrenkamp's introduction, see *Taylor and Taylorism: Public Debate and Decline in U.S. and Europe, 1900–1939*, Working Paper Logistics 21/2018; available at https://kobra.uni-kassel.de/bitstream/handle/123456789/14638/WorkingPaperLogistics_WP21_2018.pdf?sequence=4&isAllowed=y.

20 See Braverman, *Labor and Monopoly Capital*, chapter 3 ('The Division of Labor').

21 See Martin Baethge, 'Abschied vom Industrialismus: Konturen einer neuen gesellschaftlichen Ordnung der Arbeit', *SOFI-Mitteilungen* 28 (2000), pp. 87–102; available at http://webdoc.sub.gwdg.de/edoc/le/sofi/2000_28/baethge.pdf.

22 Ibid, p. 93.

23 Ibid.

6 The Capitalist World of Work Today

1 See the survey of professions that no longer exist in Rudi Palla, *Verschwundene Arbeit: Das Buch der untergegangenen Berufe*, Vienna: Brandstätter, 2014.

2 See e.g. Kittner, *Arbeitskampf*.

3 See Werner Plumpe, *Wirtschaftskrisen: Geschichte und Gegenwart*, Munich: C. H. Beck, 2010.

4 The following passage is based on Axel Honneth, 'Neoliberalismus? Eine skeptische Wortmeldung anlässlich einer Studie von David M. Kotz', *WestEnd: Neue Zeitschrift für Sozialforschung* 13:1 (2016), pp. 167–79.

5 Attempts to bring some clarity into the conceptual confusion by drawing a stricter

distinction between ordoliberalism and neoliberalism were made by, among others, Taylor C. Boas and Jordan Gans-Morse, 'Neoliberalism: From New Liberal Philosophy to Anti-Liberal Slogan', *Studies in Comparative International Development* 44:2 (2009), pp. 137–61; Andreas Renner, 'Die zwei Neoliberalismen', in Diether Vogel (ed.), *Fragen der Freiheit: Beiträge zur freiheitlichen Ordnung von Kultur, Staat und Wirtschaft* 250 (1999), pp. 48–64.

6 See Alain Supiot, *Beyond Employment: Changes in Work and the Future of Labour Law in Europe*, Oxford: Oxford University Press, 2001; Colin Crouch, *Will the Gig Economy Prevail?*, Cambridge: Polity, 2019. On the reflection of the new work regime in contemporary German literature, see Lydia Mühlbach, *Von Nicht-Arbeit erzählen: Erwerbsarbeitslosigkeit in der Gegenwartsliteratur*, Paderborn: Wilhelm Fink, 2021.

7 Crouch, *Will the Gig Economy Prevail?*, p. 72.

8 See Philipp Staab, *Digitaler Kapitalismus: Markt und Herrschaft in der Ökonomie der Unknappheit*, Berlin: Suhrkamp, 2019, pp. 97–107. However, we should not exaggerate the symbiotic nature of the relationship between finance and the rising internet companies. There are also frictions and tensions between them, as the attempts of digital currencies to become independent of traditional financial institutions have made clear.

9 Crouch, *Will the Gig Economy Prevail?*, pp. 25–34. See also Martin Höppner, *Wer beherrscht die Unternehmen: Shareholder Value, Managerherrschaft und Mitbestimmung in Deutschland*, Frankfurt am Main: Campus, 2003. On the diminished role of the trade unions as a consequence of transformations in the labour and production regime, see Luc Boltanski and Ève Chiapello, *The New Spirit of Capitalism*, London: Verso, 2005; especially part II, chapter 5, section 1 (pp. 274–96).

10 See Crouch, *Will the Gig Economy Prevail?*, pp. 36–41.

11 See Staab, *Digitaler Kapitalismus*, chapter 5. On the massive increase in digital control and measurement of individual performance, see the instructive article by Jodi Kantor and Arya Sundaram, 'The Rise of the Worker Productivity Score', *New York Times*, 14 August 2022.

12 Alwin Strothmeyer, 'Bauer in der 18. Generation im Osnabrücker Land', in *100 Jahre Landleben – Bauer aus Leidenschaft*, Documentary produced by Norddeutscher Rundfunk, broadcast 20 August 2022, available at: https://www.ndr.de/geschichte/chronologie /Landwirtschaft-im-Wandel-Vom-Handwerk-zur-Robotertechnik,landleben135.html.

13 See Andrea Bambey and Hans-Walter Gumbinger, *Neue Väter? Rollenmodelle zwischen Anspruch und Wirklichkeit*, Frankfurt am Main: Campus, 2017. Trudie Knijn, Ilona Ostner and Christoph Schmitt, 'Männer und (ihre) Kinder: Einstellungen zur Elternschaft im Ländervergleich', in Frank Lettke and Andreas Lange (eds), *Generationen und Familien: Analysen – Konzepte – gesellschaftliche Spannungsfelder*, Frankfurt am Main: Suhrkamp, 2006, pp. 189–222. A recent publication points in the same direction: Katrin Menke, *Wahlfreiheit erwerbstätiger Mütter und Väter? Zur Erwerbs-und Sorgearbeit aus intersektioneller Perspektive*, Bielefeld: transcript, 2019.

14 See Ursula Huws, *Labour in Contemporary Capitalism: What Next?*, London: Palgrave Macmillan, 2019, chapter 7 (pp. 121–40).

15 On the prehistory, see Susan Strasser, *Never Done: A History of American Housework*, New York: Henry Holt and Company, 1982, especially chapters 11–13.

16 Tanja Carstensen, 'Effizient, optimiert, alltagstauglich: Digitale Praktiken zwischen Erwerbs- und Sorgearbeit', *Mittelweg 36* 30:1 (2022), pp. 40–59.

17 See Lutz, *Vom Weltmarkt in den Privathaushalt*.

18 Weber, *Die Lage der Landarbeiter*, p. 925.

19 Edyta, a Polish woman who did not complete her training as a gardener and who today works in private care for the elderly. Quoted after Sarah Schilliger, 'Ein Leben in Sorge um andere: Dauereinsatz in der 24-Stunden-Betreuung', in Nicole Mayer-Ahuja and Oliver Nachtwey (eds), *Verkannte Leistungsträger:innen. Berichte aus der Klassengesellschaft*, Berlin: Suhrkamp, 2021, pp. 119–37, here: p. 129.

20 This follows, in part verbatim, Baethge, 'Die Arbeit in der Dienstleistungsgesellschaft', p. 47.

21 See e.g. Philipp Staab, *Macht und Herrschaft in der Servicewelt*, Hamburg: Hamburger Edition, 2014. Philipp Staab, 'Metamorphosen der Fabriksozialisation: Zur Produktion des Arbeiters in Vergangenheit und Gegenwart', *Mittelweg 36* 23:6 (2014), pp. 4–27.

22 Florence Aubenas, *The Night Cleaner*, Cambridge: Polity, 2011, p. 75.

23 See pp. 69–71 above.

24 See Crouch, *Will the Gig Economy Prevail?*, pp. 21f. See also the comprehensive study by Sophie Bernard, *Le nouvel esprit du salariat*, Paris: Press universitaires de France, 2020.

25 See e.g. the study, based on personal experience, by Callum Cant, *Riding for Deliveroo: Resistance in the New Economy*, Cambridge: Polity, 2019.

26 But for counter-examples see the preface in Cant, *Riding for Deliveroo*.

27 From Thorsten Nagelschmidt's novel *Arbeit*, Frankfurt am Main: S. Fischer, 2020, pp. 67f.

28 See the impressive account in Raphael, *Beyond Coal and Steel*; esp. chapter 1.

29 Ibid., p. 251. On the reactions in industrial sociology, see Horst Kern and Michael Schumann, *Das Ende der Arbeitsteilung: Rationalisierung in der industriellen Produktion – Bestandsaufnahme, Trendbestimmung*, Munich: C. H. Beck, 1984. Horst Kern and Michael Schumacher, 'Limits of the Division of Labour: New Production and Employment Concepts in West German Industry', *Economic and Industrial Democracy* 8 (2) (1987), pp. 151–70.

30 Herrmann Kotthoff and Josef Reindl, *Die soziale Welt kleiner Betriebe: Wirtschaften, Arbeiten und Leben im mittelständischen Industriebetrieb*, Göttingen: Schwartz, 1990, p. 29.

31 But see the warnings sounded by Daniel Susskind in 'Work in the Digital Economy', in Robert Skidelsky and Nan Craig (eds), *Work in the Future: The Automation Revolution*, Cham: Springer Nature Switzerland AG, 2020, pp. 125–32.

32 See the excellent study by Claudia Czingon, *Die Berufsmoral der Banker: Potentiale und Grenzen finanzwirtschaftlicher Selbstregulierung* (Frankfurter Beiträge zur Soziologie und Sozialphilosophie, vol. 29), Frankfurt am Main: Campus, 2019; especially chapter 6.

33 Mr Voigt, a former investment banker of twenty years' experience. Quoted after Czingon, *Die Berufsmoral der Banker*, pp. 127f.

34 On this trend, see the study by Danièle Linhart, *Travailler sans les autres*, Paris: Seuil, 2009.

35 See Hans J. Pongratz and G. Günter Voß, *Arbeitskraftunternehmer: Erwerbsorientierungen in entgrenzten Arbeitsformen*, Baden-Baden: edition sigma, 2004.

36 On this, see Baethge, 'Abschied vom Industrialismus', p. 94.

37 On the project nature of some of the new forms of work, see Boltanksi and Chiapello, *The New Spirit of Capitalism*, part I, chapter 1, section 2: 'The Development of the Management Problematic from the 1960s to the 1990s' (pp. 64–86).

38 The disembodiment of labour should not be confused with the notion of 'immaterial

labour' as used in Italian post-workerism, where it denotes a whole range of global changes in the character of work, such as the turn towards communication, symbolic operations and the mediation of relations, but does not make explicit what their common denominator is.

39 According to André Leroi-Gourhan, the transition from hand to symbol in social practices is a universal historical process that explains increasing complexity and cultural diversity. See his *Gesture and Speech*, Cambridge MA: MIT Press, 1993; 'The Fate of the Hand' (pp. 254f.). My thesis is that this transition is currently taking place at an accelerated pace in the area of social labour.

40 On 'industrial fatigue' see Chapter 3, note 22.

41 On the situation in Germany, see Nora Ahlsdorf a.o., *Psychische Erkrankungen in der Arbeitswelt*, Bielefeld: transcript, 2017.

42 See Huws, *Labour in Contemporary Capitalism*, chapters 6 and 7.

43 Thomas H. Marshall, *Sociology at the Crossroads and Other Essays*, London: Heinemann, 1963, p. 98. The term 'industrial citizenship' is not an altogether fortunate choice, because it places too much emphasis on the industrial sector. On the trend towards deregulation, see Karl Hinrichs, 'Irreguläre Beschäftigungsverhältnisse und soziale Sicherheit: Facetten der "Erosion" des Normalarbeitsverhältnisses in der Bundesrepublik', *PROKLA: Zeitschrift für kritische Sozialwissenschaft* 19:77 (1989), pp. 7–32. A good survey can also be found in the collected volume edited by Robert Castel and Klaus Dörre, *Prekariat, Abstieg, Ausgrenzung: Die soziale Frage am Beginn des 21. Jahrhunderts*, Frankfurt am Main: Campus, 2009.

44 See the analyses and personal reports in Mayer-Ahuja and Nachtwey (eds), *Verkannte Leistungsträger:innen. Berichte aus der Klassengesellschaft*; Veronika Bohrn Mena, *Die neue ArbeiterInnenklasse: Menschen in prekären Verhältnissen*, Vienna: ÖGB Verlag, 2020; Guy Standing, *The Precariat: The New Dangerous Class*, London: Bloomsbury, 2011; Julia Friedrichs, *Working Class: Warum wir Arbeit brauchen, von der wir leben können*, Berlin: Piper, 2021.

45 This point is made very convincingly in Standing, *The Precariat*, chapter 1.

Excursus II: On the Concept of the Social Division of Labour

1 Friedrich Kambartel's very interesting attempt at developing a normative theory of labour that includes unpaid, 'informal' housework also sets out from the concept of the social 'exchange of services'. See Friedrich Kambartel, 'Arbeit und Politik: Zu den begrifflichen und methodischen Grundlagen einer aktuellen politischen Debatte', in *Philosophie und Politische Ökonomie*, Göttingen: Wallstein, 1998, pp. 59–84; here: pp. 66–72.

2 See Niklas Luhmann's interesting introduction 'Arbeitsteilung und Moral: Durkheims Theorie', in Émile Durkheim, *Über soziale Arbeitsteilung: Studien über die Organisation höherer Gesellschaften*, Frankfurt am Main: Suhrkamp, 1992, pp. 19–38. An exception to this trend is Ulrich Beck, Michael Brater and Hansjürgen Daheim, *Soziologie der Berufe und der Arbeit: Grundlagen, Problemfelder, Forschungsergebnisse*, Reinbek bei Hamburg: Rowohlt, 1980.

3 See Marx, *Capital, Volume I*, pp. 131f.

4 Hegel, *Elements of the Philosophy of Right*, §191 and §§202–6, p. 229 and pp. 234–8.

5 On Durkheim's unusual position on this question, see Luhmann, 'Arbeitsteilung und Moral', p. 23. Durkheim's concept of labour is so broad that even sexual intercourse is included in the division of labour.

6 Durkheim, *The Division of Labor in Society*, p. 56.

7 Smith, *Wealth of Nations*, p. 446.

8 I ignore Smith's anthropological premise that humans have a 'disposition to truck, barter, and exchange' – a fact that he believes explains why humans take pleasure in the division of labour, which necessitates barter and exchange; ibid., p. 21.

9 See ibid., pp. 14f.

10 Durkheim, *The Division of Labor in Society*, Book 2, chapters 3–5, here: p. 346.

11 See ibid., Book 3, chapter 2: 'The Forced Division of Labor'.

12 See e.g. Hausen, 'Die Polarisierung der "Geschlechtscharaktere"'.

13 The strategy of the social 'closure' of professional fields to 'outsider' groups was already identified by Max Weber. See the section 'Open and Closed Economic Relationships' in his *Economy and Society*, pp. 341–3.

14 Paul Willis, *Learning to Labour: How Working Class Kids Get Working Class Jobs*, London: Routledge, 1978.

15 This kind of self-deselection follows the logic of an anticipatory adaptation to limited possibilities, which Jon Elster analyses under the heading of 'sour grapes'. See Jon Elster, *Sour Grapes: Studies in the Subversion of Rationality*, Cambridge: Cambridge University Press, 1983, chapter III.

16 Piore and Sabel, *The Second Industrial Divide*, p. 11 and pp. 21–6. For more detail, see Charles Sabel, *Work and Politics: The Division of Labor in Industry*, Cambridge: Cambridge University Press, 1982; especially chapter 1.

17 Piore and Sabel, *The Second Industrial Divide*, p. 15.

18 See ibid., chapter 2, pp. 19–48.

19 See ibid., chapters 8 and 9, pp. 194–250. The study was originally published in the US in 1984, at which point the authors clearly believed they were still in a position to influence the changes that had begun in the late 1970s.

20 See ibid., pp. 29–32.

21 Ibid., p. 29.

22 Ibid., p. 38.

23 Ibid., pp. 38–44; here: p. 44.

24 See Beck, Brater and Daheim, *Soziologie der Berufe und der Arbeit*, p. 24.

25 On the following, see ibid., pp. 67–70.

26 Ibid., p. 68.

27 See ibid., p. 69.

28 Ibid. (emphasis added, A. H.). See also pp. 210f.

29 Ibid.

30 Two studies by Barbara Garson show that the current intensification of the division of labour is primarily grounded in management's lack of trust in their employees' reliability and willingness to follow instructions. Garson substantiates this thesis through interviews with employees and management representatives. See Barbara Garson, *All the Livelong Day: The Meaning and Demeaning of Routine Work*, revised and updated edition, New York: Penguin, 1994; Barbara Garson, *Electronic Sweatshop: How Computers Are Transforming the Office of the Future into the Factory of the Past*, New York: Simon & Schuster, 1988.

Part III

1 Richard Rorty warned the American left about this development many years ago. See his *Achieving Our Country: Leftist Thought in Twentieth-Century America*, Cambridge MA: Harvard University Press, 1998.

7 The Politics of Labour

1 Robert Castel, 'Worin liegt die Bedeutung der Arbeit', in *Die Krise der Arbeit: Neue Unsicherheiten und die Zukunft des Individuums*, Hamburg: Hamburger Edition, 2011, pp. 76–97; here: p. 87.

2 André Gorz, *Farewell to the Working Class: An Essay on Post-Industrial Socialism*, London: Pluto Press, 1997 [1980].

3 André Gorz, *Critique of Economic Reason*, London: Verso, 1989 [1988], p. 58.

4 Yannick Vanderborght and Philippe Van Parijs, *Basic Income: A Radical Proposal for a Free Society and a Sane Economy*, Cambridge MA: Harvard University Press, 2017, p. 1 and passim. A universal basic income has even found support on the neo-republican side: see Philip Pettit, 'A Republican Right to Basic Income?', *Basic Income Studies* 2:2 (2007), pp. 1–8.

5 On this question, see the mostly critical contributions in Christoph Butterwegge and Kuno Rinke (eds), *Grundeinkommen kontrovers: Plädoyer für und gegen ein neues Sozialmodell*, Weinheim: Beltz, 2018.

6 On economists' reservations about a universal basic income, see Heinz-Josef Bontrup, 'Das bedingungslose Grundeinkommen – eine ökonomisch skurrile Forderung', in Butterwegge and Rinke (eds), *Grundeinkommen kontrovers*, pp. 114–30.

7 Gorz, *Critique of Economic Reason*, Part 1: 'Metamorphoses of Work', pp. 12–103. Claus Offe, 'Arbeit als soziologische Schlüsselkategorie', in Offe (ed.), *'Arbeitsgesellschaft'*, pp. 13–43; especially: pp. 28–36.

8 On the promotion of 'parasitic' behaviour, discussed from a Rawlsian perspective, see Muirhead, *Just Work*, chapter 1, pp. 13–29; here: p. 18. Following the arguments of Amy Gutmann and Dennis Thompson (*Democracy and Disagreement*, Cambridge MA: Harvard University Press, 1996), Muirhead points out that this effect does not necessarily mean that there should be a 'social obligation' to work, or that the state should be 'legally enforcing' such an obligation, although, somewhat worryingly, forms of 'softer sanctions' are considered. See *Just Work*, pp. 18f.

9 John Dewey coined the phrase 'social centre' for such spheres. In French, there is the expression 'grand intégrateur' (the great integrator). On the concept and function of a 'social centre' as it relates to the school, see John Dewey, 'The School as Social Centre', in *The Middle Works, 1899–1924*, vol. 2, Carbondale: Southern Illinois University Press, 2008, pp. 80–93; here: pp. 91f. On the 'great integrator', see Yves Barel, 'Le grand intégrateur', *Connexions* 56 (1990), pp. 85–100.

10 Marie Jahoda, Paul E. Lazarsfeld and Hans Zeisel, *Die Arbeitslosen von Marienthal: Ein soziographischer Versuch*, Frankfurt am Main: Suhrkamp, 1975. The study was originally published in 1933. See also Marie Jahoda, *Employment and Unemployment*, Cambridge: Cambridge University Press, 1982.

11 Anne Helen Petersen and Charlie Warzel, 'Remote, Invisible and Failing at Work', *New York Times*, 28 November 2021, p. 3.

12 I believe this also explains why John Rawls holds that the principles of political justice require a system of fair cooperation. On this complex of issues in Rawls, see my remarks in Chapter 3, note 15, and the very illuminating analysis in Ostheimer, *Liberalismus und soziale Gerechtigkeit*, chapter 2.4, pp. 70–88.

13 Richard David Precht is right to emphasize that 'without a change in attitude ... a basic income would be of little value'. But he remains silent on the question of how this change in attitude should come about. Richard David Precht, 'Frei leben!

Digitalisierung, Grundeinkommen und Menschenbild', in Butterwegge and Rinke (eds), *Grundeinkommen kontrovers*, pp. 32–49; here: p. 32. This gap in the argument is even more obvious in Sascha Liebermann's contribution to the same volume: 'Bedingungsloses Grundeinkommen: Fortentwicklung des Sozialstaats aus dem Geist der Demokratie', ibid., pp. 64–82. Liebermann claims that 'vague and open social relations' into which the individual can enter 'unconditionally' can be found only in the 'family triad' and the 'system of rule of the body politic', whereas the individual is integrated into economic enterprises and organizations only as a means to an end that is not the individual's own. Of course, in 'modern republican democracies' it is solely the recognition of someone's membership that makes him or her part of the body politic. But this does not answer the question of how to bring about a shared awareness of belonging, which is a necessary condition for individuals to understand themselves as part of a 'we', as a subject of democratic will formation. Liebermann simply passes over this question. In an article that is critical of the idea of a basic income, Ulrich Steinvorth raises this objection pointedly: 'Today, under normal circumstances, political interest only arises once one takes up a specific position within the system of social labour. Political interest here does not mean an interest in getting the greatest possible slice of the socially produced cake, but an interest in having a say in what is produced, what it is produced for, and under which distributive principles production takes place.' Ulrich Steinvorth, 'Kann das Grundeinkommen die Arbeitslosigkeit abbauen?', *Analyse & Kritik* 22 (2000), pp. 257–68; here: p. 258.

14 My claim here somewhat contradicts the assumption that democratic commitment is nourished by a broad network of civil associations, such as choral societies, sports clubs and the like – a thesis commonly associated with Robert D. Putnam; see his *Bowling Alone: The Collapse and Revival of American Community*, New York: Simon & Schuster, 2000. I would argue that Putnam's thesis must be qualified: the norms of mutual commitment and shared responsibility that emerge from such associations will lead to the formation of a sense of community only if there is also an awareness of the comprehensive cooperation on the basis of which these norms are generalized and transposed onto society at large.

15 Sometimes the revitalization of democratic commitment and the strengthening of individual bargaining power are mentioned side by side, as though the scope of these political goals did not differ markedly. See e.g. Veltman, *Meaningful Work*, pp. 92–104.

16 This was pointed out to me by Claus Offe in personal conversation.

17 Alex Gourevitch has presented similar objections to a universal basic income from a republican perspective. See his 'Labor Republicanism and the Transformation of Work', *Political Theory* 41:4 (2013), pp. 591–617.

18 See the short analysis by Boltanski and Chiapello, *The New Spirit of Capitalism*, pp. 275–342. Though based on the situation in France, this account can be generalized and applied to other countries.

19 See Axel Honneth, 'The Invisible Rebellion: Working People Under the New Capitalist Economy', in Didier Fassin and Axel Honneth (eds), *Crisis under Critique: How People Assess, Transform, and Respond to Critical Situations*, New York: Columbia University Press, 2022, pp. 387–402. In the following, some passages draw on this essay.

20 Albert O. Hirschman, *Exit, Voice, and Loyalty: Responses to Decline in Firms, Organizations, and States*, Cambridge MA: Harvard University Press, 1970.

21 See Jill W. Graham, 'Principled Organizational Dissent', *Research in Organizational Behaviour* 8 (1986), pp. 1–52. Forty years ago, I objected to the assumption that workers'

resistance must have such a morally 'principled' form if it is to count as an objection to the status quo: see Axel Honneth, 'Moral Consciousness and Class Domination: Some Problems in the Analysis of Hidden Morality', in *Disrespect: The Normative Foundations of Critical Theory*, Cambridge: Polity, 2007, pp. 80–96. Originally published in German in *Leviathan* 9:3/4 (1981), pp. 556–70.

22 Vivek Chibber comes to a similar view in his *The Class Matrix: Social Theory after the Cultural Turn*, Cambridge MA: Harvard University Press, 2022. According to his well-argued conclusion, workers' current acquiescence is a sign of resignation rather than acceptance of existing conditions. See ibid., chapter 3: 'Consent, Coercion, and Resignation'. On this question more generally, see the informative empirical study by Linda Beck and Linus Westhäuser, 'Verletzte Ansprüche: Zur Grammatik des politischen Widerstands von ArbeiterInnen', *Berliner Journal für Soziologie* 32 (2022), pp. 279–316.

23 This sketch also suggests that preferences and attitudes among employees may vary less than Richard Arneson claims in his impressive article 'Meaningful Work and Market Socialism'. As I shall show, many studies suggest that despite their acquiescence and passive perseverance, most working people would still very much like to have more say and actual influence over the organization of what they do.

24 A first impression of the privatized and often defeatist forms such discontent takes can be gained from Julia Friedrichs's book *Working Class: Warum wir Arbeit brauchen, von der wir leben können*. Her study is based on personal conversations. On the US, see the excellent study by Jefferson R. Cowie, *Stayin' Alive: The 1970s and the Last Days of the Working Class*, Book II: 'Despair in the Order, 1974–1982', New York: The New Press, 2012. On France, see Jean-Pierre Terrail's study *Destin ouvriers: La fin d'une classe*, Paris: Presses universitaires de France, 1990. The works by Cowie and Terrail focus exclusively on the individualization and dissociation of industrial workers. Data on the psychological misery caused by the massively reduced life chances of the 'white' proletariat in the US can be found in Anne Case and Angus Deaton, *Deaths of Despair and the Future of Capitalism*, Princeton NJ: Princeton University Press, 2020. With regard to individual resistance in the expanding area of 'basic' services, see Philipp Staab's very informative 'Metamorphosen der Fabriksozialisation', especially pp. 23–6.

25 See e.g. Roland Paulsen, *Empty Labor: Idleness and Workplace Resistance*, Cambridge: Cambridge University Press, 2014; Adam Reich and Peter Bearman, *Working for Respect: Community and Conflict at Walmart*, New York: Columbia University Press, 2018; Cant, *Riding for Deliveroo*. The extent to which acts of sabotage can be seen as forms of resistance is discussed in an excellent article by Friederike Bahl, 'Funktionale Informalität und verdeckter Widerstand – über zwei Seiten der Sabotage', in Ferdinand Sutterlüty and Almut Poppinga (eds), *Verdeckter Widerstand in demokratischen Gesellschaften*, Frankfurt am Main: Campus, 2022, pp. 213–38.

26 See Paul Edwards, David Collinson and Giuseppe Della Rocca, 'Workplace Resistance in Western Europe: A Preliminary Research Agenda', *European Journal of Industrial Relations* 1:3 (1995), pp. 283–316.

27 Georg Wilhelm Friedrich Hegel, *Lectures on the History of Philosophy*, vol. III, London: Kegan Paul, Trench, Trübner & Co., 1895, p. 553.

28 Workers do in fact feel that their living and working conditions exclude them from processes of democratic will formation. In an empirical study, Linda Beck and Linus Westhäuser have convincingly demonstrated that awareness of political exclusion remains an enduring element of the sense of injustice among members of this social stratum. See

Beck and Westhäuser, 'Verletzte Ansprüche', pp. 302–7. It goes without saying that this awareness can take on nationalistic and populist as well as democratic and progressive forms, depending on the cultural climate and political conditions. For an illustration of this point, see Didier Eribon, *Returning to Reims*, Cambridge MA: MIT Press, 2013, and my review article: Axel Honneth, 'Workingman's Blues #2: Ein Literaturessay zu Didier Eribon und Arlie Hochschild', in *WestEnd: Neue Zeitschrift für Sozialforschung* 14:1 (2017), pp. 169–85.

29 This position – perhaps theoretically sound, but certainly practically unworkable – is argued for in e.g. Nicholas Vrousalis, 'Workplace Democracy Implies Economic Democracy', *Journal of Social Philosophy* 50:3 (2019), pp. 259–79.

30 See Axel Honneth, 'Democracy and the Division of Labour: A Blind Spot in Political Philosophy', in *The Poverty of Our Freedom*, pp. 126–40.

8 Alternatives to the Labour Market

1 See Chapter 5.

2 The concept of 'slavery' is vague, however, and can also include other forms of bondage such as servitude, indenture or forced labour in the penal system. See Osterhammel, *The Transformation of the World*, pp. 697f.

3 The putting-out system of previous centuries, which is today staging a comeback in a slightly different, internet-based guise (see Chapter 6), represents a hybrid form between autonomous entrepreneurship and wage labour: on the one hand, it requires the individual's ownership of the means of production; on the other, however, it is fully dependent on the private capitalist client, who stipulates the rules governing the organization and remuneration of the work.

4 Michael Walzer, *Spheres of Justice: A Defense of Pluralism and Equality*, New York: Basic Books, 1983, p. 169.

5 On the following, see ibid., pp. 169–72. Debra Satz offers some striking arguments in 'In Defense of a Mandatory Public Service Requirement', in Julian Baggini (ed.), *A Philosopher's Manifesto: Ideas and Arguments to Change the World*, Cambridge: Cambridge University Press, 2022, pp. 259–69.

6 See ibid., p. 264.

7 The following draws on ideas put forward by Ulrich Steinvorth, 'Kann das Grundeinkommen die Arbeitslosigkeit ersetzen?'; see especially pp. 260f.

8 van der Linden, *Workers of the World*, chapter 8: 'Producer Cooperatives', pp. 151–69.

9 Within the workers' movement, Rosa Luxemburg was a firm opponent of cooperatives. She saw them as a 'hybrid form' between capitalism and socialism that hinders rather than supports the aims of the revolution: 'The workers forming a co-operative in the field of production are thus faced with the contradictory necessity of governing themselves with the utmost absolutism. They are obliged to take toward themselves the role of capitalist entrepreneur – a contradiction that accounts for the usual failure of production co-operatives which either become pure capitalist enterprises or, if the workers' interests continue to predominate, end by dissolving.' Rosa Luxemburg, *Reform or Revolution?*, Paris: Foreign Languages Press, 2020 [reprint of the revised second edition of 1908], p. 51. I would like to thank Ada Reichardt for pointing me to this passage.

10 Mill, *Principles of Political Economy*, Book IV, chapter 7, §6, p. 373.

11 See e.g. Erik Olin Wright, *Envisioning Real Utopias*, London: Verso, 2010, pp. 234–56. In his chapter on economic alternatives to the capitalist labour market (pp. 191–269),

Wright also discusses other forms of production, such as 'social economy' and 'social capitalism', which I shall leave aside.

12 I am very grateful to Ada Reichhart for conversations about these tensions.

13 On these structural problems, see Ada Reichhart's empirical study on a metalworking company in eastern France: 'Demokratie am Arbeitsplatz: Eine Produktionsgenossenschaft im Kapitalismus', *Westend: Neue Zeitschrift für Sozialforschung* 1 (2023). Historical examples of some of these problems can also be found in van der Linden, *Workers of the World*, pp. 154–69.

14 An exception is the Mondragón Corporación Cooperativa, whose headquarters are in the Basque town of Mondragón. It managed to overcome great hurdles to become a global cooperative company. See Astrid Hafner, 'Genossenschaftliche Realität im baskischen Mondragón', in Markus Auinger (ed.), *Solidarische Ökonomie zwischen Markt und Staat: Gesellschaftsveränderung oder Selbsthilfe?*, special edition of Mattersburger Kreis (ed.), *Journal für Entwicklungspolitik*, vol. XXV (3), Vienna: Mandelbaum Verlag, 2009, pp. 43–64. The article also mentions the cooperative's growing problems as a result of the widening gap between management and employees. On Mondragón, see also Wright, *Envisioning Real Utopias*, pp. 240–6.

15 For an overview see Pateman, *Participation and Democratic Theory*.

16 See Kuhn, *Haus, Frauen, Arbeit 1915–1965*, and Robert W. Smuts, *Women and Work in America*, New York: Columbia University Press, 1971.

17 For a brief account of Red Vienna, see Axel Honneth, 'Das "Rote Wien": Vom Geist des sozialistischen Experimentalismus', in *Die Idee des Sozialismus*, expanded edition, Berlin: Suhrkamp, 2017, pp. 169–80.

18 See the interesting article by Veronika Duma, 'Rotes Wien: Eine Inspiration für feministische Utopien', in Kitchen Politics (ed.), *Die Neuordnung der Küchen: Materialistisch-feministische Entwürfe eines besseren Zusammenlebens*, Münster: edition assemblage, 2023. I would like to thank Sarah Speck for pointing me to this article.

19 See Huws, *Labour in Contemporary Capitalism*, especially pp. 121–40.

20 See Berger and Offe, 'Die Zukunft des Arbeitsmarktes', pp. 107–14.

21 In his survey of experiments with socialist alternatives in the present day, Erik Olin Wright calls this the problem of 'faith-based initiatives'. See his *Envisioning Real Utopias*, pp. 213f.

22 One of the entries in his list of current socialist models; see ibid., pp. 234–56; here especially: pp. 237ff.

9 Improvements to the Labour Market

1 See Berger and Offe, 'Die Zukunft des Arbeitsmarktes', p. 115.

2 Guilty of this mistake are those commentators who paint beautiful pictures of workplace and economic democracy without telling us how these visions might be realized. An example would be Vrousalis, 'Workplace Democracy Implies Economic Democracy'.

3 See pp. 24f. above.

4 The difficulty arises from the need to formulate conditions for economic independence that are compatible with the conditions of wage labour, and thus with a fundamental dependence on 'private' entrepreneurs.

5 See Anderson, *Private Government*, especially pp. 48–61.

6 See Castel, *From Manual Workers to Wage Laborers*.

7 See Karl Marx, 'The Struggle for a Normal Working Day. Laws for the Compulsory

Limitation of Working Hours. The English Factory Legislation of 1833–64', in *Capital, Volume 1*, pp. 389–411.

8 Immanuel Wallerstein, *The Modern World System IV: Centrist Liberalism Triumphant, 1789–1914*, Berkeley: University of California Press, 2011.

9 On Germany, see Wolfgang Strengmann-Kuhn, *Armut trotz Erwerbstätigkeit: Analysen und sozialpolitische Konsequenzen*, Frankfurt am Main: Campus, 2003. On the US, see Barbara Ehrenreich, *Nickel and Dimed: On (Not) Getting By in America*, New York: Henry Holt, 2001. On the 'time squeeze' suffered by the precariat, see Standing, *The Precariat*, chapter 5: 'Labour, Work, and the Time Squeeze', pp. 115–31.

10 See Karin Gottschall and G. Günter Voß (eds), *Entgrenzung von Arbeit und Leben: Zum Wandel der Beziehung von Erwerbstätigkeit und Privatsphäre im Alltag*, Munich: Rainer Hampp Verlag, 2005.

11 On the reversal of the trend towards shorter working hours in the US, see Juliet B. Schor, *The Overworked American: The Unexpected Decline of Leisure*, New York: Basic Books, 1992. Schor's observations fit well with the increase in symptoms of exhaustion and burnout as a result of mentally, rather than physically, draining working conditions; see Sighart Neckel and Greta Wagner (eds), *Leistung und Erschöpfung: Burnout in der Wettbewerbsgesellschaft*, Berlin: Suhrkamp, 2013.

12 See pp. 40f. above.

13 Castel, *From Manual Workers to Wage Laborers*, p. 422.

14 See Axel Honneth, 'Recognition as Ideology: The Connection between Reality and Power', in *The I in We: Studies in the Theory of Recognition*, Cambridge: Polity, 2012, pp. 75–97; 'Organized Self-Realization: Paradoxes of Individualization', in ibid., pp. 153–68. A surprisingly frank account of the way businesses use 'commendations' as 'intrinsic incentives' to increase performance is provided in Bruno S. Frey, 'Geld oder Anerkennung: Zur Ökonomik der Auszeichnung', *Perspektiven der Wirtschaftspolitik* 11:1 (2010), pp. 1–15.

15 On the reasons behind the psychological inclination to equate inherited wealth and financial prowess with merit, and therefore afford them social esteem, see Adam Smith, *The Theory of Moral Sentiments*, Indianapolis: Liberty Press, 1982, pp. 56–66.

16 See Claudia Honegger, Sighard Neckel and Chantal Magnin (eds), *Strukturierte Verantwortungslosigkeit: Berichte aus der Bankenwelt*, Berlin: Suhrkamp, 2010.

17 On the history of this 'devaluation', see Evke Rulffes, *Die Erfindung der Hausfrau: Geschichte einer Entwertung*, Hamburg: HarperCollins, 2021. The 'aesthetization' of occupational areas with predominantly female workers can also be a subtle form of devaluation, as shown in an interesting article by Johanna Hofbauer and Ulli Pastner: 'Der diskrete Charme der Diskriminierung: Ästhetisierung von Frauenarbeit als unscheinbare Form der Missachtung', in Holtgrewe, Voswinkel and Wagner (eds), *Anerkennung und Arbeit*, pp. 219–46.

18 Valuable reflections on the foundations of social systems of esteem for occupational areas can be found in Speier, *Die Angestellten vor dem Nationalsozialismus*, chapter 7, 'Die Grundlagen der sozialen Geltung'. The significance of the current devaluation of simple and manual labour is the focus of Imogen Tyler's analysis in 'Classificatory Struggles: Class, Culture, and Inequality in Neoliberal Times', *The Sociological Review* 63:2 (2015), pp. 493–511. Further suggestions regarding the role of 'negative classification' in the context of social struggles can be found in Ferdinand Sutterlüty, *In Sippenhaft: Negative Klassifikationen in ethnischen Konflikten*, Frankfurt am Main: Campus, 2010; see

especially chapters 1 and 3. On the role and function of esteem in modern societies, see also Ludgera Vogt, *Zur Logik der Ehre in der Gegenwartsgesellschaft*, Frankfurt am Main: Suhrkamp, 1997, especially part B, pp. 65–224, and Young, *Justice and the Politics of Difference*, chapter 7.

19 See the extremely informative contributions in Mayer-Ahuja and Nachtwey (eds), *Verkannte Leistungsträger:innen*.

20 The important concept of a 'counterculture of dignity' was developed by Richard Sennett and Jonathan Cobb. See their *The Hidden Injuries of Class*, Cambridge: Cambridge University Press, 1972, p. 83.

21 The literature contains ample empirical evidence that those who do less qualified work in the production and service sectors in particular complain about a lack of recognition. To name just three sources: Mayer-Ahuja and Nachtwey (eds), *Verkannte Leistungsträger:innen*; François Dubet, *Injustices: L'expérience des inégalités au travail*, Paris: Editions Seuil, 2006, especially chapter 4, section III; Beck and Westhäuser, 'Verletzte Ansprüche', pp. 297–302.

22 Smith, *The Theory of Moral Sentiments*, pp. 121f.

23 Durkheim presents his reflections *ex negativo* by analysing what he calls 'abnormal forms' of the organic division of labour and drawing up a list of conditions that would need to be met for its 'normal' morally integrating function to be restored. See Durkheim, *The Division of Labour In Society*, Book 3, pp. 353–409.

24 Ibid., pp. 372f.

25 Friedmann, *Industrial Society*, pp. 145–8.

26 See Braverman, *Labor and Monopoly Capital*, part II, pp. 105–71.

27 See Beckert, *Beyond the Market*, pp. 114–18.

28 See the survey by Timo Luks, 'Gruppe und Betrieb: Sozialwissenschaftliche Zugriffe auf industrielle Produktionsweisen', *Mittelweg 36* 28/29:1 (2020), pp. 44–67.

29 See Kern and Schumann, *Das Ende der Arbeitsteilung?* Horst Kern and Michael Schumacher, 'Limits of the Division of Labour: New Production and Employment Concepts in West German Industry', *Economic and Industrial Democracy* 8:2 (1987), pp. 151–70.

30 See Staab, 'Metamorphosen der Fabriksozialisation', pp. 16f.

31 See Felix Hörisch, *Unternehmensmitbestimmung im nationalen und internationalen Vergleich: Entstehung und ökonomische Auswirkungen*, Münster: LIT-Verlag, 2009.

32 See e.g. Bernhard Ebbinghaus and Claudia Göbel, 'Mitgliederrückgang und Organisationsstrategien deutscher Gewerkschaften', in Wolfgang Schroeder (ed.), *Handbuch Gewerkschaften in Deutschland*, Wiesbaden: Springer, 2014, pp. 207–37; Christopher Kollmeyer and John Peters, 'Financialization and the Decline of Organized Labor: A Study of 18 Advanced Capitalist Countries, 1970–2012', *Social Forces* 98:1 (2019), pp. 1–30.

33 Spiros Simitis pointed out this danger decades ago in connection with the problem of 'juridification'. See his 'Wiederentdeckung des Individuums und arbeitsrechtliche Normen', *Sinzheimer Cahiers* 2 (1991), pp. 7–42.

34 See Oskar Negt, *Wozu noch Gewerkschaften? Eine Streitschrift*, Göttingen: Steidl, 2004.

35 Again, we must bear in mind that relatively autonomous groups can also be used to increase productivity. See Helmut Hoyer and Matthias Knuth, 'Die teilautonome Gruppe: Strategie des Kapitals oder Chance für die Arbeiter', *Kursbuch* 43 (1976), pp. 118–32. On the history and function of self-organization in businesses, see the

– perhaps overly optimistic – study by Günter Hillmann, *Die Befreiung der Arbeit: Die Entwicklung kooperativer Selbstorganisation und die Auflösung bürokratisch-hierarchischer Herrschaft*, Reinbek bei Hamburg: Rowohlt 1970, chapter I.

36 See Chapter 7.

37 Staab, 'Metamorphosen der Fabriksozialisation', pp. 16f.

38 See Paulsen, *Empty Labor*.

39 Max Weber, 'Politics as a Vocation', in *The Vocation Lectures*, Indianapolis: Hackett, 2004, pp. 32–94; here: p. 93.

Index